VILLAINS

VILLAINS

IT TAKES ONE TO KNOW ONE

PAUL FERRIS
&
REG McKAY

BLACK & WHITE PUBLISHING

First Published 2006
This editon first published 2010
by Black & White Publishing Ltd
29 Ocean Drive, Edinburgh EH6 6JL

1 3 5 7 9 10 8 6 4 2   10 11 12 13

ISBN: 978 1 84502 291 4

Typeset by RefineCatch Limited, Bungay, Suffolk
Printed and bound by J F Print Ltd., Sparkford, Somerset

The Ross Street San Toi
aka The Bowery Boys
You will never be forgotten

CONTENTS

INTRODUCTION

VILLAINS?

Who the hell am I?
Who the hell are you?

Do you ever catch yourself asking that question? Maybe in lonely, quiet moments? When things have gone wrong? When things have gone right? Or maybe just when you're too drunk or too stoned to do anything else but listen to your favourite music and think dark thoughts in the dark?

Not just your name, address, job, friends, family and hobbies but who are you really? You know, that bit of you that thinks like only you can. The bit that is truly alone at times with your successes, your failures, your regrets, your pain and your joy. Who the hell is that?

Of course, if I could answer that question, this would be the intro to a book on philosophy not true crime. But who the hell wants to read a book on philosophy? Not me.

Whoever the real you is surely is influenced by what you do and who you know. It's not the whole story, of course, but it's a bit of it we can touch, see, describe. That's my kind of philosophy.

What do I do? Well, I'm a writer now but, most of my life, I've been up to villainy. Who do I know? All sorts of people but more than my fair share of villains. That's who this book is about – the villains I have known and who have influenced me for good or ill.

Here you'll meet figures – some you'll have heard of and others will be brand new to you. They'll have somehow slipped by you unnoticed – deliberately slipped by you unnoticed – but here we tell their tales of the street for the first time.

Yes, you'll meet one or two characters I've written about before but don't turn away from them if you have read about them before. This book contains new tales – funny, tragic and sometimes very bloody ones. It's real life – real life that has made me think, made me who I am – who I really am.

With great reluctance, a few names have been changed to protect the guilty. They know who they are. So do we. But in *Villains'* case the guilty have also been helpful telling true accounts that have never been told before, often of crimes that remain unsolved – crimes the cops are still very interested in.

It seemed a fair trade-off to us to change a couple of names to get into the underbelly of these scenes. If we had refused to do it, the truth would never emerge. Burying the truth is the job of bent cops not writers like us who always stick to the principle of keeping it real.

Villains is stacked full of people who live beyond the law but they are not all the same. Why should they be? Are all footballers, bizzies, taxi drivers, working girls, homeless folk, scribblers the same as each other?

Villains isn't just about my friends. Sometimes it's about my enemies. But it's always about people I've learned from. Some taught me what is the right thing to do – others what never to do. You'll have to make your own mind up.

Villains is about the mad, the bad and the sad – all as different from each other as it is possible to be. The one thing they have in common? They are all villains. Trust me in this. Well, it takes one to know one.

1

OLD SCHOOL

Swinging lead kissed his cheek.

WhzzzzzwhoOOMP.

'Just tell us where he is, right?' The speaker stood in front of him, a hammer in one mitt, jabbing the air at him with the other.

WhzzzzzwhoOOMP.

'You're a stupid little bastard. Look at the state of you.'

They'd jumped him as he walked down a lane on his own – team-handed, like they usually did. Maybe thirty or forty – he hadn't stopped to count. Too busy fighting – and losing this time. A jagged slash ran down one cheek, the blood drying black and crusty. One eye was closed, mottled navy and purple. Skin flapped loose from a split lip. One arm was aching and useless and he held it up with his other hand, suspecting it was broken but praying he'd only ripped some tendons.

'We've given you a doing already. And we're no' finished yet.'

WhzzzzzwhoOOMP.

The lead inched closer to his face. The swinger was off to his blind side but he knew who it'd be. The lead was a heavy lump of metal used in old-fashioned sash windows. Most guys just used them as coshes but this bastard kept it on the thick cord sash and liked to swing it at skulls. He knew who the lead swinger was all right. He knew all of this big mob – every one. They were older than him – men, really – but he'd grown up in the same neighbourhood, knew what they were capable of.

'Tell us, for fuck sake, or we'll finish you.' The speaker opened his long thick coat to show his usual array of steel – a butcher's cleaver and a sword.

Next to him, one of the team laughed high and shrill, drawing a long-bladed knife. The small teenager stared straight ahead and said his usual – nothing.

WhzzzzzwhoOOMP.

He knew who they were looking for. Sinatra, a mate of his who'd jumped in when three of the team had been beating up some old guy. Nobody messed with Sinatra and the three had come off very much second best. To add insult to injury, Sinatra and his mates had turned over an illegal gambling joint that this mob were meant to be protecting. Now this was a revenge raid – payback time. All they wanted was to know where Sinatra was. He knew. Their wee group always knew each other's whereabouts. But his wee team didn't work with anyone else – not the cops or ugly mobs like this lot, no matter what they threatened. The small teenager stood, staring straight ahead, and said nothing.

WhzzzzzwhoOOMP.

'YOU LOOKING FOR ME, YA PRICKS?' The shout came from the end of the lane. It was Sinatra and his other mates, tooled up and teamed up. Well, all four of them were there, hefting open razors and meat cleavers. Some passing citizen must have given them the word on the small teenager's predicament and, as usual, they'd dropped everything and come running to help a pal.

He looked around, seeing fear in the eyes of the big mob. All they'd hoped to do was ambush Sinatra on his own but now they had the whole team to face – thirty versus four. Bad odds? He turned towards the lead swinger and kicked him swiftly in the balls. It was now thirty against five. He knew who he'd bet on and he wasn't proven wrong.

Once upon a time, there were five wee boys – pals as close as you can get. None of them would ever be described as tall – ever. But big men they were all – so big they were going to change the face of organised crime. In the hungry 1930s they were just nippers, scraping to get by in the hard-lands of Glasgow. It was never easy – never easy for anyone. But they had a plan – they were going to stick together.

Ross Street was their pitch. Just off the Gallowgate, round the corner from Saltmarket, walking distance from the Green. It was old Glasgow, reeking of the gallows, prisons, slaughterhouses, pub after pub and the outdoor hustle-bustle of the Barras market.

It was the kind of area you could catch anything – diphtheria, pleurisy, TB – and too many did, perishing young. Not these five amigos. They might have been wee but they were tough and had parents who made sure they took their cod liver oil and orange juice supplements. They'd live till they died and that was some time away.

It was a violent place where kids learned to battle with fists and feet as soon as they could walk. Brutal? That was the way of the place. You either battled it or bottled it and, once you bottled it, you'd be relegated to the bottom of the food chain. Permanently. Not a good place to be in that place in those days.

As individuals, this lot learned to handle themselves very well, thank you. Poverty had seen to it that Glasgow was a city of small people. But, even among that tiny urban tribe, these five were smaller still. No matter – they just fought harder.

No one can recall how they came together as a group but come together they did and, by their teens, they were well known as one of the most feisty gangs on the streets. So well known that they were given a name – the Ross Street San Toi among themselves and close associates. In the annals of Glasgow street life, they'd be given their other name – the Bowery Boys.

There was John 'Sinatra' Sawyers, who got his nickname for looking like Ol' Blue Eyes himself but he was one of the best street fighters in a city of street fighting men. Sinatra came from a long line of brothers, each as well known as the other. Now he was going to take their endeavours on to a new, higher plane.

John 'Pudden Pen' Clarke was so called because his family came from that part of Glasgow's infamous Garngad area. Pudden Pen was a hard patch and he was top boy. The nickname was a badge of honour, in other words. God help the individual who thought it had something to do with stodgy sweets.

James 'The Gent' Cannon had a suave, mannerly approach with the ladies and no little success but, if anyone thought he was just a fanny bandit, they were in for a big shock. The Gent was a gent with the ladies and would be a smooth operator with the whole world – till someone crossed him. That was a different matter entirely.

Jimma 'Swiftly' Hill was sallow skinned with jet black hair. Some folk thought he was Spanish or Italian but he was as Glaswegian as the River Clyde. No mistaking where his street handle came from. The boy could sprint faster than anyone – a handy skill when you're involved in street battles and a bit of day-light robbery. By all accounts, with an easier upbringing and a bit more money around the house, Swiftly could have been a com-petitor of Olympic standard.

Last but not least was my old man – Willie Ferris. Funnily enough, though he wasn't the shortest of the group, he was always referred to as 'Wee Ferris'. Maybe it had something to do with his readiness to tackle anyone no matter how much bigger or older – something that never left him. Right from the start, Wee Ferris was fascinated by cars – even in those days of very few motors. He became the group's driver – the best in the city, so they said.

If some talent scout had scoured the streets of Glasgow to come up with the best gang possible, they would've recruited the same five boys. The Ross Street San Toi were the tops and no mistake.

From an early age, they got organised. They had to. In those days, the Billy Boys, the Norman Conks and other mobs num-bered hundreds among their members. They were five boys.

That day in the lane, it had been a battalion of the Billy Boys. There was nothing sectarian about this even though the Billy Boys identified with Protestants. It was street warfare, simple as that, and the Ross Street San Toi were well outnumbered. They had to be organised.

They got organised in another way. This fighting for fighting's sake malarkey wasn't for them. They wanted to make a few quid and went about it in their usual way – with planning, cunning and sheer audacity. Warehouses, banks, offices on payday, the Ross Street San Toi never missed a trick. The turning-over of an illegal gambling den that had so infuriated the Billy Boys was another familiar trick. They knew the folk in charge couldn't go to the cops. All they should have had to fear was the Billy Boys who were taking a protection tax from the place every week. Yet the Ross Street San Toi feared no one – and this was when they were still too young to vote.

They were the envy of other players, some of whom grumbled about how the Ross Street San Toi never got caught. Well, they did but it was seldom and, when they did, they never got shopped. Apart from being good, they had a major weapon in their armoury – a moral code.

They never gave trouble to those who didn't deserve it. They helped weaker folks when they could. They protected women, children and oldies. They never dealt with the police, preferring instead to dish out their own form of street justice. They minded their own business and expected other people to mind theirs. They didn't boast or show off. They were as close as blood brothers and would go to the line for each other, not needing to be asked.

Call it old fashioned? It certainly is now. Old school? Certainly. But it served them well. Want a good reason to stick to the code? They rarely got grassed. People, even ordinary citizens, liked and trusted them.

The Ross Street San Toi were villains all yet they lived moral lives and knowing that helped me through the darkest of times – villains, sure, but good guys too. It's easy to get a guide from a good person's example. But not all villains have good sides – I learned that from them too. One right bad bastard's coming your way now.

2

NO SCHOOL

It didn't look like the Devil's Lair but that's how some people thought of it. A small flat in the Anderson area of Glasgow, close to the cop shop, most people would rather die than pay it a visit. But some things in life are just so important you have to take action. Me, I was going into the Lair.

There was trouble on the street – not that there was any big surprise about that in Glasgow at any time and there wasn't back then, around 1990. The decade before had been a wee bit fraught.

I'd opted for a life of crime rather than a life of grime, shifting cases of booze into hotels, clubs and the like. After a short period of freelancing in jewellery-shop robberies with some mates, I got diverted by some payback. A big ugly mob called Welsh had stolen my childhood by their violent bullying. So, now that I was in long trousers, I got them back – a throat slashed here, a bit of a scalping there.

Arthur Thompson, the so-called Godfather of Glasgow, was impressed. He'd been fighting a twenty-five-year feud with the Welsh clan that had resulted in much bloodshed and many deaths, including that of his own mother-in-law in a car bomb. So the Thompsons recruited me. I thought I'd joined the big league.

There followed a few years as their bagman and equaliser, being chased for a score of attempted murders, tried for a shooting and finally being set up with drugs by the police and proving that in court. They were busy years but then I walked away from the Thompsons to do my own thing, certain that Arthur's son, Fatboy,

6

had grassed me to the cops. Well, who'd hang around in that company?

Out on my own, I teamed up with Bobby Glover and Joe Hanlon, fine guys you could trust all the way, and the city's street players, as well as the bizzies, were a wee bit worried. I didn't have to go looking for trouble. But this was personal. Not mine, you understand, but of two close pals of mine – same thing really.

Neily the Bomb was top man in Glenochil Detention Centre when I had served a spell in there. Through him I got to know his brother Kevin O'Neil really well and I liked the pair of them. Their middle brother William, known as 'Wid', I didn't know so well but he was connected so that's all that mattered to me.

Wid had gone to some house to buy temazepam – or Jellies as they're called on the street. Not my kind of recreation but so far so good. In spite of what you see in the Hollywood version of life, visiting a drug dealer is more often like visiting a pal than some sleazy transaction. If you're going to buy drugs, then do so from someone you know, someone you trust – just as you would in other aspects of life.

So no doubt Wid was standing there, his new purchases stashed carefully away, swapping banter with his dealer. Then everyone went silent. The Lord of the Rings had just walked into the flat. Also known as Hammy the Poof and worse, his mammy knew him as Martin Hamilton. I'm sure she loved him dearly. Aren't our mammies just so bloody unconditional in their love no matter how badly we act? Want a homage to mothers everywhere? No better example than Hammy's mother. He was worse than bad. He was pure evil.

There was no problem in my mind about Hammy being gay. There are just as many gay men – and women – on the street as anywhere else. But Hammy liked extras with his nookie, especially when it involved him inflicting pain – a lot of pain – and he fancied Wid big time.

The pair of them had been in the same jail at the same time. Hammy in jail is like a pig in shit – right at home. He'd take over the drug dealing, ensuring that his need for a massive daily intake of Valium or Blues was met and he would be on a good earner as well. By 1990, the jail dealer was king – simple as that – and, as everyone knows, it's good to be king.

In my too many years in jail, I've only chanced upon two guys who paid for sex. One liked to think of himself as the original Essex Boy but really he was a fat, steroid-poisoned backstabber by the name of Jason Vella. The other was Hammy.

Hammy would watch the new, young boys come in and decide who he fancied. No courting rituals from him, just stark choices – it was a blowjob for a tenner bag of smack or get kicked into hell and raped for good measure. The Lord of the Rings didn't make idle threats.

In jail, he'd made it obvious that he fancied Wid O'Neil. Young Wid ran for cover and used references to his brothers, Neily the Bomb and Kevin, to keep the sadist off his back – literally. But now they were both out and in the same dealer's flat and Hammy was making his wishes plain.

'A grand,' he said, eyeing up young Wid.

'What?'

'A grand for a blowjob.' And Hammy smiled – well, what he passed off as a smile.

Wid O'Neil was out of there in a flash. Before he cleared the close, he was ramming Jellies into his gob like they were jelly babies. He'd bought them to sell on at a profit but now he was using them to blur out the vision of Hammy's rampant knob and his evil smirk.

Wid knew Hammy wouldn't take no for an answer. Not now he'd made such a direct approach and offered him money for sex – even if he'd only been joking about the grand. Joking – that was about as close as the monster would get to foreplay. He just took what and who he wanted.

Wid wasn't a fighter but his brothers were. Neily the Bomb understood his wee brother's predicament instantly when he phoned. There was going to be big trouble. Neily contacted me for help and I was glad to. Wid O'Neil was in big shit and no doubt. Hammy had this habit of taking young guys hostage, stripping them and repeatedly buggering them over a period of days and nights. He didn't admit to being gay – in fact, he denied it – but he'd let the world know what he'd done to his victims, adding this stigma to their already deep-seated problems.

His game wasn't new. Ron Kray had done precisely the same thing many years before. He denied being gay too at that time. Like Ronnie Kray, Hammy was feared but no one respected him.

Our first task was to get hold of Wid. If he was with us, then we'd stop Hammy's evil plans. Me and a guy called The Hamster – no relation to Hammy, of course – an all-round good guy, swept up to the Wid's house in Balornock in the north of city. No sign. Fearing that the young bloke had already been lifted by Hammy, we drove at speed to the only place I knew you could usually find the beast – his mammy's house. The man who terrorised the streets was definitely a mother's boy. Nothing wrong with that but it seemed to contradict the rest of the way he lived his life. After all, I'm sure his old dear knew nothing about his rapes.

It was just a bog-standard wee flat in Anderston but people – hard people – really thought of it as one of the most dangerous places in Glasgow. Maybe it had something to do with Hammy always packing a gun and never hesitating to use it. To be honest, there were other places I'd rather have visited but a pal's wee bro was in trouble. Walking away simply wasn't an option.

With The Hamster planted outside under strict instructions to come bursting in if I wasn't out in twenty minutes, off I trotted. When Hammy opened the door, the look of shock on his face was a picture.

'Whit the fuck do you want?' he asked and I could tell by his voice that, just by turning up there at his mammy's house, I had unnerved him. First blood to Ferris.

'Want a word, Hammy,' I replied. 'Can I come in?'

Hammy let me in and, as he showed me into his room, I could hear his mother moving about in the kitchen. With the curtains pulled tight shut, there was hardly any light in Hammy's bedroom but, as my eyes adjusted and I began to see properly again, I couldn't believe what I was seeing. The place dripped with icons of saints, holy medals and rosary beads. The beast had religion big time.

'Paul, what do you want?' His eyes shifted from side to side, nervous as hell as that I had turned up at his place – not a common occurrence.

'How you doing, Hammy?' I said sitting down, uninvited a few feet across the room from him. It's nice to be nice. And that's what it was like for five or ten minutes – just small talk. You didn't rush guys like Hammy. He was likely to go off on one. I wanted to resolve the issue for sure but with the minimum trouble. As we spoke, I could see that lying beside him was a big revolver. It would be the real thing and loaded for sure. Hammy was like that.

After a few minutes, I got to the point. 'I hear you've been speaking to Wid O'Neil.'

'So what?' he got as close to a growl as that shrill voice of his would allow. As he spoke he moved his hand, edging the revolver closer to him.

'Well, there's a problem,' I replied slowly pulling a knife out of my waistband.

His eyes widened and his jaw tightened.

'Aw, don't worry, Hammy,' I reassured him, 'I'm no' going to use it. Just showing you this is all I'm carrying.' I held the blade by its handle, dangling it in front of me.

Hammy must have thought I was mental, walking into his pad to raise an issue armed with just a knife. There are those who would've agreed with him. But time had been of the essence when Neily belled me and I hadn't been carrying. No problem, I reckoned.

'Is Wid some pal of yours then?' Hammy asked.

'Me? No, no. Hardly met the guy.'

'So whit you pushing your nose intae ma business for?'

'His brothers are good friends of mine,' I replied, picking at my nails with the point of my big chib – well they needed a manicure – and letting my last words sink in. 'Very good friends.'

Hammy knew what that meant – mess with them and theirs and he was messing with me. If he was going to go off on one, now was the time.

'Give us a look at your shooter,' I asked.

'Whit?' You'd think I'd just asked to sleep with his mother such was his tone of horror.

'Just give us a wee look.'

'Naw.'

'What's the problem?'

'I don't trust you.' That was rich coming from him and for the first time I noticed he was shaking – still looking as mean as fuck but his fingertips were quivering and there was a tremor in his fat lips. 'And my ma's in the next room.' That was a white flag. Hammy was telling me there would be no trouble from him. Given his psycho nature and the imbalance in weaponry, I took that as him backing down.

'Fair enough but the point is this – Wid O'Neil better not be harmed, Hammy.'

'He's no'.'

'What?'

'He's no' harmed. He'll no' be harmed.'

'Where is he then?'

'Fucked if I know, Paul. Haven't seen him since I bumped into him this morning in that flat.'

Endgame.

Outside, The Hamster was waiting for me as I knew he would be. He reckoned he was two minutes away from coming crashing through the door. Just as well he didn't. I wouldn't have wanted Hammy's mammy to get a big fright. Poor woman had enough to contend with. Later, we caught up with Neily and Kevin. They had found Wid all right, safe and sound – at least safe from Hammy.

Wid had been found on Clyde Street in the city centre, running flat out as fast as he could. It was the terror of Hammy, no doubt exacerbated by the Jellies. He was in a hell of a state for days, weeks.

Funny thing was the brothers had found Wid before I'd knocked on Hammy's front door. I'd taken the risks for nothing. Not that I expected any gratitude. It was just one of those things you helped mates with and they'd help you in return. But the bold Wid was arrested a short time later on a robbery charge. He is the world's worst robber, always ending up in the nick, always broke. This time he offered to trade with the cops – he'd give them information on me if they'd go easy on him.

Wid O'Neil didn't have any info on me apart from what he'd read in the newspapers and rumours he heard on the street. That's not the point, though, is it? Biggest mistake he made was telling his brothers about his proposed trade with the cops. They promptly disowned him and told me. That would be the last time I'd help Wid O'Neil. Mind you, where he was going I couldn't help him anyway. Twelve years in the jail for a failed robbery. Some big-time criminal, eh? But certainly a man of his times – no code, no friends, no loyalty, no standards, no bottle, no school. Maybe I should just have left him for The Lord of the Rings. They'd make good company for each other.

But there were better people about the street, that's for sure. And sometimes people let you down big time without meaning to. They just couldn't help themselves. You can learn from both, as we'll soon see.

3

ALL THAT GLITTERS

'It's a fucking goldmine, Paul.' Mobina, one of my Asian pals, was holding his large Jack Daniels in both hands, leaning across the table and talking to me in a conspiratorial whisper – in spite of the fact that there was only him and me in my flat.

'Gold?' Of course I was interested. 'There's gold there?'

'Aye. Aye, there is some gold,' his emphasis all on the word 'some' and his sour expression explained the rest. 'But it's the stones, man. You should see the fucking stones.'

'What? Diamonds?'

Mobina nodded his nut like it was in danger of falling off. 'Big fucking diamonds. Like you've never seen.'

Now I was very interested.

Mobina had some family working in a top-secure Customs and Excise facility in London where they held a lot of valuable goodies confiscated from people entering the country through Heathrow and Gatwick. For the obvious reason of it posing too much of a temptation, its location is kept secret even within The Knock, as the Customs call themselves after their code for action. But he claimed to have inside contacts and, even better, they wanted to make an extra wage for themselves. Perfect.

Mobina was getting drunker by the minute but he still managed to explain that his relatives' place of work was a store for all the confiscated valuables taken off mule passengers flying in from South Africa, Nigeria, Japan, China, all over the world. Whatever they got caught with, only things of extreme value were lodged in the store and the stuff was left there sometimes for years. We're not talking some cheap gold jewellery from the Canaries here but lumps of gold, big jewels, rare art, ancient artefacts.

As he explained late into the night over his umpteenth drink, 'It's a fucking Anadin's cave, Paul.'

'Aladdin's cave,' I said gently, not wanting to upset the guy.

'A what?'

'Aladdin's cave – the bloke in the story was called Aladdin.' He gave me such a disbelieving look I was tempted to add, 'And Anadin is a fucking painkiller, you wanker.' I resisted.

'Whatever,' he dismissed my comments and went on raving about the possible heist.

It seems that the whole place was loaded with goodies but the best of the best was kept in a big cage in the middle of the compound. It so happened that one of Mobina's relatives had occasional access to the cage but never on his own. In addition, the whole store was rife with security, of course, but not so rife as to prevent a little smuggling.

It was going to be a difficult one but not so difficult as to rule out the action. There are many men in this country who apply such intelligence, cunning, skill and bravery in carrying out big heists that you just know that, if they'd walked a straighter line, they'd be successful as doctors, engineers, lawyers even. Old-time, big-time robbers are among some of the most intelligent people I've met. By the time I'd bid goodnight to a wobbly-legged Mobina, I'd already decided I was going to need some help from the old good boys.

First thing the next morning, I was at work. Funny how a bit of business gets rid of a hangover better than any so-called cure. There was only one place to contact about a load of hot gems – London and my mate Onity.

I'm not using Onity's real name for good reason. For thirty years, the man had been one of the most daring robbers Britain has ever witnessed – so good we'll tell more of his stories later. Here's a wee taster.

Hatton Garden in London is the centre of the jewel-trading world. On any given day, there will be millions of pounds' worth of jewels floating about those street. When Onity and some mates decided to hit one of the top traders, they decided the only get-away car they could possibly use was the only make of car that was seen in the place – a Rolls-Royce. Anything else was going to stick out like a con at a cops' ball. They nicked the Roller, of course – no problem to those boys.

On the day, the job went slickly enough. It was executed, as planned, during the busy opening hours when the place was hoaching with customers and the streets were, of course, full of their Rollers. Afterwards, Onity was driving smoothly away in his Roller with a boot-ful of jewels, feeling totally anonymous, when he heard a siren – then another and another. The cops seemed to be coming from every direction. Onity was in big shit.

Later, it transpired that someone hadn't done their homework. The place they'd hit had a silent alarm button installed – a direct line to the cops – and it was working. Time to leave and fast.

Hatton Garden can get very congested, as it was that day. Flooring the accelerator wasn't Onity's best idea but it was the only option available to him as, in his rear view mirror, he saw the first cop car arrive at speed. A few hundred yards down, already beginning to lose the bizzies, his car swerved and sideswiped another Roller before crossing the street and whacking another. No problem – he just kept on booting it.

With the Roller dumped – a few panels battered but otherwise whole – Onity changed cars, stowed the loot and headed home. He had a good night in with his girlfriend, a few beers and a relaxed time. In spite of the close call with the cops he was sure it had been a good, safe day's work – till next morning, that is.

Sitting at his breakfast, reading the newspapers, as you do, his eye was attracted to a big article with a picture of a bashed Roller – his bashed Roller. Next to it stood the rightful owner – top comic and mimic, star of the *Royal Variety Show* at the London Palladium in front of the Queen, Mike Yarwood. Back then, Mike Yarwood was like royalty himself. Never mind the big haul from the jewellers, every cop in London was going to be hunting the blokes who'd wrecked Yarwood's car. It was time for Onity to get on his toes.

Along with another stack of big, audacious robberies, Onity has never been convicted of the Hatton Garden robbery. Now that's why I can't use his real name. But back to the Customs storage . . .

Onity was definitely interested. 'Cut or uncut?' he asked in his direct manner.

I didn't have a clue what he could mean.

'The gems – are they cut or uncut?' He had to explain that there was a big difference in trading such gems. The cut ones were easier but, with the uncut, you needed an expert jeweller to transform them into glittering jewels. It so happened that he knew a man who could work the magic – just as I knew he would.

First we had to glean as much accurate info from Mobina about the content of the cage. Having told him this, weeks went by and only dribs and drabs came through – enough to convince shrewd, cynical Onity that there were at least several million pounds' worth of uncut gems in that pot yet not enough info to set up a job.

Mobina was hot on issues like the details of the kitty. Here was a guy who knew what was worth a dollar but who was sloppy on issues like the position and angles of the CCTV cameras, the number of guards, their time rotas and so on. It was like he had approached people he thought of as professional robbers and expected us to somehow magic the goods away. Like much else in life, robbery is about preparation, preparation, preparation. Mobina was more ogle, ogle, ogle.

But Mobina ogled everything, including what wasn't in the cage like masses of ivory and rhino horn. Both were illegal, of course, and, between you and me, I agreed with that. Elephants and rhinos are beautiful creatures and should be given a chance, even if that means protecting them. But these poor sods were dead already and their highly valued products were going to waste away in C&E storage. Better that we made a few quid.

Mobina got us a photocopy of all the goods stored outside the cage. Rare vintage wines, bottles of whisky worth thousands of pounds and more Cuban cigars than you could shake a roach at. No interest. The ivory and rhino horn were a different matter. Ounce for ounce, those were the real gems.

Onity immediately pooh-poohed the ivory. 'Too much fucking weight for too little dough,' is how he expressed it. 'But we'll shift a bit. What we want, though, is that rhino horn. A little bit of that gets yer pecker up – worth a fucking fortune.'

From the inventory it was obvious that around 250 kilograms of rhino horn was in the less secure area. Rhino horn fetched £1,000 per ounce on the black market which mainly served the massive population in the Far East who believed it was an aphrodisiac. You do the sums. There was a fortune lying there waiting for the taking.

A tiny sample was smuggled out and passed to some of Onity's Chinese contacts – serious people. After they had a chemist test it, they advised us, in matter-of-fact, low-key terms, that they'd buy the lot. But they meant the whole lot – there'd be no deal unless they received the full 250 kilos. Anything less wasn't worth the bribes and other associated costs of getting the gear into the Far East countries where they operated. They'd take the ivory too – as much as possible.

'No fucking problemo,' said Mobina, confidence oozing from every pore. 'But it will take a few weeks to get all that horn out as well as the ivory you want and I'll have to be based down in London for delivery. They'll only pass the gear to me.'

It made sense so we moved Mobina into a top London hotel. Onity would foot the bill till the job was done then deduct the costs from Mobina's share. The thing was Mobina brought his whole family – well, he said they were his family.

After a few weeks, only a small proportion of the horn and ivory had been handed over. Then there were numerous phone calls of complaint from the hotel manager to Onity, who'd booked the deal. Mobina's 'family' were drunk most of the time and running up a hefty bill. Meantime, the Chinese group were pressing for results. They'd agreed a deal for 250 kilos of rhino horn and expected delivery. When asked, Mobina then demanded payment for the small consignments he'd passed on, totally disregarding that he'd been told it was the whole deal or nothing. Onity was beginning to feel a pressure he did not like.

When he got the bill for Mobina's short stay at the hotel, Onity's face fell. Itemised was vintage champagne, wine at over £100 a bottle, five-course dinners and so much room service Onity wondered if Mobina was feeding his London relatives as well.

The bill came to well over £6,000 for a short stay – a hell of a lot of money in those days. As ever, Onity didn't hesitate to express his displeasure.

'Phaa,' spluttered Mobina with a dismissive flick of his wrist, 'what's six grand? Six fucking grand when I'm going to bring us in a fortune. That's me that's bringing us in the payday. Me.'

'It's six grand out of my pocket,' growled Onity, 'not yours.' He already knew that Mobina was skint. We'd even had to pay for his flights to London.

'I could pay, you cunt,' Mobina snarled back. 'You know I could pay.'

Onity sighed, knowing exactly what was coming next – he'd heard it so often before.

'Just pay me now for what I've delivered.'

Onity had received several small deliveries of rhino horn totalling around twenty kilos, nowhere near the full load. Some ivory had been delivered too. He'd already asked his Chinese contacts if they'd pay for that lot upfront and the answer was no. But Onity decided that something had to be done. There was a very bad smell about this deal.

At the hotel's reception, Onity was about to pay the bill and say that Mobina was booking out when the manager appeared and declared very politely and quietly, 'Thank you, sir. We're sure your guests will be very happy at their next hotel.' Message received loud and clear. But, since Onity had planned to move them out anyway, he didn't ask the manager why he'd delivered it.

Onity's plan was to move Mobina in to his own home. But he didn't fancy that for too long, so he would have to go back to the Chinese pronto and ask again if they'd buy the available consignments. Onity can be a persuasive bloke and he was optimistic of success – always a bad state of mind.

The very next day, he met with his Chinese contact in London. Bad news – the Chinese New Year had just begun and his contacts in the Far East took that very seriously. It would be at least two weeks before they'd be available for business.

Onity went home feeling deeply depressed. It didn't help when he found Mobina drunk as a jakie again. In fact, he couldn't remember ever seeing him sober. He had no problem with drinking but Mobina was a loud drunk and was getting on Onity's nipples. Late that night, when they were alone, Onity's girlfriend told him that Mobina had pissed the bed the night before. This wasn't good. Was that why the hotel manager had been so insistent he moved on?

Next morning, Mobina rose late and, as he downed some Jack Daniels for breakfast, he immediately launched into a tirade about getting paid for what he had delivered. Onity was explaining, yet again, about Chinese New Year when his girlfriend came into the room and whispered to him that Mobina had wet the bed again.

'That is fucking IT,' screamed Onity storming upstairs, throwing all Mobina's clothes into his case. Downstairs he yanked the front door open and chucked the case out on to the street.

When he made it into the living room, Mobina sussed what was going on and lay down on the floor banging his fists and feet, screaming. 'Give me my money, you English cunt. What do you think I am? A daft Paki?'

The Onity I know would have given the man a right slap for suggesting he was a racist. Instead, he didn't reply but lifted Mobina up by the scruff of the neck one-handed and hoisted him bodily out of the house. 'FUCK OFF FOR EVER, YOU SCROUNGING PRICK.'

Once upon a time, Onity had been an extremely fit and strong man, capable of all sorts of daring feats – climbing into so-called secure buildings and the like. He had kept up his fitness regime. This was a man you didn't mess with. Even pissed, Mobina sensed that. Off he went without a grumble, not even asking for some of his rhino horn or ivory back.

On the phone to me soon afterwards to explain everything that had happened, Onity had calmed down a bit and said, 'You know I said to that drunken bastard that I wasn't even sure he'd delivered rhino horn to us. I mean, how the fuck would we know, Paul?'

I had to agree but I reminded him that the tiny early sample passed to the Chinese dealers had passed their chemist's test. End of conversation.

A good few years later, I met up with Onity again and he had a small confession to make. He and his woman had a rich and varied sex life that often involved a few lines of charlie. Onity found himself out of cocaine one night but definitely in the mood for some sheet wrestling. Yet didn't he just have a load of good old rhino horn? It had to be top gear as an aphrodisiac if people were willing to pay all that dosh for it.

So, late that night, he sat on his own slicing a piece of the rhino horn and carefully grinding it into a fine powder. It was tough going, wearing out three razor blades. Then he snorted it, just like he did with coke. He didn't know if that's what you were meant to do with rhino horn but it seemed to work with most things.

Upstairs in bed he lay down beside his ready and more-than-willing lady and waited. And waited.

'Know what fucking happened, Paul?' he asked. I was beginning to regret him starting the tale. There are some things you don't tell anyone, even pals. 'Nothing. Then more nothing. Then something did.' He paused and drank some beer. 'My fucking nose started to bleed. I don't mean dribble, I mean Niagara. Wish to fuck it was Viagra. Bled for four days solid. I knew we'd been sold crap. Took the whole load and dumped it in the garbage.'

Trying to stifle my laughter but not trying too hard, I asked him, 'Do you know what ivory looks like?' He thought for a minute then said, 'Fuck me. You mean I was snorting elephants' stuff?'

'Sounds a bit like it.'

'That little cunt Mobina – wait till I get my hands on him.' He was growling but also laughing. 'You seen him lately?'

The answer, of course, was no. Nor have I seen him since. Some players do that. One day, they just disappear. As we'll see, it happens to bigger fish than him. Much bigger.

4

HERE TODAY . . .

Frank the Yank was a smoothie, all right – silver hair, a fit man in his sixties, with smart and expensive suits – and could he talk? What is it about me that I never can quite trust someone who is so bloody suave?

My good friend Artorro introduced us. Artorro was a London man, well known to all the big firms and the best of faces. But to Joe and Jessie Public? No way – just proving how clever my pal was.

Definitely old school, by the early 1990s, Artorro was in his sixties. Almost from the minute he stepped into long trousers, he was a skilled and successful robber. By his early adult years, he was one of London's top men on bank jobs, specialising in cracking safes respected by all the faces, all the top firms. A man who could be trusted, he was so professional that, one time, he had tried to count up the entire wardrobes of clothes he had destroyed and the houses he had given up in order to cover his tracks but he'd had to stop halfway through – it was taking too long. Small and wiry, like so many Glaswegians of his generation, Artorro was also distinguished. Though he never wore fancy suits and preferred roll-ups to ready-made fags, folk meeting him for the first time and clueless about what he did sensed his power – a top man, in other words. A top man in many people's book.

Frank the Yank was in London on business – big business, worth millions – but not quite legit business so he needed help. Who better than the much-respected Artorro?

Bearer bonds were in Frank the Yank's possession. Now, by the 1990s, I considered myself well versed in the ways of the street and of straight business and finance but I didn't have a clue about bearer bonds.

Artorro and Frank, however, were well up to speed. 'Y'see, Paul,' Frank started, with much more of a drawl than I can write, 'they are issued by governments in times of need – when they have to raise funds and in a hurry.'

I knew all about that state of affairs.

'Usually in time of a major international conflict.'

'You mean war, Frank?' I asked, taking the piss a bit.

'War? Yes, indeed, war would create the kind of economic climate I'm referring to.'

He fitted that American stereotype – no sense of irony.

'Bonds would be offered at certain values but always large sums with the government undertaking to pay compound interest on them.'

That I understood. It meant big bucks especially if they weren't cashed in for a long time. As Frank the Yank continued to tell me about bearer bonds, I'd cast innocent looks occasionally towards Artorro and, by the slightest movement of an eye – the way he drew on his fag, the movement of a hand – he'd tell me that the guy was on the straight and narrow with his story. So far.

The most interesting thing about these bearer bonds was that, once they were purchased, they simply belonged to the person who had them – thus bearer. As Artorro explained to me later, when we were alone, over the years, these bonds would be sold on – a handy way to raise some dough without the authorities knowing. Occasionally, of course, they'd be stolen from people careless enough to leave them outwith bank safe deposit boxes. Surprise, surprise, they'd also get copied – big time.

The bonds themselves weren't that complicated or secure. A skilled counterfeiter could soon run a few hundred off and a lot of them did. So, when someone like Frank the Yank turned up looking to sell some, you had to be suspicious.

Artorro, as ever, suspected the worst – a set-up. He'd served some time, for sure, but many cop files on robberies were still open and he knew the cops had his name marked down for them sometimes decades later. He was good – very good – so, when Frank the Yank had made contact with him, Artorro was curious but cautious, even though they had been introduced by a third party who he trusted. That's why he brought me in. A second pair of eyes and ears and as big a dose of wariness as he had.

At a special meeting with more subterfuge than a James Bond movie, Frank the Yank displayed his four bearer bonds to me and Artorro. They were Anglo-American and had been underwritten by the US government in 1941, the early years of World War Two. More interesting, their numbers were in sequence – something like 17348, 17349, 17350, 17351. So far, so good.

Artorro had seen and handled bearer bonds before – the real thing – and he confirmed these looked genuine. But that, by itself, wasn't enough. What interested Artorro was a receipt stapled to one bond indicating that the compound interest had been cashed in. It wasn't solid proof, of course, since receipts and government stamps and seals can be counterfeit too, yet it did take Artorro a step closer to accepting the bonds as the real deal.

The two of them sat and chatted about the bonds, types of interest and so on. At least it sounded like a friendly chat though I knew that the bold Artorro was actually grilling Frank the Yank. With the bonds, I was well out of my depth but I kept listening to every word. All learning is good and maybe worth a few quid as well. Bonds I didn't know but people? They were a different matter. And Frank the Yank was intriguing me big time.

'Frank, how did you get these?' I asked when there was a lull in their conversation. It was a bit direct at a sensitive time in the discussions but this guy was a stranger to us, having appeared out of the blue from New York – or so he said.

'Yeah, I appreciate the inquiry, Paul,' he replied, saying my name in a long, whiny transatlantic way I was already beginning to hate.

'The short answer is that I was left them by an . . .' He left the sentence unfinished. 'By an associate.'

'That was good of him,' I said, trying to make sure there was no sarcastic tone in my voice. 'Close were you?'

'Close?'

God knows what that word meant where he came from. Isn't it really inconvenient as well as interesting how the same words in the same language can mean totally different things to different people? 'Aye – friends – you know?' I explained. 'Like good buddies.'

'Yeah, OK. OK. Yeah, we were close as friends and . . . um . . . business associates.'

'So, why come all the way over here to cash the bonds in?' I was getting to my point so pushed ahead. 'And why through people like us? Why don't you just go to a bank or some finance man?' Frank the Yank had offered an explanation before, of course, but it had been all too vague for my liking.

'My associate wasn't . . . um . . . How d'ye say? Was not official. How d'you guys say it again? He was not legit – not entirely.'

'So are the bonds ripped off?' This stranger had come to two well-known players, after all, not the Boy Scouts.

'Ripped off?'

It was funny but I thought 'ripped off' was something we'd borrowed from the Americans but he didn't understand it – either that or it was my accent.

'Stolen,' I explained and noticed Artorro throwing me a wee look out of the corner of an eye.

'Yeah, I appreciate your directness, Paul. I like that in a man. But it's a bit more complex than that.'

By my side Artorro threw a look that I knew meant that he was expecting this – that it's always more complex with bearer bonds.

By their nature, Bearer bonds were for handing over, trading, and this meant they were wide open to stealing. Each bond was just like a bank note – whoever possessed it owned it – but worth a fortune. Artorro agreed with Frank the Yank that his bonds were worth several million pounds – if genuine. So, by stealing just one of those bonds, you'd be in clover. The bearer bonds had been around for so long, passing from person to person, that it was almost impossible to know if they had arrived in your possession by an entirely legitimate route – even if they'd come from an otherwise totally straight source. So Frank the Yank had us at a disadvantage. Or at least the bearer bonds put us in that position. But I was still curious as to why he flew all the way to London from New York to do business.

'You not welcome back home, Frank?' Any Londoner would have known that I meant 'wanted by the cops'. God knows what he made of my choice of phrase but he answered by question nevertheless.

'Y'know, Paul, this puts me in a difficult position.'

Just as I reckoned, he was going to tell us sod all.

'I have no desire to be unfriendly but I can't tell you the whole story. My position is . . . yeah . . . awkward. Y'see I work for certain agencies,' he hesitated and allowed the word 'agencies' to sink in, 'that are – hmmm – let us say secret in their work – their national work.' This time the emphasis was all on 'national'. 'So, y'see, I cannot be seen to be participating in such financial dealings back home. If they found out, there could be the most dire retribution.'

So Frank the Yank was hinting loud and clear he was in the FBI or the CIA or whatever. Come to think of it, his hints could almost be attributed to the Mafia as well but we knew that wasn't true. Artorro had that checked out through an old mate of his, Joey Pyle, Don of Dons in London and the main man in England as decreed by the New York Mafia families.

Frank the Yank was passing muster so far and Artorro didn't want him to be vulnerable or public in any way except ways he chose. So Frank booked out of his plush hotel and moved to a safe house in Battersea, in a big mansion that Artorro owned and, indeed, where one of his old uncles lived. You couldn't get safer than that and it was a measure that Artorro thought there was a chance of a big earner through The Yank.

Artorro did some other checking on Frank the Yank, of course, using sources he didn't reveal to me. It wasn't because of a lack of trust – just how you have to treat some contacts. You can't reveal them to anyone, even your most trusted friend, since what he might do is share that with his most trusted friend who in turn shares it with his most . . . and, before you know it, every street player in the country knows about your contacts.

The reports back to Artorro were reassuring. Not on Frank the Yank – it seemed no one knew anything about him, either that or they weren't willing to reveal what they knew. But they knew about the source of the bearer bonds – the bloke who'd left them to Frank – and he would only have had kosher bonds, apparently.

So, eventually, Artorro took the next step and began to introduce Frank the Yank to certain faces, big-time boys now gone semi-legit and with enough money to be interested. The Yank started out by saying he wanted around 70 per cent of the bonds' face value for a no-questions-asked cash sale. He was soon advised that his cut would be a lot less than that and, if he wasn't happy, he could go and see a broker.

These faces trusted Artorro, of course, but still asked Frank a load of questions. Well, there was a lot of money at stake here. Several times, he hinted again at his involvement in some arm of the security services back in USA. If he was trying to impress these guys, he'd have to try a lot harder. Then again, he might just have been telling the truth.

It got to the stage where small sums of money were paid by some of the faces – goodwill money to keep the deal on. Not so much as they'd miss it and not so much as to make Frank a rich man – far from it – but enough to embarrass certain people because, just at the point where the big deals were to be struck on the bearer bonds, Frank the Yank disappeared. One minute, he was happily living there, in the old mansion in Battersea – the next, he was gone. He didn't even leave a message but did leave clothes, shaving gear, even money. Only he and the bearer bonds had gone.

Word was put out among the London firms who can usually trace anyone in that city in a blink – even those who go underground. No sign.

Years later Reg and I wrote a novel, *Deadly Divisions*, and used bearer bonds as part of the plot. I'm eternally grateful to Artorro for the knowledge he passed on. We also paid a little homage to Frank the Yank by having an American on the loose in Glasgow – though there the resemblance ends. The fictitious Yank met an unfortunate end at the hands of a hooker and her pimp and ended up in the Clyde.

The real Frank the Yank? Well, he and the bonds haven't been seen again. Maybe the Met cops should be dragging the Thames? Then again, maybe he wasn't bullshitting when he claimed to be employed by the US Secret Service and the spooks came to take him home.

Who knows? Someone does; but, for the rest of us, it will have to remain a mystery. Isn't that just like real life?

Whatever happened to him, wherever he went, I hope Frank the Yank is OK. Whether he was working some scam or not, telling some porkies, I felt he was a decent man. I'll never learn if I was right or wrong – all I know is that I sensed the man was OK, the way we all make judgements about other human beings.

Some people turn out all right in spite of the trickiest of starts – like the next old-time guy I'm very fond of. You'll have to make your own mind up – all we'll do is tell you how it is.

5

IN THE NAME OF THE FATHER

Boss – Hugo Boss. The name always struck me as a good alternative to James Bond. It also passed that crucial vowel and S test. Well, how could you ever do James Bond without Sean Connery's speech impediment?

Me and a pal we call The Man Who Knows were in the Hugo Boss shop in Glasgow's city centre sometime in 2004 – one of my favourite shops, as it so happens. There I was looking at shirts and the word 'BEWARE' kept rattling loudly through my brain.

Pick a top men's shop, any shop where it costs a few quid for the gear, and that's where you're likely to bump into other faces. Well, they have the money, the time and the inclination so why shouldn't they shop at the best? But, if one or two of them bumped into me, they'd forget their wardrobes in a whisper and be on my case. Not good. It would upset the staff. Can't have that. So I was on the shifty-eye lookout.

There was another good reason 'BEWARE' was screaming in my nut. It might have been twelve years before but it still hurt. Still haunted. In 1992, I had a stack of gear. Whatever was in fashion, I'd try it. I'd bought a shirt by Versace, I think it was. Great shirt – well made but bright, highly patterned. At the time, it was the bee's knees. Honest.

Then I was tried for Fatboy's murder and a host of other charges. The cops, so confident of a result, kept me banged up in solitary and took me to court everyday in a cavalcade of force. Necessary? No. Bad publicity for me? Yes. Good publicity for them? Yes. Did they look like arseholes when I was found not guilty on every charge? You fucking bet.

Immediately afterwards, I was being hunted by every bugger from the media so I offered an exclusive to Steve Wilkie, a big bloke I knew who worked at *The Sun*. They had done all right by me in the past so I could trust them. No payment – just get me the fuck out of there. All the attention from the public was a compliment but, in truth, I was embarrassed – couldn't handle it – so off I went to an anonymous hotel in a fast car.

Every day, they interviewed me. Every day, they took more snaps. One morning, I crawled out of bed, hung-over as usual, shaved, showered and put on that bloody shirt for the day's photos. For some reason, that pic worked. Well, they thought so – while I thought I looked like I was wearing somebody's bad taste in wallpaper. Not only did *The Sun* use it but, for twelve solid years, every other newspaper did so too. In fact, they're still using it now in 2006.

The shirt is long gone, passed on to a gay pal of a pal. The shirt is gone but haunts me still. So, that day in 2004, I was wary of making the same mistake of having a bad shirt day – that and of lurking hit men and stalking coppers.

And that's when he spoke to me. 'Paul?'

I looked up from the hangers into the handsome face of an older guy, maybe in his fifties, but fit, strong. He had silver-grey hair and a strong barrel chest. At a glance, you could tell that the sleeves of his suit weren't empty but full of rock-hard bicep and tricep.

'Do you no' know me?'

'What?' I threw him a sour dismissive look. 'Did you arrest me once or something?' I'd marked him down as a retired cop – one of the Serious Mob who were always more impressive than your average PC Plod. After all, smartly dressed as he was, what was a man of his age doing in Hugo Boss? He was on my tail. Those bastards never retired.

'What?' He looked back at me, hurt all over his face. Then a smile cracked the side of his mouth and lit up his eyes – a handsome fucker, right enough. 'You think I'm the polis?' A bigger grin spread across his face as he enjoyed the thought. 'Oh, Paul, I knew your da and ma when you were . . .' He manoeuvred his flat palms in front of him trying to decide what size of baby I'd been at that time. 'When you were young. See me?' he went on, obviously responding to my sceptical grimace. 'I'm your uncle – your honorary uncle.'

'Right you are and I'm the Chief Constable of Strathclyde Bogies.' Who did the old cunt think he was fooling?

'Right. Aye, I've been posted missing for a long time,' he looking almost thoughtful as he glanced downwards at his highly polished shoes. 'But phone Jenny and ask her. It's time to make amends. Tell her . . .' and he told me his name.

Jenny is my mum's name and, outside on the pavement, mobie clutched against one ear, a lit Kensitas Club in the other mitt, I spoke to her.

'A lovely man,' she was telling me. 'Your father got on that well with him. You'll be OK with him.' Want a recommendation with me? Get Jenny Ferris to say you're OK.

Back in the shop, under the ever-watchful eye of The Man Who Knows, I walked up to my new honorary uncle and shook his hand warmly.

We spoke and spoke that day of the old times – the times when my father and the Ross Street San Toi were still very much alive and on the hoof. My new uncle was younger than my father but had gone on to work with him on a few jobs as well as socialising with him. It was as if the world of my dad, a world I'd lost, had suddenly been opened up to me. I'd gone looking for a shirt and had found a bit of my own history. Greedy for it? You bet but could I trust this man?

Looking back, the whole scene was a bit spooky. I'd gone into the city centre for a meeting but, with some time to spare, I'd decided to do a bit of shopping. Not having lived in Glasgow for many years, he'd travelled quite a distance for a rare meeting with an old pal but, arriving early, he'd decided to do a bit of shopping.

Independently, we'd both decided to go into Hugo Boss. Yet we didn't find new clothes – we found each other. Serendipity – I love it when that sort of thing happens.

We moved out of Hugo Boss to chat. Well, that place is just so quiet people can hear what you're thinking never mind saying. Sitting in my new uncle's car, I could see he was doing very well for himself. The scent of leather and walnut filled the interior of the top-of-the-range, classy four-by-four. You weren't going to get much change from fifty grand for that motor.

It was also plain that we didn't need to leave the shop. In fact, we could've made an announcement to the world that we were about to have a confidential chat and invited them to listen. Or gone to the Pitt Street HQ of Strathclyde Police and sat with a squad of plainclothes in some interview room dripping with bugs recording every word. They still wouldn't have had a clue.

Many people in my world speak in a kind of code. It's a wise habit, some say. For most, it's a mixture of prison talk, street slang and initials. My companion did all of that and also mixed in some Jockney rhyming slang, old street words and nicknames he and only he had for some folk. For the general population, he might as well have been talking in tongues. For the sake of comprehension, I've not used our lingo here.

Taking precautions always impresses me but I wasn't yet totally sold on the old guy. He might well have been friends with my mother and father and a good friend too but people do change, as I've learned too often to my cost. So I pushed the boat out a bit further and asked him about how active my father had been in his younger day.

'As active as they get,' he replied, 'and good, very good. Come on and I'll show you a place we did when we were really young.'

That's what I wanted to hear from him. He drove through the busy city centre streets till we hit the old quarter near the Cathedral and the Royal Infirmary. Driving down High Street as careful as any Sunday driver in a brand new motor, he pulled in to the pavement. 'That's one we hit,' he said, nodding his head to the side. We were parked right next to a shop that had been there for as long as I could remember – even when I was a kid, it looked old, ancient. Trouble was it was a shop that sold religious goods – a Roman Catholic shop, selling holy medals, rosary beads, bibles and the like.

'You didn't rob the holy shop,' I said. It was one of the few times in my life I can recall feeling shocked.

'The what?' he asked, turning to look at me, confusion wracking his face.

'The fucking holy shop,' I repeated, nodding past him to the place's dusty window.

For the first time he turned round properly and looked. 'No, no, no,' a big smile cracking his face, 'not the fucking holy shop – not enough money in there.'

'So where?' I asked, feeling a bit relieved. I don't hold at all with religion but that doesn't mean I think any church should be ripped off.

'There,' again he nodded his head only slightly – this time not to the side but slightly down the High Street. 'Three down,' he muttered out of the side of his mouth not in the plain English used here but in his code. 'There was one of the biggest jewellers in Glasgow. Broad daylight. Panned in the window, filled our sacks and got the hell out of here.' As he spoke he put the car in gear and pulled gently away from the scene.

'How long ago was that?' I asked, also being impressed at any robbery there. That was a part of town that was always heaving with cops.

'O-o-o-h, must be over forty years ago at least.'

'Can you still remember the getaway route?'

He turned and looked at me with contempt. 'Of course I can.'

'Take me round it.'

'OK.'

And, with that, he skilfully indicated and steered the car into a U-turn – no mean feat in that busy street – and then headed on the old getaway route, talking me through every stage.

Driving was my skill and planning getaway routes my business, once upon a time. The man knew what he was talking about and no doubt. Over forty years later and he remembered every detail. This was no slouch. Even more impressive had been the confusion outside the shop. That had also all been down to him being so careful. It was an unsolved crime after all and he didn't want to run any risks. Not now that was all behind him. Not ever. Forty years later and still taking good care? I could see why my old man worked with him and got to love him like a brother. This was my kind of man.

He was a man who could link me back to a time before me – to my father and his generation. Help me understand who brought me into life and who gave me my values.

'Do you want to know anything else, Paul?' he asked, having driven and talked through the getaway route twice.

'Yeah, tell me about you,' I asked.

'About me?'

'About the young you and the folk around you then. Tell me how it was. How it really was.'

'OK.'

Some tales they are. Here come the stories never before told. Stories of a time before this – a time that made us all and influenced our world. The stories of one villain I have come to love not as an honorary uncle but as the real deal.

Three short chapters where my name isn't mentioned follow. But am I there? As sure as if I'd been along side him, pulling some scam. Here is my past and a strong clue to my present. Here is the echo of a generation now almost gone. Better times? Worse times? You judge.

Here comes The Shark.

6

THE SHARK PUP

The Shark. The man who never sleeps, never stops and never misses a trick.

He was one of a big family – they made the best upbringing they could on the rough streets of Glasgow's east end. They were going to prosper even if that meant fighting, kicking and robbing all the way and that's just what they did.

By the time The Shark was a young man in the late 1950s to early 1960s, he had left behind the need to box every challenger in sight. All he wanted was a living – enough money to move away from the cramped squalor of a single-end in a tenement full of overcrowded single-ends. A reputation as a fighter was fine and he worked every day to be fit, strong and ready – very fit and always prepared – but a fighter's reputation was limited in its currency. What he needed was cash.

Two London men arrived in Glasgow looking for a bit of business. They had some watches to sell strictly off the record. Not a box of watches just four special ones – so special, they were looking for a couple of grand each. Even at that, it could be a quick profit for the right man with the cash to buy and the customers waiting to pay a decent price. The Shark had the latter but not the former but that wasn't going to stop him. All he needed was the watches.

A meeting was set up in the Royal Hotel in West Nile Street in the city centre. The two Londoners were cautious, almost paranoid, and insisted the meet take place in a windowless room deep in the basement – a very dark room. Checking that there was no one outside in the corridor, closing the door securely and jamming a chair against the handle, one of the Londoners finally revealed the timepieces, gently laying them on a table.

The Shark and his companion knew nothing about jewellery. Where they came from, there was hardly enough money for grub never mind baubles. But even the two teenagers could see that these were beautifully crafted watches and they were heavy – very heavy, made out of solid gold.

The two Glaswegians lifted the watches up carefully and made a great show of examining them – knowledgeable buyers needing to be convinced they were the real deal.

'It's too dark in here,' said The Shark, 'I can't see the pieces properly.'

The Londoners weren't happy with this call. They had spent a lot of time setting up a secure meeting place and now here was this Scottish youngster wanting to move to a place with better light. But the Londoners had a weak hand – they were desperate for the money and to ditch the watches, obviously white hot from some robbery.

Eventually they agreed that The Shark would be accompanied to a better-lit part of the hotel but The Shark's pal would stay in the basement with the other Londoner.

'It's still too dark in here,' said The Shark when they'd reached a room upstairs.

'Well, we're not going any farther,' replied the Londoner now with a shiny, damp upper lip and his eyes darting from side to side.

'Well, you can forget the deal,' declared The Shark.

The Londoner's eyes widened. This was not good news.

'You can't expect me to pay out all the shekels without seeing the goods properly. Well, can you?'

Again the desperate Londoner conceded and the two men moved to the hotel's foyer.

'Nah, still no good,' declared The Shark, after holding one of the watches close to his face, screwing his eyes in concentration, looking for fine detail he didn't know existed. 'I'll just take them to the doorway,' he declared and before there was any discussion The Shark had ambled over. But he didn't stop there. In a flash, he was through the door still holding the watches up to the light. But he kept walking faster and faster then took to his heels just as the Londoner emerged into the sunlight.

No one caught The Shark. Even a professional sprinter would have had a problem – that's how fit he was.

Back down in the basement the Londoners turned on The Shark's friend.

'He's done what?' the young Glaswegian shouted in horror. 'The dirty bastard, so he is. And he's away with the money as well. My fuckin' share too. Fuck.'

The panicking Londoners grumbled and moaned but they were amateurs compared to the teenage Glaswegian.

'Whit direction did he go in?' he demanded as he collared the Londoner who'd been outside. 'Up or down?'

The Londoner didn't understand.

'Up or down the fuckin' street? It's on a fuckin' slope, man.'

'Eh, up,' the Londoner finally replied.

'Aw that's fuckin' done it. He'll be in the Gorbals before you can blink. That cunt's got so many pals there, he'll be well holed up by now.'

Of course The Shark had no great connections with the Gorbals and that area was in the opposite direction but the young Glaswegian had gambled rightly that the Londoners didn't know that. He sat slumped on a hard, straight-backed chair his head in his hands. Even to the upset Londoners reckoned he looked a picture of despair.

'It was all ma money,' he finally spoke up. 'Had to borrow a good bit of it. What the fuck am Ah gonnae dae?' the sentence finished in a wail.

The Londoners had enough to deal with in coping with their loss. They were buggered if they were also going to have a distraught Scot on their hands. Worst of all was that the more upset he became the more incomprehensible his accent got.

'Fuckin'-bam- so-m-urr,' the Glaswegian boy moaned. 'Jist-a-fuckin'-mental-bam-annat.'

That was it. Now he was clearly delirious, raving, and that was his problem not theirs. They showed him the door.

'How much you reckon these are worth?' he asked The Shark in the pub two blocks away from West Nile Street where they had arranged to meet.

'A grand – maybe a grand and half for a quick sale,' answered The Shark, shoving the pint of export across the table to his friend. He then took a large swig of his orange juice. The Shark didn't smoke, didn't drink and, if drugs had been readily available back then, he would have run a mile. 'They give you any hassle?' he asked, nodding to one side.

'Naw, I think they felt sorry for me,' his mate laughed. 'Besides . . .'

'I know,' interrupted The Shark, 'they were Fagans. Reset guys. Hands as soft as bank clerks. The pair of them would have problems giving a paper poke distress.'

The two pals laughed, excited by their success.

'A grand and a half each,' said The Shark's mate. 'We're fucking rich, man.'

'No' rich yet,' said The Shark, his face going serious though warm. 'But we're on our way. We're getting there.'

But would he?

7

HUNTING ALONE

'It's a beautiful stone as you can see,' said The Shark, passing the ring box over.

'Aye, aye,' the grocer was talking breathlessly, excited little pants peppering his words.

'Was that the kind of ring you were looking for?'

'Aye. Eh, aye, well maybe,' the grocer had regained his composure, drawn himself up straight, trying to act a little standoffish.

The Shark knew this man's style. They had done business before. Now he was getting ready to negotiate. The Shark knew the grocer wanted the ring – wanted it badly but only at the lowest price possible, as usual.

'Well, there's only a few like it,' The Shark went on. 'I got it from . . .' he hesitated, 'well, I can't really tell you where I got it from. Let's just say it's a Jewish family, diamond dealers in London. Top dealers. Been at that game for generations.'

The grocer was holding the ring up to the light, marvelling at the glints and rays thrown out by the stone as he turned it this way and that. 'Well, it's not as big as I thought you'd said it was,' said the jeweller.

Now The Shark knew the man had started negotiations seriously. Always the same. Obvious lust followed by a cooling and some negative observation then into the hard bargaining.

'Right,' said The Shark looking all thoughtful. 'I could get you another one. Not the same but very good and a bit bigger.' He let that hang in the air for a couple of seconds to see if there was a reaction.

None.

'A lot more expensive too. That's diamonds for you.'

'Aye, right enough, and how soon could you get that other ring?'

'It would take a week or two,' said The Shark, knowing that would be too long.

'Ah, pity,' replied the grocer. 'Our anniversary is next week. It's a special one. Want to get her something a wee bit special.'

'You don't get any more special than a beautiful diamond ring.'

The grocer was still playing with the ring, weighing it in his hand, holding it back up to the light.

'Especially at such a good price.'

'How good?' the grocer snapped back, turned abruptly and eyeballing The Shark.

'It retails at five grand but you can have it at three thousand,' replied The Shark.

He knew what was coming next – the barter. After some good-humoured haggling, they settled on two and half thousand. The grocer was well chuffed. Not everyone could get The Shark to reduce his prices.

The transaction was completed right there and then with the money handed over in well-thumbed bank notes and the ring passed the other direction. Everyone was happy.

Two weeks later, The Shark decided to pay the grocer a visit. The man ran a licensed grocer shop out in Twechar, an isolated mining village in the middle of Lanarkshire. It was the only licensed grocer shop in that town and back then, in the 1960s, people didn't have the cars or the motivation to travel anywhere else. The grocer was sitting on two licences – one to sell booze, the other to print money.

As The Shark pulled up to the front of the shop in his Jag, he saw workmen with their vans and equipment digging up the road. They were just ordinary workies and he thought nothing of it.

Inside the shop the grocer seemed in not such a good mood, though sometimes that was hard to notice.

'How did your wife like the anniversary present?' asked The Shark.

'Great,' replied the grocer. 'Loved it. I was right in the good books for days,' he winked a knowing wink, probably meaning he got his leg over for the first time in months. 'But, eh, see the workmen?' the grocer asked, thumbing over his shoulder.

'Yeah. You can't really miss them.' The Shark wasn't joking. There were six big vans and at least twenty men, all busy.

'Searching for the diamond.'

'What?'

'The diamond fell out of the ring last night when she was washing the dishes.'

'Oh, for Christ's sake!' cried The Shark with great sympathy.

'She blames herself,' said the grocer sadly. 'She usually takes the ring off when she's washing up.' He shrugged. 'Forgot, didn't she? Hasn't been able to force herself out of bed all day. I'm worried for her, she's that depressed.'

At that, the shop door opened and in strolled a man in a donkey jacket and muddy boots with a half-smoked roll-up hanging from his lip. He was the gaffer of the workmen and he'd come in to report that they had cleared all the drains and searched them as thoroughly as they could but no joy. They could try further down the drain system but they'd have to get the local council's permission and that would take time and cost a bit. It wasn't looking good for the grocer and he knew it.

The grocer was a hardman in business. He treated his customers like shite but his wife ruled. He doted on her. Spoiled her. Danced to her every whim. She was humanity's revenge on the grocer. He didn't see it that way, of course. He thought it was love.

'What can I do?' moaned the grocer looking wistfully in the direction of his bungalow next door where his wife lay in a darkened room, the curtains drawn, not speaking to anyone, least of all him.

'I'm really sorry,' said The Shark. 'Truly sorry but . . .'

'I know,' butted in the grocer, 'you shouldn't take risks with fine jewellery – that the setting is the weakest part of any decent ring.' He fancied himself as knowledgeable in such matters.

'Aye. Sorry,' apologised The Shark sadly, 'I know you know.'

The grocer was nodding his head in agreement. 'Och, you know, she just gets so down,' the grocer was looking in the direction of his house again. 'I'd do anything to fix it for her. Even buy her another ring. What's money, eh? What's money?' said one of the meanest men The Shark had ever met. And that was saying something.

'Would you go that far?' asked The Shark.

'Aye, in a blink.'

'You know,' said The Shark, 'I wasn't going to come here today. Meant to go elsewhere but something told me to pay you a visit.'

The grocer was looking at him with dull, disinterested eyes.

'Mind I said that the ring came from a limited edition of five rings?'

The grocer nodded.

'Well, I had two. Still have the second one. Almost identical. Not identical though. No two stones are ever the same.'

'Do you have it on you?' Now he was interested.

'Strange enough, aye. I came here to show you some fur coats I've got. Lovely coats at a great price. Knowing how much you like to treat your missus well. But I put the other ring in the car thinking I'd go on and see somebody else that might be interested.'

'Is it . . .'

'In the car? Aye, I came here first.'

Half an hour later, a very happy grocer had bought another ring from The Shark, this time paying the asking price of £3,000 without negotiation or question – insisting that he paid the asking price. For good measure, he bought a fur coat for his wife, forking another £1,500.

'A wee treat for her,' he said to The Shark. 'She's been that down all day.'

With the deal done, money and goods exchanged hands, The Shark was leaving the shop when he stopped and turned.

'Remember and tell your wife . . .'

'I know,' said the grocer, 'I know. She'll be taking that ring off her finger every time she goes anywhere near soapy water and a drain. Once bitten, eh?' he said, shaking The Shark's hand vigorously as he happily showed him out the door.

'Aye, once bitten right enough,' laughed The Shark walking away with a cheery wave.

Towns like Twechar have eyes that outsiders don't see. The place will look deserted of folk but the folk see you, the outsider. The Shark had often wondered about that, comparing it with his own city background in Glasgow where, in overcrowded areas teeming with folk, people could pass right by some accident or murder and not see a thing. But Twechar was different. That's why he kept a straight, sober face as he drove the big Jag carefully and easily till he was miles from the place. Then he started to laugh. And laugh. Till the tears were streaming down his face and he thought he'd have to pull the motor over to avoid crashing.

'Serve you right, you wee fucking miser,' he spluttered out loud through his chortles, 'serve you bloody well right.'

The year before, the grocer had conned The Shark on a deal and then committed the cardinal sin of denying that he'd done so. Now he was trying the same con again – The Shark had found that insulting. So, when the grocer revealed that he wanted a ring, a special present for his wife, The Shark knew he had just the rock for him. It looked like a diamond all right – looked like the real thing. There was just one problem – it disintegrated when put in warm water and detergent. The Shark had picked the rings up in a job lot for a few quid. Now the grocer had paid thousands for rubbish – twice. He wouldn't fuck with The Shark again. It was payback time.

The Shark was getting there all right. But where would it lead?

8

SHARK WATERS

It was a crisp, clear day in Glasgow – the kind you get in spring or early winter that takes you by surprise, reminding you of the smell of the city. A green smell, even among the traffic. The Shark had no time to stop and sniff the breeze. He had business and he suspected it was bad business. He had a man to see about money.

The millennium had passed and gone and, with it, forty years of The Shark's life since that incident with the grocer and the rings. A lot had changed since then. Well, it does, doesn't it? He was still upright, straight-backed, big-chested and strong looking with bright clear eyes. He'd remind friends of his age because he was rightly proud of it. He knew he looked a good fifteen years younger than he was and he was as strong as an ox, with a heart like a lion. He'd earned that sparkle, that youth.

Even in his sixties, he worked out harder than the hardest workers-out of all – aspiring young boxers. He'd give most of those a good square-go for their money – just like he used to do decades before. As a snotty-nosed kid, sitting in that single-end in the east end of Glasgow, he'd promised to achieve two things in his life – physical strength and enough money to get out. He was a winner on both accounts.

The Shark was rich now and stayed in an all-together better place – had done for years. Even better – he was legit. No dodgy dealing for him. That was part of his past when it was the only way he could see to take that next step on the ladder.

Now and then but not often, he'd think of that hundred-yard

dash up West Nile Street with the watches stuffed into his jacket. Within a couple of days, he had his start-out money and he used it well. Did he feel bad about the men who he'd ripped off? Why should he? They knew the watches were blagged, for sure, and they'd have cheated him too – if he'd any money for them to steal.

The Londoners and the henpecked grocer who had conned him and tried again weren't the only ones he had put in their place. The list seemed endless. It was a hard world on the street but he reckoned it was even harder among the so-called legal business-men. They'd happily ruin you for a few grand and sleep well at night mumbling their mantra of 'business is business'. Where he came from, a using was a using and a user had to be put in their place.

The Shark had put a lot of users in their place. Not something he was proud of, though not ashamed either. That was life. And life goes on. It was now a new millennium and, unlike most of the folk he grew up with, he wasn't dead or booze addled or sitting at home regretting lost years spent in jail. He was out there, active, rich and, even better, legit.

But that fine crisp day in Glasgow he wasn't reminiscing or even thinking of retiring. He was on business and he smelled a rat. A local businessman who owned a flash hotel had entered into a deal with another bobber and weaver, a huge man weighing at least twenty-six stones. The deal had been set up by The Shark and he, in turn, had brought in some of his business associates – pals they were, as well, and trustworthy.

The deal was all above board and they had each invested heav-ily at around quarter a million. It had worked and it was now pay-day with most expecting returns of around two million – except nothing was forthcoming.

The Shark went on the case. He knew The Fatman was an expert at all sorts of financial shenanigans – legal, of course. He knew the hotel owner was nothing but a con merchant wrapped up in expensive suits. The man had run with the top gangsters in Glasgow when young but then so had so many of his type. Some habits he hadn't lost, especially where making a few quid came into it.

The Fatman and the hotel owner were meeting up, The Shark's sources told him. That day, he was on his way to interrupt them, confront them. He had introduced good friends who had put money up in good faith on his word. The Shark couldn't let that go. Who could?

The meeting must have ended early because there, coming down that city-centre street, was The Fatman, striding out in that arm-swinging, waddling walking way of his. The Shark was in front of him in a flash.

Words were had. Polite words – that was The Shark's way. But he always knew when he was smelling shite and that was what The Fatman was giving him. Worse, he thought he could get off with it.

There, on that busy city-centre street full of shoppers and office workers on lunch breaks and *Big Issue* sellers and buskers and traffic wardens pretending to be busy, The Shark did one of the things he has always done best. He swung a punch at The Fatman and knocked him to the deck. The Shark was over him and on him in a flash. One punch didn't make a reckoning in his book. As he pummelled into the prone body, The Fatman reached up and did all that he could do, wrapping The Shark in a bear hug and clinging on for life. With twenty-six stones of humanity gripping and pulling him down with the strength only terror can bring, The Shark, even at half his age, would have been struggling. That day, aged over sixty, he struggled too – but he managed.

Somehow pushing a hand and an arm free, The Shark got hold of The Fatman's face. 'Game over,' he thought to himself and it was. He gripped and ripped and tore. The Fatman's bear hug disintegrated and, in an instant, The Shark's other hand grabbed hold of his other chubby cheek.

God knows what the city-centre pedestrians made of it all. Two grown men – one vastly overweight, the other silver-haired – lying on the pavement, as one howled and the other tore his face from his skull.

As The Shark stood up, tidied himself and began to walk away, he turned and looked down. On the pavement, The Fatman's knees were twisted and both hands seeped blood and skin as they held the sides of his head, his mouth hanging open in a silent scream.

The Shark had made his mark, just as he had been taught to do by his older brothers all those years go in the east-end schemes.

'Well, he cheated me and worse,' The Shark said later. 'He cheated my friends. We eventually got the money we were due and that was all legal. But that day on the street was personal. It was about principles. Guys like The Fatman are used to legal battles – that's their territory. Some kinds of human behaviour deserve more – deserve the old rules, the old justice. Street justice. That's what I gave him. That's my territory.'

The Fatman's still in business. Word has it he has spent a fortune on plastic surgery on his face. It worked but not entirely. If anyone notices the scarring on his face, these days he just says he had been involved in a head-on crash. He's not lying.

The Shark is still in business, still super fit and still looking decades younger than he is. He hasn't ripped any faces off lately. It's not something he hopes to do soon. But would he do it again in the same circumstances? When I asked him this, after that chance meeting in Hugo Boss, it seemed to be a different man I was talking to – a successful businessman, bright, smart, articulate and powerful.

But, as he took a sip of his chilled mineral water with a slice of lime, he didn't hesitate in his answer. 'Yes, of course,' he said. 'It's one of the things I was taught on the streets as a kid and it's right. Never forget your roots – that's rule number one.'

It's a rule someone else should have learned, as we're about to see. Especially when they tangled with the most feared men in Glasgow.

Meeting The Shark got me thinking of tales other people of my generation had told me and thinking not just about where my own values came from but also about certain people who influenced me big time – sometimes by trying to harm me. There was one guy in particular who fits this category. For the rest of my life, my name will probably be linked to that of Arthur 'The Godfather' Thompson – mainly for the worst. Why was it that my father and my uncle Bertie felt able to warn me about working with him all those years ago? What was it that made him more dangerous than men who were even more powerful than he was?

What made Thompson Thompson? Here's some insight into his early career – young Arthur Thompson as never seen before.

9

DAN, DAN THE DESPERATE MAN

Mendel Morris was a man about town – had been for years. To the outside world, he was a straight player, a successful entrepreneur, a man going places. And he was all of that – problem is he kept bad company.

Running illegal casinos, bookies, gambling dens, legal boxing bouts and bare-knuckled unlicensed scraps and all sorts of other enterprises were all part of Morris's business empire. It was during a one-foot-on-the-pavement, one-in-the-gutter period when many young men with gumption fought their way into respectability – if not for themselves in their lifetime, then certainly for future generations.

If Morris hadn't hired muscle, he would have gone under from pressure from the gangsters, the protection racketeers and those who just wanted to rob him. There was a queue, a very long queue.

Having acquired a good living, Mendel Morris hired the best. In the post-Second World War years, the best was a guy called Samuel 'Dandy' McKay, so named because of his taste for smart suits. If there was such a person as the Godfather of Glasgow in those days, McKay would have been a top candidate except for one thing – he worked for others. When Morris offered him good money for doing what he did best – wreaking havoc – McKay didn't hesitate.

Better that Morris lived with the devil than fought him. It was the only choice he had. Dandy McKay was a hardman extraordinaire. With blade or cosh, he'd tackle anyone and long before, back in his childhood, he had learned the secrets of fighting first and fighting dirty.

A measure of Dandy McKay can be seen from one wee tale. Morris had a very successful illegal gambling operation but he was concerned about competition from another that was run by one Peter Fox in his place, the George Hotel. Fox was no gangster and he didn't use threats or violence but running an illegal gambling den meant that he had to play the game in that seedy underworld he had joined so he hired his own muscle – a young man by the name of Arthur Thompson.

At that time, Thompson was known as a hardman himself who had been a bouncer and bagman for moneylenders. While Morris and Fox competed fiercely, they would never use violence themselves. But their troops had other ideas.

One day, Thompson came across Dandy McKay's brother. Without reason or hesitation, he grabbed him by the throat and pulled a razor down his face twice. Why? Because he was Dandy's brother.

It was an insult and injury that Dandy McKay couldn't tolerate. Thompson knew that and he was probably deliberately trying to provoke McKay. He succeeded but, if Thompson was expecting a straight challenge to him, he was sadly mistaken. Dandy McKay was as cunning as he was callous.

At that time, Mendel Morris was one of Britain's big boxing promoters – as big as the legendary Jack Solomons. As such, he was friendly with many characters from the boxing world, including Bobby Neil, a diminutive Scot who, by then, in 1959, had just won the British featherweight crown. Bobby had an impressive record of winning by knockouts.

Neil had sent Morris a box of his favourite cigars. Expensive ones they were and they came in a quality wooden box. Morris wasted no time in puffing his way through the bogies and the box was left lying around empty. These were solidly made boxes and people used them for all sorts of things like keeping special mementoes or photographs in or for their secret plank of dough if they didn't trust banks or couldn't declare their money officially. Dandy had other plans for Morris's box.

One day in 1959, a parcel arrived for Peter Fox. He sat at his desk and unwrapped the brown paper to discover a box containing . . . Now he was no expert, had never seen one before, but even Fox could see it was a bomb. All very clever, all very deadly, apart from one thing – it didn't explode. It could've been the end of Peter Fox for sure and the end of Mendel Morris's problems. Instead, Fox was very much alive and Morris's problems were just beginning.

Later that same day, Morris was at Ayr races, working at one of his legal activities as an on-course bookie. As usual, he was standing on a box so the punters could see where he was when they fancied a bet. He was marking up the odds on his blackboard, reading the tic-tac signals from his spies down by the horses and taking bets from the gamblers. As ever at Ayr, it had been a good day's business for him. Then he was punched right off his feet. Morris had barely scrambled to his feet when he was punched again.

'See you, you murdering bastard?' screamed Peter Fox, punching Mendel again. 'I'm going to fucking murder you!' And he punched his competitor again. It was the best entertainment of the day – or so the punters thought. Morris the bookie getting hammered all the way round the grounds. Some thought it justice – well, Morris was a bookie and bookies didn't have friends.

Those who knew Peter Fox thought it was well out of character. A hard businessman, sure, but he was no man of violence. Then again, they didn't know about the bomb. But how did Fox know it had anything to do with Mendel Morris? Just a wild guess? No. It was more to do with the label on the side in Bobby Neil's best handwriting – 'To Mr Mendel Morris . . .' with his home address and details.

Dandy McKay might well have been vicious but he lacked an eye for detail. There were going to be a few changes in Mendel Morris's camp. The question is would they be for the better?

10

THE CLOWN

Dandy McKay was in big trouble. Some guy who'd been creating hassle for Morris had been seen to – a little shotgun blast did the trick. Trouble was the cops were on McKay's tail.

All the backhanders Morris had been paying to certain polis wouldn't wash now. There were certain crimes that just had to result in a conviction. Besides, Dandy McKay was getting out of control and the cops wanted him off the street. So did someone else.

Mendel Morris had known nothing about Dandy McKay's plans as far as the bomb to Peter Fox were concerned – that simply wasn't the way Morris wanted to do business. But you couldn't sack guys like McKay. That was like inviting them to be your enemy – not a good call. So Morris let his cop contacts know that he wouldn't be too bothered if McKay ended up in jail and then sat back and let the mobster hoist himself with his own petard.

Morris told McKay that he wanted the hassling guy sorted out good and proper and then waited. Sure enough, the heavy went too far, as Morris knew he would. Now, with McKay being chased by the cops, Morris's next move was easy – do nothing.

Realising Morris wasn't for helping, McKay had no choice but to get on his toes. Glasgow soon proved to be too hot so he moved out to pals in Ayrshire. A few weeks later, they were feeling too nervy so he was off again – this time across the water to Ireland. But it wasn't far enough and Glasgow cops trailed him there and brought him back to face a trial.

With Dandy McKay jailed for ten years, Mendel Morris needed some help. He didn't have far to look – Arthur Thompson would do the trick. Loyalty? There didn't seem to be much room for that in Morris's world. He was about making money and would do whatever it took, hire whoever he needed. Besides, as lethal as Dandy was, he was a bit crude in his approach. Thompson was brutal all right but he had more of a brain and more staying power. Thus the working partnership of Mendel Morris and Arthur Thompson was formed, a partnership that many would see as the basis for Thompson going on to be called The Godfather of Glasgow.

Even in those early days, when he was still in his twenties, Arthur Thompson was active. He was robbing banks up and down the country – something that was easier then with the lack of security. But he was mainly working on what he'd need if he was going to be a strong street player – a solid base in Glasgow.

He had guys like Scadger Bain who ran messages for him and would tackle people like Charlie Elliot who was a police informer. There have always been grasses, just not as many then as now – drugs have seen to that. Thompson himself would go on to be a police informer and even work with MI5. But this was Thompson the young man, before he picked up those bad habits.

In those days, he did earn a reputation as one of the Glasgow faces who applied his brain as well as his brawn. One time, he was determined to shoot this guy but he couldn't get close enough to him. The bloke had eyes all over the place and, on the first sign of Thompson, the red warning flags were waved. But Arthur wasn't going to give up.

Every year, the university students in the city had a big charity fundraising day. On a particular Saturday, the city streets would be teeming with folk in fancy dress, rattling collecting cans. That would do nicely.

Thompson got hold of a collecting can – not that difficult in those days when charities were barely regulated. A clown's outfit and full-face paint completed the disguise. With his favoured Beretta tucked into his shirt, off out he went, heading for a pub where he knew his target was likely to be.

The city centre was engulfed in a carnival mood with a procession of brightly coloured floats winding its way through the main shopping streets, coloured streamers in the air, music blaring and the pavements invaded by fun-loving characters in costumes as varied as they were numerous. It was a day that brought a feel-good factor to the whole city centre and it was enjoyed by the public as much as the young students themselves. What they didn't know was that in their midst was a hit man in a clown outfit, ready to start blasting as soon as he spotted his target.

As an ambush, it was perfect. Who – even an ultra-cautious gangster – would suspect any threat to come from a clown? If he pulled the job off then took to the streets, how would they find him? There were hundreds of clowns about that day.

It was a dangerous manoeuvre though – not for Thompson but for the public. The streets were packed that day. One stray bullet could cost an innocent life. It would be like shooting into a barrel stuffed full of fish. Already Arthur Thompson was beginning to show that he didn't give a shit about others – something that would stay with him all his life.

Great planning, true cunning, ace disguise but sometimes all of that isn't enough – especially when the target doesn't show. The Charity Day hit didn't come off. If it had, it would've been way up there in the annals of true crime and been called something like the Clown Killer.

But there were those who thought that Thompson was a different sort of clown all together. Here's one incident that explains what was fast becoming his style.

Jim Strachan was a local entrepreneur who had grown up in Glasgow. In fact, as a teenager, he'd been a close ally of the Ross Street San Toi, particularly Sinatra and Willie Ferris. But Strachan had moved on, preferring to keep company with other businessmen – some legal, some not.

There was trouble brewing between Mendel Morris and Strachan and Thompson had put it about that he was going to give Strachan a seeing-to. It's the type of message you had to sort and fast if you wanted to keep your reputation. One day, Strachan was driving in his car with John Banks, a well-known bookie in the city, when he spotted Thompson. Pulling his car over and winding down his window, Strachan demanded, 'You looking for me, Thompson?'

Arthur Thompson, an angry sneer across his face, turned and looked down at the man. 'Why the fuck would I be wasting my time looking for you?'

'I hear you're putting it about that you're going to sort me out.'

'So whit?'

'So what about it?'

Two minutes later, a square-go had been agreed. A square-go is the term in Glasgow, in London it's a settler and other cities give it other names. It's still the same thing – a fight with fists and boots, the winner being the last man standing.

Inevitably bloody, brutal affairs, there are just a couple of rules – unwritten, of course. No weapons are to be used. No one else is to interfere. That's it – not exactly Marquess of Queensberry standards – and, what's more, even those two basic guidelines are all too frequently broken. Always best to bring along some insurance.

Jim Strachan didn't have such men hanging around him any more. He'd left all of that behind him but he knew where to look – back near where he had been brought up in Ross Street in the Gallowgate.

For the night, he hired two likely-looking characters by the names of Miller and Devine. Big, heavy-built guys with a face full of chib scars each, they'd scare the horses with just one look. With the two heavies right behind him, Jim Strachan parked his car and started walking the last few hundred yards towards the venue.

The square-go was going to be held at the White City in Govan. It was once the top greyhound racing venue in Scotland but had fallen into semi-redundancy, having been overtaken by the bigger

Shawfield Stadium. On the way there, two men hefting shotguns jumped out on Strachan and his minders. This is exactly the situation he had paid his two gorillas for. They took one look down the barrels of the shooters, turned on their heels and scarpered.

So much for looking the part – they turned out to be a pair of cowards. Jim Strachan had lost touch with his roots and, when he went back there, didn't know who was the real deal. Any street player in the Gallowgate could have told him to avoid those two. In street fighting, sometimes the smallest, most innocuous, fresh-faced man is the most vicious, best street fighter, with the heart of a lion. Appearances mean fuck all on the street. Jim Strachan had known all that but he'd forgotten it.

It was a costly error since he couldn't go to the square-go alone as it would be too dangerous. And now he was on the back foot with Thompson. As for Arthur Thompson, he had, of course, hired the men with the shotguns to carry out the ambush. He had never any intention of the square-go going ahead. That, apparently, was typical of the man from early on.

It wasn't that Thompson couldn't fight. He could but, compared with some street fighters, he was no match. In square-goes, there's no hiding place. Thompson didn't like that at all, especially since they were always watched by a large crowd, gathering together to see who was the toughest man, taking bets and taking sides.

Often the build-up lasted longer than the fight itself with excitement growing minute by minute among the spectators till it burst out in screams and yells with the first punch. In two minutes – sometimes even less – the square-go might be finished but what was for sure was, in that short time, the crowd would have witnessed extreme brutality. Many hardmen have been left permanently disabled as a result of a square-go.

If you bottled it in such a contest or if you were hopelessly beaten, the whole city knew about it before bedtime. Arthur Thompson wasn't willing to take that risk. He knew that Jim Strachan had been a top street fighter in his day and that day hadn't been too long before.

As the gunmen ambushed Strachan and his girls' blouses of handlers, Arthur Thompson was in the White City declaring that Strachan had crapped out. It was a no-show – that's how scared he must be of Arthur Thompson.

There were some who weren't fooled by Thompson's ploy and immediately marked him down as suspect. But the majority fell for the propaganda and he took another step towards becoming a top man. In street life, as in many other walks of life, it's often what people think of you that matters rather than what you have actually achieved. Fear is fear and Thompson wanted to be feared – no matter how that was achieved.

There were plenty, though, who didn't fear him – most famously, the Welsh Family who fought a bloody feud with him for over twenty-five years. When, in the 1960s, Thompson's car was blown up, killing his mother-in-law and injuring him, there was no doubt that the Welsh crew were behind it.

Thompson put the word out that he'd only sustained minor injuries. Even though they were enough to keep him in hospital for a long while, most people bought the line. In fact, his injuries were more serious than he ever let on.

Associates of Thompson were told that he been blinded in one eye and the sight in the other was impaired – damage to eyesight is common in bomb blasts. As he recovered in hospital, some of the guys decided to help him bit – as you do when a friend has had a bad time. At The Hanover club, owned by Willie 'The Milkie' Mortimer, a bloke called Jimmy Hendry had passed round a sheet for folk to sign up to for collecting money for spectacles for Arthur – or so he said. In those days, decent glasses cost a lot of money and, though Thompson could well afford them, it was a wee sweetener. The punters gave generously of course but Thompson didn't see a penny.

When he was eventually discharged from hospital, someone told him about the collection. Furious, he stormed round to The Hanover with some men and handed out hidings to the tea leafs. It wasn't the principle – it was the money. Thompson believed that cash had been given for him and, therefore, Jimmy Hendry had stolen from him. No one stole from Arthur Thompson.

Then again, maybe that was Arthur Thompson's principle – maybe *cash* was his god. In some ways, he was ahead of his time. By putting the old values behind him and being willing to rip off anyone, work with anyone, tell anyone what he thought they needed to know – as long as he got richer – maybe he was forging a new way of operating.

It was an approach that would see Thompson climb in the power stakes and live a long life till he died in his bed as others perished helping their friends or rotted in jail because they weren't willing to rat on their mates. It served him well all right – if money and fear is what you want. But, if you value friends, allies, people who will see you through, Arthur Thompson was the poorest man in the world.

As we'll see, there were others who had different values – tough men who earned respect. One, in particular, did it the hard way – that was the only way he knew.

11

COUSIN JOHN

The car snaked slowly through the Manchester streets. Passing through Eccles, skirting Cheatham Hill into Mosside, near the heartland of that great city. No one paid the car any attention. Why should they? If only they had known what was coming.

It was a good, class motor though not flash, didn't rev its engine or speed around the streets. A trouble-free, anonymous car – just as its occupants wanted everyone to believe. In fact, one of its occupants actually did believe it.

In the driver's seat was a guy called John from Glasgow. Temporarily down on his luck, he had phoned his cousin in Eccles, Manchester, and he immediately told him to come live with him for a while, do some work for him – just a bit of driving now and then, nothing too demanding.

The two men didn't even know if they were really cousins. A complex, messy extended family with as many honorary aunts and uncles as there were real ones saw to that. But they got on well so had never bothered to ask. Maybe you can actually choose your relatives – well, some of them at least.

The old buildings of Eccles looked like a mirror image of those in Maryhill in Glasgow where the two men were born and raised. John still lived there and he intended to go back when he got himself on his feet. His cousin didn't just live in Manchester, though – he ruled its streets.

Back in the early 1960s, when Glasgow was gripped by razor gangs, he had first made his mark as a teenager. In a city full of sword-waving, cleaver-swinging, chib-stabbing desperadoes, his was a name to be feared. Born into a poverty-stricken background, by rights he should have been sickly and weak. Although not tall or broad, he was still somehow gifted with a body and determination of remarkable strength and endurance. How does that happen? Just the luck of the draw? Or is it a result of coming from a long line of folk who'd struggled simply to live in terrible conditions? Many didn't even make it past infancy. Only the strongest survived – the special ones who defied the odds. Those were his people – just like my old man and even Arthur Thompson. Our man was younger than my dad and ages with Thompson but they all knew each other. Glasgow was that sort of place.

In the early 1960s, someone died in a gang fight against his mob. The cops had been hunting him since he was a nipper and he'd already been through every sort of institution and jail they could lock him up in. He'd even done time in borstal for a crime he didn't commit. Mind you, some folk might think that's fair enough since he'd never been done for other crimes he certainly had committed. The way he saw it was that the cops had him as a marked man and he was going to get chased for, maybe even set up for, this gang-fight murder. And that's when he skipped town to Manchester.

There was no reason to choose Manchester other than it seemed far enough away. Too many Scots on the hoof go as far as Blackpool and for good reasons. For years Scots, particularly Glaswegians, have been heading there for weekend breaks. During the public holiday in September, walking along the front, teeming with bodies, talking and laughing, you'd be forgiven for thinking you were in Glasgow. My folk simply take over the town. Over the years, many Glaswegians have forgotten to go home from Blackpool and, in dribs and drabs, they've ended up running so many pubs, hotels and clubs as well acting as the bouncers on every door – a home from home almost.

When, in the 1980s, my brother Billy went on the run after more than twenty years in jail for a crime of passion, that's where he went. He lived there happily, openly, with a woman and her kids, even working and being protected by the folk around him. He might have still been there to this day if he hadn't got nabbed.

But our man wasn't just getting away from the cops – he was also getting away from Glasgow and Glaswegians. The polis would have paid dearly for the info on his whereabouts and he was known to every single street player and gang member there was. Some were just as likely to pop down to that seaside resort for a break with their families or a weekend away with the boys. So Blackpool wasn't for him but Manchester would do. It was close but not that close – simple as that.

Most asylum seekers keep their heads down and act low key – not our man. He was simply incapable of it. 'If you stay still, you die' was his mindset and it was matched by a restless energy that would keep him on the go for days at a time without sleep – sometimes this was a dangerous thing for a street player on someone else's streets to do.

Even in this age when people flit from city to city all the time, players don't like someone else muscling in on their space. Back in the 1960s, it was even worse with gangs believing they owned their part of a city. Maybe they didn't own it but they certainly ruled it and what's the difference? That didn't faze our man one bit. He went straight to Manchester's top teams and faced them up without a flicker of fear. Why should he be scared? Manchester or Glasgow – one gang is very much like the next. Gangs had been his business for most of his life, one way or another. It must have spooked the hell out of the Manchester mobs but it worked. They left him alone and he prospered and stayed.

That had been almost thirty years before and he had stayed in Manchester ever since, only going back to Glasgow on visits to his family or to spook the hell out of guys like Arthur Thompson. By then Thompson was called the Godfather of Glasgow – that was a title the media gave him. Our man knew that and he also knew that he could take Thompson's power, position and money any time he wanted. He didn't want to – ever – but he wasn't going to let Thompson know that now, was he? He liked to play those sorts of games.

But a lot else had happened in those thirty years. Too many of his friends had died, too many bloodily. His own son had died and it had broken his heart. For a while, he had been almost a recluse, not answering his door or his phone, not caring about business deals that were going belly up.

When he eventually re-emerged, he had changed. He still looked smart, fit and hard and, somehow, he'd managed to keep his hair and its colour. That kind of grieving can wear someone out faster than life but he had a new habit – cocaine.

For years, he had hated drugs but, locked away in that house, he had decided to see what all the fuss was about, why people sacrificed their lives just to support an addiction. As ever, he did nothing by halves. His coke pipe was in use from the minute he woke up till the minute before he crashed. He didn't smoke coke for a high, fun or a buzz – he smoked it to live, to get by, to blot out his grief. He needed coke just to get him through the day. Maybe he still hated drugs. Maybe he hated life.

As Cousin John was driving him through the Mosside streets, he sat slumped in the passenger seat stoned out of his box as usual. John didn't seem to mind and certainly would never say anything to him. Besides, there were positive sides to his new-style cousin. All of his life, he had moved from one potentially explosive scene to another but not now. He was quieter, more at peace, safer to be around. Well, he was also getting on in years so it was time he was taking it easy – that's how Cousin John saw it.

'Pull in over there,' our man instructed, stifling a yawn. Those days he was constantly tired from the coke kicking out sleep till eventually he was driven to take some smack to help him pass out for a few hours.

'At the pub?' Cousin John asked.

'Yeah, down there.'

Cousin John knew what he meant – park at the side of the pub, not in view of the pub door but not too far away. Make sure the car was parked and pointing in a direction that they could leave in a hurry if they needed to. During the time John had been in Manchester, they had never needed to. But old habits die hard, he reckoned, having a wee smile to himself.

'I'll not be long,' said our man, stirring himself in the passenger seat and opening the door. Standing on the pavement, he pulled the collar up on the ankle-length leather coat that he was wearing as ever. Leaning down and putting his head through the passenger door, he added, 'And keep . . .'

'I know, I know,' Cousin John laughed, turning to face him, 'keep the engine . . .' The sentence died in his mouth and his jaw fell open as he saw inside his cousin's open leather coat and spotted the Uzi dangling there from a strap.

'Back in a minute,' said our man, slamming the car door and striding towards the pub.

Rab Carruthers was paying a wee visit – and it wasn't a social one.

12

A WEE VISIT

It wasn't like in the movies. When Rab breezed through those pub doors with the Uzi under his coat, the place didn't fall into deadly silence. A few folk turned to eyeball who had come in and turned away again, back to their pints and pals. Then Rab let loose hell.

Standing by the door in the packed pub, he swung the gun out of his coat and started blasting. Smoke and noise shattered the place. It only lasted a minute but, for the boozers hitting the deck, falling behind tables and chairs, their hearts thumping in their chests, it must have been the longest minute ever. They weren't to know Rab was firing into the ceiling and they weren't going to stop and ask.

'LISTEN UP, YOU CUNTS,' Rab roared once the noise of bullets had stopped, leaving a total and eerie silence now. 'My money better be down here by nine o'clock the night. I'm coming to collect.' With that, he rattled his last few bullets into the ceiling, slid the Uzi back into the cover of his coat, turned on his heels and marched out of the pub.

Cousin John in the car was close enough to have heard all the shooting. By the time Rab slipped back into the passenger seat, John's mood had changed from laid-back to wired to the moon.

'What the fuck was all that about?' asked Cousin John, crunching the gears into first and jerking the motor away at speed.

'Calm the fuck down, John,' Rab soothed. 'Just easy with the motor, eh? Nice and easy now.'

Not a player and not having had any previous experience of all of this, John just didn't understand that, when driving away from such scenes, you took your time, driving carefully and within the law. All that TV stuff with screeching tyres was like having a big sign over the car declaring that you were the bad guys.

'What was all that about, Rab?' John asked once they were well on their way.

'What? That? Just a wee bit of debt collecting.'

Behind him in the pub there was chaos. So many bullets had been fired into the ceiling that it had collapsed, filling the air with choking white dust. Slugs had also peppered the actual roof, sending broken slates, ripped felt and chunks of wooden rafters down onto the heads of the shaken drinkers. Even as Rab was driven quietly and slowly away from the scene, the effects of his handiwork continued behind him.

The pub was the base of a big black Manchester crew who had risen to prominence against the traditional white mobs. They were renowned for being brutal, vicious and quick to use shooters. In the whole of Manchester, there's not likely to be a more dangerous place to go and shove your weight around. But some of them did owe Rab money for a consignment of guns and ammo and the payment deadline was long overdue. He had tried polite and then tried assertive, with no results.

'I thought they might be taking the piss,' Rab told me a while later. 'A big mob versus me – they probably thought they could get off with it.' As usual, Rab had his coke pipe going and stopped for a blast. 'Just went down there to show them that they weren't dealing with some useless fanny of a toothless old man.'

And showed them he had. Make no bones about it, at 9 p.m. that night, Rab Carruthers would have gone back to that pub – on his own but tooled up to the gunnels. He would've known it very likely that the gang would have been waiting for him and not to shake hands. But Rab had learned long ago that, on the street, you don't let others push you around, no matter how strong they are, and you don't make idle threats. Besides, he'd been in hairier situations in his life. What was one more?

As it happens, Rab didn't need to go that pub. While he was sitting at home cleaning some of his massive collection of guns, the doorbell went. It was one of the main parties and a bagman with Rab's cash. Not only were they there to apologise to him for the delay, they were also there to congratulate him. A very practised shooter, Rab made sure every shot had hit the ceiling. It wasn't in his plans to hurt anyone – that visit.

Guns are always dangerous – Rab, above all folk, knew that. It's just that, when he used them, he didn't care too much. According to his visitors, he'd shot a guy in the pub in the skull. He was badly done – alive but critical. Yet there they were in Rab's house shaking his hand. Had he not cooked his coke properly, he wondered. This just wasn't making any sense.

It turned out that, the day before, the man in question had shot and killed some kid on a pushbike – just for the sport. The local people were naturally up in arms and the street players weren't very happy either. They had been thinking about what they should do in terms of punishment, wary that the bloke in question was a crazy one and that it would be difficult to damage him without there being some swift retaliation from his equally mental mates. In other words, no one was volunteering.

The gang had been contemplating drawing straws to see who'd deliver the punishment when Rab came in with his Uzi blazing and blasted the guy in the skull. Word had quickly spread around Eccles that Scots Rab had punished the shooter of kids. That's why he had set up that scene at the pub. It was nothing to do with money owed. Everyone knew that that mob paid their dues, didn't they? It was a front for shooting that bad bastard, that's all.

All the while the two guys had been talking, Rab had been handling a magnum, making sure they could see it was loaded. Now he laid that aside – but not too far away – and searched out his coke pipe. That wasn't too far away either – never was.

One of his bullets must have ricocheted from a metal beam or the like on the roof, come back down and caught the guy fair on the skull. Rab understood that but it tickled him that people thought he had been the avenging angel of street justice. In fact, he had been so immersed in his own world, too busy packing his pipe and staring at the wall that he hadn't even heard of the shooting of the kid. If he had, he would've gladly done something about it and the bad bastard wouldn't have been critical – he would've been in the morgue.

So what to do? Tell the truth? Nah, Rab just let it ride and had a laugh every time somebody mentioned the hit on the kid shooter. It was his bullet that had crashed into the guy's skull after all and, if he had known about it, he wouldn't have pussyfooted about like the team. Besides, Rab liked a laugh.

One time I was in his house when this local Manchester bloke came in and brought up the shoot-out at the pub, yet again. 'Would you really have killed them that night?' the stranger asked.

'No fucking problem,' Rab replied, looking all distracted and straight-faced. 'But they should know that they were lucky bastards,' he added, not looking up.

'Why?' the bloke wanted to know.

'I should have had my specs on.'

The guy nodded seriously at Rab's answer, paid some money he owed him and then left.

As soon as the bloke was far enough away from the house, Rab started to laugh. 'Kill them? There was no fuckin' danger of that,' he told me. 'Mind, I might just pay them another visit and put my specs on for a giggle.'

Rab had a few laughs over that wee incident and he had succeeded in something else. No one in Manchester, no matter how young or how wild their reputation, ever again thought of him as a tired old man who might be turning into some easy touch. Never again did he have to chase a debt. Instead, the up-and-coming young teams treated him like the senior player he was. These were some of the most efficient street gangs in the UK who feared no one. Their respect for Rab Carruthers was a mark of the measure of the man.

The man who walked away from Glasgow was a much-revered figure in Manchester. No wonder a Liverpool crew came up to ask him for guns to trade with the authorities to buy the freedom of drug dealers John Haase and Paul Bennett. Who else would the Scousers go to? Later, Home Secretary Michael Howard authorised a royal pardon for them. A fuller account of the ins and outs of this appears in our previous book, *Vendetta*, published in October 2005.

Cousin John had a sudden change of fortunes. Having left Glasgow because he was down on his luck, he suddenly had to return home for reasons that were never made clear.

Years later, the poor guy would admit to me that the incident at the pub had scared him shitless. Cousin John thought that's how it was going to be on a regular basis and didn't fancy becoming the getaway driver for some tooled-up desperado – even if he was his cousin. Little did he know that that one incident had made things so much easier for Rab – removed a whole load of strife from his business.

Unfortunately, the rest of Rab's life wasn't going to be so easy.

13

TOO PROUD

Prison can be the loneliest place on earth in spite of being over-crowded with men. The last thing you'd wish on anyone you were fond of is for them to be locked up. Yet it's one of those con-tradictions that, in the pokey, a fond, familiar face turning up is a gift.

It was 1999 and I was holed up in Full Sutton Prison for gun-running. It was the first time I'd been in the English prison system and it was a very different set-up from back home in Scotland. People think that one jail is just like another – far from it. Because you are enclosed with so many people, living on top of one another, having to put up with their smells and noise . . . because one governor's rules are so different from another . . . because you spend so much time in your cell . . . because of a hundred reasons more – the smallest change, difference or shortfall looms large in jail, unlike in the outside world.

Outside, if some guy has chronic, foul flatulence, you just avoid him, right? What if you have to share a cell with him for months on end? Or even just work next to him? Or someone else whistles those aimless wee tunes through their teeth every waking hour. You end up wanting to smack them, right? In jail you're stuck with them.

There have been prison riots over things like the kitchens run-ning out of chips or a minor change to visiting times. From beyond the walls, it might all seem trivial and, by themselves, they are. But it's everything else that lies behind those triggers that cause the tension. It's the same with being surrounded by strangers. Not a good place to be, no matter how much they accept you.

So, when Rab turned up in Full Sutton, I was both delighted and sad. Sad that he'd got fourteen years in jail for possession of drugs – a hefty load being added on because of who he was, not what he'd done – and delighted that an old pal was close by. Don't get me wrong, a whole heap of English prisoners were very good to me. Joey Pyle had seen that every London face in there serving time knew that I was OK. Also, every now and then, a familiar Scot would breeze in. But Rab was a good pal I had spent a lot of time with up in Manchester.

In the world of crime, we always know who's up to what and who has gone down for what yet the authorities never let on where someone will be sent to serve their time. This is probably because they fear escape plots. With top-risk Category A prisoners like me, they very often move you in the middle of the night. Unsettling? Bloody right. But, from the other perspective, it means you sometimes went to your bed one night with one neighbour and woke up in the morning with an entirely new one. There's good and bad in that, of course, but what they always try to avoid is placing friends or foes close to each other.

Of course, they knew all about Carruthers and Ferris so we were kept well apart – for some reason, this didn't apply to gym time so we used to meet up then. I was delighted to see that Rab hadn't changed much and he looked as strong as ever.

On only the second day Rab had been in Full Sutton, he arrived in the gym and handed me the heaviest towel I've ever lifted. Inside were chicken breasts, steaks and all sorts of other goodies half-inched straight from the jail freezer. Nerves of steel – or should that be steal? – and taking care of his mates. That was Rab Carruthers for you.

A short while later, I was moved on to Frankland Prison in Durham and, by his own request, Rab was moved into the Scottish prison system. That might seem strange for a man who had lived most of his life in Manchester but Rab had good reasons. His brother Jim, who I had originally been friendly with, had died some years earlier. After the death of his son, Rab was left with only his mother, who he doted on – always had. His old dear was getting on in years and didn't enjoy great health. It was very unlikely she'd survive the length of his prison sentence and he wanted to see her again before she died – tragic but true for so many prisoners. And some folk say jail is too soft, eh?

As expected, while he was in Shotts Prison, Rab continued never showing that jail was getting to him and working every line in the book. He was still managing to get a steady supply of all the drugs he needed and, unlike others, he had no ambitions to turn into some jail drug dealer – the top man in any prison, some reckon. As ever, Rab just wanted to blot out reality.

Then things got worse. Rab's mother died and he went to pieces. Many grown-up people do so why should it be any different for a street player? For Rab it meant only one thing – more and more drugs. He knew fine well it was wrecking his health but he just didn't care. By then, I had been released from prison and was visiting Rab regularly. After his mother died, he refused to see me and many other old pals too. Things weren't looking good for Rab.

One day I got a phone call from the screws at Shotts nick. Rab was critically ill, had been rushed to Monklands General Hospital and had asked to see me. Would I go along? A battalion of the SAS couldn't keep me back.

Driving straight there, I wandered through the corridors of the big modern hospital, following the directions I'd been given at the reception. Why do these places too often look the same? So damned anonymous. They're the easiest places to get lost in – except in Rab's case. There was a wee clue to where he was.

The uniformed screw sat in a chair in the corridor outside Rab's room. I told him who I was but there didn't seem to be any need. My picture had been spread across newspaper pages for years, in attempts to blame me for everything from murder to running smack factories. But he didn't hesitate to let me in. Good man. Those lucky enough not to have served jail time may wonder why

I considered that screw to be a good screw. Simple – I've known too many similar situations where the screws have forbidden even wives and kids to see their menfolk in hospital even though they were dying.

Down in Frankland, one guy took a massive heart attack. The poor bloke was struggling for life – even a layman like me could see that. Still he was handcuffed to two screws as he was driven to the hospital. There he lay in intensive care, his life hanging by a thread for days as his wife and kids paced the corridor, worried sick. They wouldn't let them in to see him. What did they fear? An escape? It looked like the only place that bloke was going to was out, in a box. Thankfully he survived and returned to the jail, only to be released a few months later, pending an appeal. It seems like the bloke shouldn't even have been in jail in the first place yet he might well have died a lonely death without his loved ones, just a screw handcuffed to either wrist.

The screw guarding Rab's hospital room was a good screw. He insisted I showed him some ID – those are the rules and the guy could get sacked just for not following them – and opened the door. I was prepared to find two more screws in there but what shocked me was Rab. His hair had turned grey and so had his face. Weight had dropped off the poor guy so that loose skin hung in folds. It had also caused his eyes to become too big and they were popping out of their sockets. The whole transformation of Rab Carruthers from hard to vulnerable was completed by the oxygen mask strapped across his mouth.

When I saw him lying there, I almost turned and quietly tiptoed out of the room. He just looked too weak. But he spotted me and slipped off the mask, giving that old wide grin. A sip of water later and he was chattering away about the old times as if we were sitting in his kitchen down in Manchester. Rab had pneumonia and was dreadfully ill. It was the type of illness that would bring most folk crashing to their knees. Physically frail he might have been but Rab Carruthers' brain was alert as ever. The man was made of strong stuff. For a whole hour, Rab chatted away. It must have been an exhausting marathon for him but he knew the screws would allow us an hour together and he wasn't going to sacrifice one second.

With a long embrace, I said my farewells and headed for the door. As I stepped through, I looked back into the room and Rab was sitting there smiling. The poor bastard must have been desperate to get that oxygen mask back on but he wasn't going to do that till I was well out of the way.

As I drove home, I reflected on the Rab Carruthers I had just spent time with. He was a sorry sight, for sure, but did I feel sorry for him? No way. Rab had chosen a road that he knew would lead to that kind of end – if a bullet didn't get him first. Besides, he'd crack my jaw if he suspected one ounce of pity was heading his way from me – from anyone.

We'd made an arrangement for me to visit Rab again by the end of the week but, before I could, he was returned to Shotts Prison and his old ways. Rab had been told by the docs that the drugs would kill him in double-quick time but he kept taking them all the same. Maybe that's what he wanted.

Again, he cut himself off from me in jail because he now needed a wheelchair to get from his cell to the visiting area. Rab Carruthers couldn't allow himself to be seen like that, especially in jail. I feared that's exactly where he'd die. Then, because he was so dreadfully ill, the authorities released him to go home, to his mother's empty house – home to die.

Shortly afterwards, Rab Carruthers passed away – a man who had lived on his own for the last few years of his life even when he lived in a crowded jail. Lived on his own but not alone. The man had so many friends. He knew that. If that was how Rab wanted to bow out of life, we all respected it. He'd earned our respect many years ago. Some tabloid headlines crowed, 'MR BIG DIES LONELY JUNKIE DEATH'. The journalists didn't know or understand Rab Carruthers at all. His departure was more like the Red Indian who, knowing his time is coming, walks off to die alone. No fuss, no bother.

Rab's funeral was going to be a gathering of faces from Manchester, London, Liverpool and all over Scotland – in some cases, there would be a volatile mix of feuding teams. If some of these guys started trouble, someone was going to get hurt and hurt badly. The unwritten rule is that there should be no trouble at funerals. But these days, drugs and big money seem to have taken precedence over any kind of standards or code. Sad times.

Some other well-known faces and I agreed that, for the sake of peace, we would stay away and pay our respects later. As it happens, even that didn't stop the trouble and, after the funeral, a good mate of Rab's was stabbed. Again the media had a field day with that but, in truth, it had been a simple misunderstanding. In the straight world, a misunderstanding might lead to an argument but, on the streets, sometimes it's a stabbing.

Not long after Rab's death, he was to come back and haunt me. Earlier this year – 2006 – I was told by my lawyer John Macaulay that the Metropolitan Police wanted to interview me in connection with a national inquiry. To be truthful, I was scratching my noggin thinking back because, by then, I'd been on the straight and narrow for over four years. Turns out I hadn't to look that far back.

In *Vendetta*, we detailed the background to the then Home Secretary Michael Howard authorising a royal pardon for drug traffickers John Hasse and Paul Bennett. We also drew attention to how Paul Bennett seemed to have floated about the country dishing out the kiss of death . . . how he turned up in Belfast and the Loyalist groups started battling over dealing drugs . . . how he hid in Glasgow with Thomas 'The Licensee' McGraw, a well-known collaborator with the authorities . . . how, wherever Bennett went, men seemed to go down for serious charges like murder and major heroin dealing . . . how they all went down but he walked free, never even being interviewed.

The whole story is told in *Vendetta* so we won't go into it here. Suffice to say that, in spite of an outcry at the time, Hasse and Bennett walked free. It was only after the book hit the shelves that the authorities acted. See the power of the pen? I should have taken up this malarkey years ago.

Now the Met wanted to interview me with regard to all those shenanigans. After a blether with Reg, I realised that my new life brought new standards. As a writer, no way would I reveal my sources if they didn't want to be revealed. It's very similar to not grassing. There are no in-between states, no compromises. It just won't happen from my lips. End of story. So that's what I told my lawyer to tell the Met. So far it's working but they have a lengthy list of folk they want to see. Maybe, by the time this book hits the shelves, they'll have come back for me – maybe for Reg too.

And where did all that business start? One day in Manchester, as I hung around Rab Carruthers' house, some Scousers came for advice on buying £50,000 of guns. Even beyond the grave, the bold Rab Carruthers is rattling my cage. I hope he's looking on and enjoying every minute of it.

As far as I am concerned, Rab Carruthers was a likeable villain. His enemies will think otherwise, of course. Even though I've moved on in life, I still recognise characteristics of Rab's that I appreciate in any human. A courageous man of his word – what more can you ask? A loyal friend who lived to the max, every day of his life. With that approach, you either end up in jail or dead. Poor Rab had both courage and loyalty in full measure. You need special individuals in all walks of life and, without them, the world is definitely a poorer place.

We are about to have a look at just such a man – one who's a good deal younger than Rab and still alive and kicking, thank you very much. While we're at it, we're going to solve a mystery. He's wanted under warrant in a score of British courts including the Old Bailey but the cops can't trace him. If they can't find him, then surely he doesn't exist. Or does he?

14

MOST WANTED

Dark figures moved slowly and methodically through the early-morning mist, picking their way between the massive gravestones and gothic statues. It was a search party in a cemetery. After all, where better to hide a dead body?

The cemetery in question was the Necropolis, one of the oldest graveyards in Glasgow and it shows. Built on a hill, the gravestones are huge and ornate, with each grieving family competing to display its wealth even after the death of one of them. Huge slabs have also been laid across the biggest plots to keep the grave robbers out. Now there's something I've never done – rob a grave, that is.

On one side stands the back of the Cathedral and the Royal Infirmary with the hospital looking even spookier than the imposing church. It's an ancient area with the city's oldest house and pub nearby. But, typical of the city, it's also a new area with the other side of the Necropolis being flanked by a brewery, all shiny metal, tubes and clouds of steam like some huge spaceship ready for take off. Now the cops were in the Necropolis and they were looking for something much more sinister than a spaceship.

Somehow, some deer have found their way into this cemetery that is almost at the dead centre of Glasgow. I wonder what those gentle beasts thought of the bizzies slowly making their way, foot-by-foot, grave-by-grave, through the Necropolis. I know what I thought – it was as funny as fuck.

Reg and I had written a novel, *Deadly Divisions*, while I was still in jail. One part of the plot involves two guys going to carry out a hit on another player who's laid up in the Royal Infirmary. He susses that they're coming and takes to his heels with them on his tail. They catch him and kill him in the Necropolis. They have to dispose of the body, of course, but where better than in a grave-yard full of bodies? So they steal some tools from the caretaker's hut, lever up one of the anti-grave-robber slabs and sling the stiff under it before slamming the slab down again. It's a novel, OK?

Strathclyde Police bought a bundle of copies of *The Ferris Conspiracy* and went through the book with a nit comb. Mind you, that was probably their lawyers wanting to see if we had actually named any of the corrupt cops. The publisher's lawyers wouldn't let us – yet. *The Ferris Conspiracy* was factual and covered real events but *Deadly Divisions* was a novel, pure fiction. What possible interest could they have in that?

Quite a lot as it happens. They had obviously read the book and, deciding that both Reg and I were devoid of any imagination, they reckoned it had to be based on real events – well, some of it any-way, especially the stiff being hidden in the Necropolis. Silly bas-tards. That was entirely made up though I wouldn't be surprised if it's a trick someone has pulled at some time – just not me or any-one I know, right? Thing is there were some real clues in that book but, as usual, the bizzies were looking in the wrong place for the wrong thing – or person, to be more accurate.

The clue related to a man. A man they have been searching for for over twenty years. A man they have failed to find and have decided doesn't exist? Oh, no.

The car took off down Greenside Street in my patch of Blackhill. It was a black Cortina Ghia 2.3 automatic and it was impressive – but not just for those reasons. It was the speed, the control, the utter bloody smoothness of it all. Whoever was behind that wheel could drive and then some. Then the cop car appeared at the other end of the street, blue lights flashing coming the driver's way fast.

The Cortina squealed to a halt quick time with only the slightest shimmy of its arse end. The cop car, on the other hand, was weaving all over the road as the driver slammed on the brakes. Effortlessly, or so it seemed, the Cortina hit reverse and was driven fast back along the road till it widened enough for a handbrake turn. Yanking the car round precisely and neatly in exactly the opposite direction, the driver was off again, leaving the polis motor way behind. Well impressed I was. At sixteen years of age and a bit of a driver myself – or so I thought till that day – I stood there watching the cop car take off hopelessly after the Cortina and wondered who the hell was driving the obviously stolen motor. I didn't have long to wait.

A couple of weeks later, up in the Balornock area at the northern edge of the city, I spotted the guy who'd been driving the Cortina so I brass-necked it and walked right up to him. I introduced myself by way of saying what a good performance he'd put on that night in Greenside Street. The man already knew that. Everybody in Glasgow knew he was the best driver of the lot. Still young, he was legendary and known far and wide. I introduced myself and it gave me a buzz when he said he had already heard of me. Then he added, 'You can just call me Addison . . .' pausing for effect and changing the accent into a very bad Sean Connery playing James Bond impersonation, 'James Addison.'

James Addison? I was pissing myself laughing. That was the name every car thief and joyrider in the north and east of the city gave to the cops when they got nabbed. The polis had more warrants out for Addison – Addie to all his friends – than any other single person.

Addie and I crossed paths every now and then and always spent a few cordial minutes together. If there was anything I could do to help him and vice versa, we would, but we never worked together as a team or any of that Hollywood crap.

It had been a good few years since I had last seen him. When I was down in Manchester around 1992, staying with Rab Carruthers, I had pulled in at a petrol station near Liverpool Road in Eccles and paid for the fuel. Distracted, I was heading back to my motor, my mind somewhere else entirely.

'Whatsa matter, son? Ye no' got any Irn-Bru?' Any time, anywhere accents from home sound out, they turn your head and grab your attention. I swivelled round to see the smiling gob of the speaker as he leaned casually on the bonnet of his motor.

'No Irn-Bru down here no matter how much you offer to pay,' I answered dead serious, like. 'But, while I'm at it, how the fuck are you, Addie?'

The pair of us burst out laughing, big embraces going both ways.

Addie had recently skipped out of Glasgow because things were getting a wee bit hot for him following a bank robbery. He had a house in Liverpool Road not at all far from where Rab stayed and where I was hanging out.

When Addie had paid for his petrol we sat in his car, an innocuous-looking Rover 3.5 V8 that I knew he could make perform tricks even the manufacturers hadn't dreamed of. We just sat there and blethered for an age and the subject of that night in Greenside Street came up.

'That was a pure Rockford, man,' Addie said laughing, probably remembering his moves and leaving the cops railing behind him. For those who don't know, *The Rockford Files* was an American TV show about a private detective, starring James Garner, and every episode had at least two superb car chase scenes. For our generation 'a Rockford' became widely accepted slang for a slick manoeuvre in a car at speed.

Addie never asked me why I was in Manchester and I never asked him – that was a strict no-no – but I found out through other sources about the bank robbery and his very sound suspicions that one of his team wasn't watertight. Safety first in these things was always how he performed. That was one reason the cops had a problem getting hold of him. Had the shit hit the fan – and the cops were obviously wise to what he had been up to – Addie would have known exactly the source. The loose-mouthed player in Glasgow would have been a dead man in double-quick time, I reckon.

As we parted, I knew exactly what Addie's next move would be – flit houses. It wasn't that he didn't trust me – I'm certain that he did – but that was his style. The only person who really knew about James Addison was James Addison. That's why James Addison stayed out of jail when so many other clever players went down. But it wouldn't be so long before our paths crossed again.

Next time it was a matter that concerned sex, guns and taped confessions – never a dull moment with Addie.

15

THE SPECTRE RETURNS

I thought I was a dead man. What else do you think when men in boiler suits and skip caps smash the window of your car and pull you out into the street into a circle of their pals all training guns on you? I'd been expecting it for a long time.

Even when I heard someone roar out, 'POLICE!', what I thought was happening was a hit. That's the best cover in the world for a killing – as long as there are no real cops around. Besides I already had the cops in Glasgow on tape talking about shooting me. Nah, I was a dead man all right.

Does your life flash in front of your eyes? No idea – those bastards didn't give me the time to find out. They were an efficient mob for sure. That's because they were trained, highly trained – just as you'd expect the police to be. Especially the top boys like the NCS (National Crime Squad), the British equivalent of the FBI – like those bastards were.

A little of this story – a story also about villains, I suppose – has been told elsewhere so, before we reveal the new parts and the role of Addie for those who haven't read about it, here's a brief summary. It was 27 May 1997 in London and I was being arrested for gunrunning. Really I was there at the house of a man called John Ackerman to pick up plates to produce counterfeit money to test them out. It was a scam that, if it came off, would be worth a few million pounds to me over a couple of years – more than enough to go legit. Instead, I was caught handling a box of Mac-10 submachine guns, weapons that could rattle off hundreds of rounds a minute.

Ackerman was one of the best-known illegal gun dealers in Britain. I knew that but he dealt in many other things as well, including counterfeit dough. I picked up the box of goods and swiftly delivered them to the boot of a waiting car driven by Constance 'Connie' Howarth who immediately drove it off as I went back into the house for a chat. It wasn't that I'd turned sociable. I didn't know Ackerman – just of him – but along with me for the ride was a good old friend of mine, Arthur Suttie, who happened to be Ackerman's cousin. Not that they were close but nice to be nice, eh?

The cops hit my car as Arthur and I drove away. They hit it well and were so chuffed by the result that they lined up for a class photograph with me already cuffed and dressed in a white forensic suit. The NCS had been formed only a short time before and their boss, Roy Penrose, announced that I was his biggest fish to date. Funny, it didn't feel that way where I was sitting.

The bottom line was that it was soon evident that MI5 and the NCS had been trailing me for over two years. Apparently, I was a big national security risk. Yet, over the same period, I had been more law abiding than in any similar period in my entire adult life. All I wanted to do was earn enough dough to support my kids. The counterfeit plates scam was just too tempting. One last big job and I could have walked away forever. So where were the Security Services getting all their strange notions from? I reckoned it had to be the cops in Glasgow who were still bitter that I was found not guilty of killing Fatboy Thompson and that they'd failed to set me up with heroin.

Whoever or whatever put MI5 on my tail, it was now a fact that I'd have to live with. My defence was that I *was* there to commit a crime – the counterfeit plates – just *not* the crime I was charged with. Arthur Suttie said he was along for the ride – that was true – so had no involvement in any crime. Connie Howarth was a real stalwart and said she was there to pick up and deliver a box but I'd never asked her to pick up guns. Then Connie raised another slice of information about her boyfriend – some bloke called James Addison.

The bold Addie had appeared on the scene out of nowhere. Connie was telling the cops that she had never been part of the set-up but had stood in at the last minute because her boyfriend couldn't make it. When asked she volunteered her boyfriend's name as James Addison. Most experienced cops wise in the ways of Manchester street folk would have been asking serious questions there. Connie Howarth played the game by the rules. She was the type who wouldn't tell the cops the time of day even if would save her life. Yet here she was volunteering an actual name. The bold Addie was at it again.

As it happens, Addie did have some involvement with Connie. The NCS had been on the trail of a whole range of people they believed associated with me. As part of that surveillance, thousands of photographs were taken, including one of Addie at a bar in the Angel area of Islington, London. The Addie I knew was too smart for that. Was he playing cat and mouse with the NCS?

While I was held in Belmarsh Prison awaiting trial, a prisoner unknown to me sidled up one day. You have to be alert in these circumstances. It's a big bad world out there and life in prison is cheap. Some of my enemies might well have managed to take a jail hit contract out on me. I braced myself.

'Gotta message for you, mate,' said the bloke out of the side of his mouth.

What message? A blade in the guts?

'From a guy called Addie,' the messenger continued. 'He said you'd know.'

The poor bloke must have thought he was dealing with some mad man. No surprise because I was pissing myself laughing. I'd been dragged in by the NCS and MI5 to face major gunrunning charges and here I was, holed up in the middle of England's most secure prison, yet Addie had still managed to reach me – and this is the man the Glasgow cops thought didn't exist.

Addie was making me an offer. An excellent offer, to my ears. A get-out-of-jail-free card maybe.

The man the cops couldn't find would get me to phone him at one of the few numbers passed by the Home Office. They limit the sanctioned phone numbers to prevent guys like me – even when untried and therefore still innocent – from contacting whoever they want. Addie would go up and pay my partner, Sandra Arnott, a visit and take the call there at an agreed time and date. Of course the phone call would be taped but that just suited us fine.

Loud and clear, Addie would ID himself and make it clear I had no knowledge of the guns. That he was responsible for that package and that Connie, Arthur Suttie and I had no knowledge of it at all. It was a generous gesture and a brave step. For most people, it would've been suicidal since the cops would have lifted them in a jiffy. Addie wasn't most folk, though.

When I met with my English solicitors, Paul Robinson and Lisa French, they didn't seem quite as excited by the offer as I was. They were concerned that the introduction of such new evidence could run the risk of contaminating other defendants, particularly Connie, as having been part of some conspiracy to transport illegal weapons. Obviously that risk wasn't acceptable.

The phone call was never made but I did get a message back to Addie that the security services had his photograph on file – not good since a warrant had already been issued for his arrest by our trial judge at the Old Bailey.

With Addie's ploy having fallen, I told Connie and Arthur that I was willing to take the full blame for all charges. This seemed only fair to me since neither of them would've been caught up in that trial had it not been for me. Also, why should three of us spend time in jail when one would do just as well? Strong people that they are, they both steadfastly refused. But they did allow me to take most of the heat. That was only right. As it happened, John Ackerman the gun dealer had turned QE and was gabbing Olympic standard. Maybe that was why the NCS and MI5 had been on my case all along? Maybe it was a set-up from day one?

The authorities had their day when I was eventually sentenced to ten years. Quite rightly, Connie and Arthur got much less. Then my sentence was reduced to seven years on appeal. It was still a long time but it was a result.

Every now and then money or a package would arrive for me in jail or through a friend. Other people sent in gifts for me and they were always greatly appreciated but these were a bit special – they were from Addie.

Not only is the Old Bailey warrant for Addie still lying there collecting dust but at least several other police forces in the UK want to get the man. He knew that the information he passed to me would be used at the Old Bailey trial and was used several times over to help others. James Addison knew what he had to do next – leave the country. Just abandon everything and all his friends and family and go. It's a hard move but it's a safe move.

No stranger to that manoeuvre, he had done it many times before. To my certain knowledge he has been to Rotterdam so often he knows it just as well as Glasgow. But then, knowing Addie, I know I do not know all that he knows. That's his style.

Police forces up and down the country will continue to search for James Addison now and then. Fat chance. They'd be better employed searching the Necropolis for fresh stiffs.

In our novel *Deadly Divisions*, we had a character who was walking the streets of Glasgow, carrying out hits on bad bastards who deserved it. No one knew who he was and the cops had never got near him – a wee bit borrowed from Addie there. But the name we gave the character? James Addison. On police wanted lists up and down the country, yet that most unsubtle of clues passed the polis by. With cops of that calibre, I don't think Addie has much to fear, do you? Power to him wherever he is.

A very powerful man closer to home than Rotterdam once opened my eyes in a most unusual way. But keep this one to yourself. We don't want to ruin his reputation.

16

POSTED MISSING

'Where's Jaimba?' It was an unusual way to hear my pal's name. Usually Jaimba was always around so that question didn't come up. Not for me. Other folk in the city were more used to hearing other statements like, 'Jaimba's coming,' and they'd shiver with fear, no matter how hard they were. I've written about Jaimba before but, don't worry, this is a side to him never revealed before. Something happened in the late 1980s that shocked even me. Shocked, then educated me – eventually.

I was very active at that time. Having walked out on the Thompsons for setting me up and decided I wanted nothing to do with that collaborator The Licensee, I was out on my own – well, along with some very good friends, Jaimba McLean included.

The first time I met him was in jail. I was young but a full-blown, hairy-arsed adult and I'd been dumped in the pokey several times by then. He was underage, maybe fourteen or fifteen, but so dangerous the authorities wouldn't put him in the usual locked, secure units for kids – juvenile prisons really – and he had to go to the real thing.

Being surrounded by adults and big rough screws didn't faze Jaimba at all. He kicked, punched and rebelled every hard inch of the way and he was doing OK. Except I knew it wouldn't last. I'd been there before and, in spite of him being a big, tough fucker, I knew they'd take him down. Harm him badly if necessary. Even just for fun. The boy needed some advice so I offered him some. To be honest, I wasn't sure if he'd lash out at me as well. For some people, their first spell in jail turns them into a cornered animal and all they can do is bite and fight whoever comes near. The young Jaimba listened, heeded the advice and had been right by my side ever since.

Out on the street, Jaimba was ferocious and second to none. With all that power and anger channelled and directed, when he turned up, grown men wept and some had been known to wet themselves.

As team players went, Jaimba was always up for a bit of business. Not only did he never refuse a job during quiet spells, he would repeatedly ask when the next action was coming up. Then suddenly he wasn't available on Tuesday nights – every Tuesday night.

It took us a good few weeks to work this out. The light bulb finally sparked into life on a Tuesday night, of course, when he'd told us that he couldn't take part in a certain piece of work. We were gathered together getting ready for the job and someone said, 'Strange Jaimba no' being up for this.'

'Aye, he's involved in every fucking thing,' said another guy.

'Gets really fucking angry if he gets left out.'

'He's always available.'

'Except that time, mind, when we had to go and see that mob creating all the problems in Barmulloch.'

'Aye,' everyone agreed, thinking hard.

'But there was that other time, remember,' someone piped up, 'when we paid a wee visit to that south-side pub?'

'Aye,' everyone agreed, thinking hard.

'Then, when you paid that visit to that Licensed cunt, Paul, and we came along as back-up.'

'Aye.'

We were a small group – five or six at most, usually smaller. Jaimba had a special place in the team. It was unsettling when suddenly he wasn't available for business, even some of the time.

'Ah've fucking got it,' said one guy and we all turned, giving him all our attention. 'This is Tuesday night, right?'

'Aye, right. So what?'

'So were the other times when Jaimba couldn't make it.'

'Nah, ye're fucking aff yer nut,' someone growled.

But I was thinking. The guy who said that it was always a Tuesday had the type of brain that's great with details, numbers, dates. So I was thinking, thinking hard, but I wasn't sure.

'Tell you what,' I suggested. 'Let's just pretend we have some business next Tuesday and see what happens.'

All the guys were grinning. They were all different kinds of blokes but they shared some things – joy in a little intrigue, pleasure at a set-up and a hoot at a send-up especially of a close pal. That's the Glasgow way.

The following Tuesday I belled Jaimba. 'Something's come up,' I said, not spelling anything out and I knew he wouldn't expect me to. You never knew who was listening. 'Can we have a meet tonight?'

'Tonight?' he replied, his voice full of puzzlement, as if I'd said yesterday.

'Yeah, tonight.'

'What time?' He was sounding worried, rattled.

'About seven – earlier if you want.'

'How long's this gonnae take, Paul?'

'As long as it takes,' I answered in a pissed-off tone since the guys should never ask that question. It was part of how we all related to each other. Work took as long as work needed and our women and kids had to understand that. I couldn't remember Jaimba ever asking that question ever before.

'Paul, Ah'm sorry, no can do.'

'No can do?' I was deliberately speaking quietly, sending him the message that I wasn't too chuffed.

'No, Ah'm sorry. Later aye. Earlier easy. The morro – no problem. Any other time of the week and Ah'm up for anything. You know me, Paul.'

I did indeed know Jaimba and this was very worrying.

That night me and a couple of the boys were on a mission. From early evening, we were sitting in a borrowed car around the corner from Jaimba's home. Sure enough, just before 7 p.m., we spotted him driving out. After waiting a wee while, we were on his tail. As we weaved through the east end I was worried for my pal. I knew all too well no one was so tough, so hard, so fearless that they couldn't get into some trouble. What was even more worrying, Jaimba's wife was with him.

Hard and uncompromising as Jaimba was as a street player, he doted on his wife and kids. It's often the way with the top boys. You could pull Jaimba's nails out with pliers, drill his gnashers without anaesthetic, dangle him from the ceiling by a fishing line tied round his balls and I doubt if you'd get any change out of him. But harm his wife or wee ones and, in a flash, that would have him coming at you kamikaze style or waving the white flag, wanting them safe.

When he pulled into the busy car park, my worry factor doubled. It was just the kind of place for a wee private chat without any bizzies listening in. Folk who watch too many Hollywood movies believe those kinds of meetings take place in some isolated spot or derelict building. Not at all – you're too easily spotted. Quite the opposite venue is chosen and car parks are great for quick getaways if necessary.

'Paul, ye'll never fucking believe this,' one of the boys spoke up, interrupting my thoughts. But he was right. I didn't believe my own eyes.

Ten minutes later, I was standing watching Jaimba, the big guy oblivious to my prying eyes, getting on with the business at hand. I still couldn't believe what I was seeing. It was show-up time.

'Evening, Jaimba,' I said, suddenly appearing in front of his table.

'Fuck's sake,' Jaimba stood up as if he'd just been shot at close range. 'Fuck's sake.'

'Having a good time?'

'Fuck's sake.' He was blushing. Jaimba McLean, the most feared man on Glasgow's streets, was blushing. That was a first and a last, I reckoned.

'Here ye go, James, son.' We'd been interrupted by a small woman with a heavy-set silver perm, scarlet lipstick and a loud floral frock. She was hefting an overstuffed handbag. It was impossible to guess her age but she'd been cashing her pension for a good few years. 'It's ma lucky one – like I promised ye last week,' said the anonymous granny.

'Oh, aye. Aye, thanks, Agnes,' said a still-blushing Jaimba as he took the marker pen Agnes was offering him, before turning back to face me.

'James?' I asked. I hadn't heard him called that in public except by some authoritarian screw or cop.

'Aye, well,' Jaimba blurted back. 'She's a good old soul. And she's right – this is lucky. She's won a fortune with it, Paul.'

I was listening to this open-mouthed, not believing what I was hearing.

'You need money, Jaimba?' I asked, already knowing the answer. We were all doing very well for ourselves at that time.

'Naw, naw . . .'

'Jaimba, what the fuck are you doing at the bingo?'

That's where he had been going every Tuesday night with his wife and he was getting right into the social aspect of the game, surrounded by women old enough to be his granny. They saw beyond his fierce looks and had taken him into their fold. Gossiping, moaning about family, sharing operation stories that would turn most folks' stomachs and loaning out lucky markers. Debating how many books they'd play that night. Bitching about someone who always won the jackpot house. Jaimba didn't just go to the bingo – he'd joined the club.

We slagged him rotten for weeks, of course. Our mothers and grannies played bingo but our mates weren't meant to. He took the slagging in good spirit. Well, it was just his turn. It would be ours another day.

When we were alone, Jaimba would try and explain to me why he had become a devotee of bingo. At first, he said it was a good night out – the patter of the oldies was great and his wife really enjoyed it – but I knew there had to be more to it than that.

Eventually I could see what Jaimba was about. That he loved his wife there was no doubt though you'd never catch the young hardman using the L-word, ever. In spite of how much street players feared him, Jaimba also liked people. He liked ordinary people and he made a good neighbour and a great friend – the kind of guy old dears living down the street might go to for a bit of help with some practical problem.

'Forgive me for being normal,' an old street-player pal of mine used to say. And most of us were just that – despite of our lives of crime. Jaimba was no different. Business was pretty hectic at that time – the type of business that meant you had no real life of your own. When something needed doing, you jumped and did it day or night and you didn't finish till it was done – no matter how long that took. It was like signing up for the army during wartime – relationships with your partner, kids and family suffered and no doubt.

Jaimba was just reclaiming a bit of his life he loved – end of story. Could he admit that to any street player without losing face? The bold Jaimba McLean off to the bingo with the oldies? No way. So he carried a secret from men like me – team mates like me whose number-one rule was no secrets. But I could see why. Jaimba went up in my estimation for his bingo nights – though you'll never find me playing the game. His reasons I reckoned were good reasons, the best of reasons – to be with his wife and the folk he belonged to. No bad thing.

A short while later, a job came up for the boys. It was important and would bring in a few quid. We were all sitting round in the Cottage Bar working out the how. That done, there was the when to consider.

'Tuesday night would be the best time, Paul,' suggested one of the guys and I knew he was right. I didn't need to think.

'Nah, we'll make it Thursday,' I said. 'Think we'll give Tuesdays a body swerve for a while.' As we got up to leave, I caught

Jaimba's eye and gave him a wee wink. The big man smiled back. Enough said.

In the years to come, Jaimba McLean went through hellish trials in life. Close friends would be gunned down in the street – killed. He claimed that cops drugged him and this sent him off his nut and led to many years in Carstairs State Hospital. He's still not well yet – probably never will be. A couple of years ago, he was shot in the chest at close range by Billy McPhee, then a heavy for Thomas 'The Licensee' McGraw. It would have killed most. But not Jaimba McLean.

Jaimba is retired from street business now. A lot has changed about his life but one thing hasn't – he's still with his wife and kids. No mean feat for a street player as active as he was. Damn few others have ever achieved that. Well done, the bold Jaimba.

Sometimes a man can be right even if he goes about it the wrong way. But, as I found out a few years later, sometimes a man can be wrong even when he has the best possible intentions. Also, now and then, two wrongs do actually make a right.

17

ARTORRO'S TOURS

The car's speed never wavered but drove on right past my hotel. I was being taken hostage and not for the last time.

I was in London in late 2005 to meet with the Metropolitan cops. It wasn't a social visit, of course, and I wasn't too chuffed about it either – bloody irritated might be a kind way to sum up my feelings.

A few weeks before, the Met, along with their sidekicks from Strathclyde Police, had raided the home of my ex-partner, Sandra Arnott. We'd separated by mutual agreement a short time before and were still on very good terms. Our son, Dean, lived with Sandra but I often went round to see him and he frequently spent weekends with me at my place. Did it upset me that the bizzies had raided Sandra's house? Fucking right it did.

From what I could gather they were looking for financial papers, letters with my name on it and anything else. They had a warrant and, despite a thorough search, it did them no good. Not that I'd been too clever for them. It was a lot simpler than that – I wasn't up to any tricky business. Full stop.

The Met were soon on my case, demanding that I make myself available for interview. My name had come up in a multimillion-pound fraud investigation. It was a serious matter and they weren't going to take no for an answer. After consulting with my lawyer, John Macaulay, it was clear that, if I didn't make myself available, then they'd lift me. Sod that.

Though I'd given up my criminal career, I still had principles. High up on the list of those is that I do not cooperate with the police. But I'd learned long ago that the bizzies, especially the ones from Glasgow, looked for any excuse to lift me so they could have it plastered over all the front pages. Some cops have long bitter memories.

Something else I'd learned was that, once the polis had their mitts on you, they were reluctant to let go. I've done enough jail time for one lifetime, thank you, and I wasn't about to risk extending that when I'd broken hee-haw laws. One other thing I'd known for years was that, on the slightest excuse, the cops wouldn't just come after me – they'd go knocking down the doors and wrecking the homes of folk who knew me. I'm not talking here of known street players but my parents, Sandra, my sisters. Though I'd moved away from crime, they'd still go through that rigmarole if I didn't show up for interview. As ever, they'd hurt me by hurting the folk I loved. That was a price I wasn't willing for them to pay so off to London I went.

Before departing, I'd belled the bold Artorro, a London man who knew the city like the back of his hand. Being in his backyard, I wanted to arrange to meet up with him as you do with friends and he could give me useful advice on which hotel was most convenient for Snowhill Police Station, where I had to attend for interview. Turned out to be the Tower Bridge Hotel – funnily enough, it was right next to Tower Bridge and round the corner from The Tower itself where many a good Scot had been jailed and executed. I hoped it wasn't a bad omen.

Artorro, being old school, picked me up at the airport and drove me to my hotel. I was very grateful and told him so. For a few days before the trip, I'd had next to no sleep due to work and other business matters. Not to put too fine a point on it, I was knackered and told Artorro so.

All the way in, we chatted about his family and, for some reason, he started telling tales of his active days – all very unusual. Once a job's done, that's normally the end of it – no chat, no reminiscing, no comparing notes. But I knew that everything Artorro was telling me would be spot on. He was that kind of man and I felt honoured that he should tell me. Then he drove straight past the Tower Bridge.

'There's the hotel,' I said to him and got nothing in reply. He just kept driving. 'THERE'S THE HOTEL!' I said louder, remembering that he was a bit corn beef due to being in the close proximity of dynamite and gelignite explosions too often – usually with a big safe at the sharp end.

'I know that, you daft cunt,' he said, disgusted that an outsider thought he'd missed anything in his home city. 'I just want to show you a couple of things.'

We were in central London surrounded by huge and very prestigious old buildings that were obviously dripping with security. But things had changed since Artorro was active. That part of London had been full of financial institutions – millions of pounds, dollars, francs and deutschmarks just waiting in big fuck-off safes to be nabbed. These days, they are offices, working the money in the cyber world – not real in other words – but still I spotted guards at each front door, security grilles and CCTV cameras covering every angle.

Artorro pulled the car over and pointed to the massive frontage of an impressive building. 'That one over there, we took about £260K and that was about thirty years ago – probably the equivalent of several million pounds now.' It would have been a big job and no doubt – definitely one for the tooled-up mob.

'I didn't take you as an armed robber,' I said to him, curious to learn more.

'You're right. I'm not. Never carried a shooter. Never needed to, mate. The worst we had to worry about was coppers on bikes – no radios or fuck all – just bicycle clips in case they shit themselves.' The pair of us had a good hoot, somehow finding the image funny. 'So no shooters but I did like stealing money,' he continued, a wee smile at the side of his mouth.

'So . . .'

'Piece of piss,' he gave a wee laugh. 'All we done was gain access to the sewers, worked our way round until we came underneath the building and calculated where we were in relation to the interior. Then we dug our way up to the goodies and it was how's your father.'

I was sitting there marvelling at how the old-time boys would put so much effort into a robbery when it would have been easier just to walk in through the front door with loaded guns – easier but potentially much more lethal to bystanders.

But Artorro was in the mood to reminisce. 'Me and a group of really tight mates used to work together,' he continued, with an almost melancholic look on his face. 'It was the only way to stay out of jail. We had all the gear – kit bags, cutters, rope ladders, miners' helmets with lamps. And the team had all the skills – safe cracking, explosives, electrics.' What he was describing sounded more like a crack commando unit than a bunch of blaggers.

'You guys must have been fit,' I offered sincerely.

'Fit? Oh yeah, we kept on our toes but we needed to bring in muscle now and then – for the liftin' and the heavy work, you know.'

I looked at Artorro – at barely over five-foot tall and with not a pick on him, I understood what he meant.

'Getting into that place, we had this new boy with us. Big as fuck and strong as an ox, he hadn't been down the sewers before. "'Ere,' he says, "there's fuckin' huge rats down 'ere and there's fuckin' hundreds and hundreds of them." Shaking, his big face was stretched with fear. Some folk are like that with rats but they've never bothered me. 'Course, there were rats but it didn't seem to me there were any more than usual. "Look at the size of the bastards," said he, nodding at the stream and staying as far back as he could. "Fucking swimming in packs. Bastards." Well, I didn't like the sound of that – not one bit.'

Artorro said he had stopped to see what the new boy meant, worried that maybe something had disturbed the rats and they were coming their direction team-handed. Finally, Artorro turned to the big man who was heading fast towards a panic attack and said, 'That ain't rats, you daft cunt – we're in the sewers.' Jobbies, turds call them what you will, they were floating past by the thousand. 'I mean, Paul,' Artorro said, through a laugh, 'what did the stupid cunt think he'd find down there? Fucking rose bushes?'

By then Artorro was driving through the city traffic, cutting back on himself towards my destination.

'There it goes,' I said.

'What?'

'My hotel.'

'I fuckin' know that, don't I? Need to show you something else.' Sure enough we sailed past the Tower Bridge Hotel towards this other impressive building where he proceeded to tell the tale of another daring heist.

'We'd worked our way into the building from the usual route – the sewers – and climbed up to hit the target first time,' he explained. 'Thing was we were faced with the fuckin' biggest old vault I'd ever seen and that's saying somethin'. It wasn't so much a safe as a fuckin' armoured chamber. It had been around for a long time and I reckoned if old Hitler had managed to flatten London all that would've been left standin' was that fuckin' massive vault.'

They had another new man on the team that day – the gelignite man. Though young, he'd come highly recommended as one of the best. As he set up his charge, the rest of the team prepared a room next door, pushing cabinets and the like against the wall adjoining the room with the vault to create extra barriers just to be safe.

'Stupid cunt,' muttered Artorro, clearly remembering the scene as if it were yesterday. 'BOOM!' He suddenly slapped the dashboard hard to emphasise the effect. 'Stupid cunt. Stuffed so much fuckin' gelly in it everything went up, including us next door. Lucky none of us were killed really.'

I thought I'd taken some risks in my time but the thought of hanging around as a load of gelignite exploded gave me the creeps.

'Once we'd picked ourselves out of the rubble we still had problems. Couldn't see fuck-all because of the smoke or hear fuck-all for the ringin' in our ears. When we eventually got our senses together, we realised that not everything had caught the blast – like the fuckin' vault. It was just dented. Stupid cunt.'

The team went back down to the sewers to take stock. Most were all for chucking it, especially when word came from their eyes on the street that the cops were sniffing around, obviously alerted by alarms set ringing by the explosion. Five tense minutes later, they received the all-clear. The bizzies had tried the door of the building next door, looked up at the windows and, satisfied that everything was OK, they'd swiftly buggered off.

Most of the crew were still all for calling it a day but Artorro and another guy thought they could carry off the job. Besides, it was near Christmas and they could all have used a leg-up. So, with the others gone, Artorro and his mates set about the vault with cutting gear.

'And did you pull it off?' I asked, laughing at the tenacity of the guy.

"Course we did,' he smiled, 'and lifted a lot more than we'd bargained on.'

'A good Christmas then?'

'You bet – and for the other geezers too.'

'You cut them in?' Can you imagine that happening these days?

'Oh, yeah – it was only right,' he said, in a matter-of-fact tone, 'but we got a better sweetener than they did. That was only right too.'

Yet another bloody time, Artorro drove straight past the Tower Bridge Hotel to show me another scene of some daring robbery.

'You're like that Mad Frankie Fraser with his Gangster Tours,' I laughed through my exhaustion. Fraser had been taking tourists on an open-topped double-decker round the east-end crime scenes like The Blind Beggar pub where Ron Kray killed George Cornell, one of the Richardson gang. Most folk laughed at Fraser in a 'how the mighty have fallen' sort of way but not Artorro, who had known Frankie for decades.

'You ever think of taking up the tours, then?' I asked.

'Fuck off – but good luck to Frank. At least he's still pulling an earner.'

At the fourth time of trying, Artorro did eventually stop at the Tower Bridge Hotel. In my room, I lay back on the bed, rolled a big fat joint and pulled deeply on the aromatic smoke. As the exhaustion and the dope brought deep relaxation, I thought of Artorro's tales of his early days and I missed them. I had no right to, of course, not having been as much as a glimmer in my old man's eye when Artorro had started in the business, but, to me, they seemed tell of a better time – a more noble time, a time when people worked to some standards and you could trust people. Trust even thieves at least to do the right thing by the public and by their mates.

I fell asleep happy, thinking of those times and feeling honoured to know a good man like Artorro who trusted me enough to share those memories. He could take me hostage any time he wanted.

I fell asleep happy but also a wee bit sad. Those days would never return – as I was about to find out the next day. A rude wakening lay ahead.

18

POKEY IN THE EYE

Waking up in a hotel room is a wee bit like waking up in a prison cell – at first, you wonder where the hell you are. Then, as it begins to dawn on you, the business at hand grips your guts for better or worse. Some days, even in the best of hotels, you can't be entirely sure which is about to occur. That's where the similarities end, of course. No matter how bad things are for you in that hotel room, at least you're still free. That morning I wasn't too bothered but you never can tell what a visit to a cop shop is going to throw up.

As arranged, I met with my lawyer from a top London firm recommended to me by Joey Pyle. I reckoned that, if Joey Pyle rated the guy, he had to be the best. Come to Glasgow and I'll tell you the best legal bods there. That's the type of knowledge that comes with the business.

The lawyer was impressive right from the off. On the phone, we'd agreed that he would try and get the cops to make a full disclosure. That would mean them laying out the case and why they wanted to investigate me. Some folk may find it hard to believe that the cops can disrupt your life, lose you friends and worry you like hell but still aren't obliged to spell out why. Yet that's the way it is.

At first, they had agreed to full disclosure and then said no. My immediate guess was that they were trying to protect someone and I reckoned I knew who – an old friend who'd turned adversary big time.

After the bogeymen went crashing into Sandra's house, they left some paperwork to do with the warrant to search the place, including a list of names of those involved. One was a Glasgow guy, Paul McCusker, who, in my opinion, ran his security businesses in a really dodgy way. McCusker had asked me to carry out some consultancy work for him. That was one of the things I did for a living after I was released from jail in January 2002.

At first, I'd been happy to take on the work but I'd later found out that he'd left too many of his stewards unprotected and uninsured. He also forced them to rent houses from him and then claim housing benefit till he sacked them and evicted them at the same time. Not my kind of guy so I told him to stuff it.

For some reason, McCusker took it personally – no idea why. He did various things to try and make my life uncomfortable. It was like being dive-bombed by a fly – irritating, that's all.

Also on the list was the name of a man I used to consider a close friend – Ben Alagha. Alagha was the grandson of the Shah of Iran. He'd been exiled to Britain when the Ayatollah and his crew threw the royalty out. He wasted no time showing his colours when he got nabbed trying to swindle the Iranian government out of millions of pounds. So far, no problem to me.

I'd met Ben while I was just a young man through my brother Billy, who was serving a life sentence for murder. Ben had befriended me and offered me chances to earn a fortune and get out of the crime game. One time, down in Wandsworth jail, Billy had saved Ben's neck. When both he and eventually Billy were released, Ben, a very wealthy man, swore to look after Billy for the rest of his life – a life for a life.

By that time I was in jail for gunrunning, down in Belmarsh Prison to start with. My family always tried to keep bad news from me while in jail. Most prisoners' families do the same. Even at that, I was getting the feeling that Billy felt he'd been dumped on by Ben – that the Shah's grandson wasn't keeping his word. As ever, I resolved to make my own mind up when I was free. That's when I learned that Billy hadn't told me half of it.

Ben was involved in rape, several international cons, the slave trade and worse. He had been involved in massive tobacco smuggling with some Russian Mafia and had cheated them big time by carrying out a raid on one of their warehouses with his team dressed as Customs and Excise men. Cheating on his own partners – that was his style. But that wasn't good enough for Ben. He was also trying to set up Billy to take the fall in something he had no part in. Being on licence for the rest of his life for the murder conviction, if Billy had gone down he might never have seen beyond the jail walls again. Ben Alagha, the man whose life he had saved, was going to put him away for the rest of his life.

When I started dirty digging, I found out that Ben had tried to raise hit contracts on women and children and some hairy-arsed adults such as me and his former housekeeper. But he'd made too many enemies and one brought us an affidavit signed by Ben and witnessed by a lawyer wherein he admitted that he had been a registered informant of Scotland Yard and MI5 for over fifteen years.

I've written about all of this in more detail in *Vendetta* and there's more, much more. By the time of my visit to London, *Vendetta* had been published and I reckoned Ben was out to get revenge. Well, his cover had been blown with a picture of him and all.

I reckoned the Met cops had changed their minds about full disclosure to protect Ben Alagha. So, because they weren't going to fully disclose, the lawyer advised me to have a no-comment interview. I'd no problem with that – never have a problem in not talking to the polis.

There we were, sitting in the interview room, two plain clothes on one side of the table, lawyer and me on the other, saying . . . well, nothing, aside from 'No comment' and that can get boring after a few goes. A few questions in, it was obvious that what they were investigating was a massive fraud of a bank. We're talking millions of pounds. Then it suddenly got interesting.

One of their questions was whether I'd gone to some little, sleepy village in the Lake District to meet a man to discuss the

fraud – a man by the name of Ben Alagha. OK so now I was paying attention. Did I go there on 21 May 2002? Screw the no-comment interview – I wanted to scream out.

Alagha had told them that, at my arrangement, we had met
there and gone into some detail about what I had been proposing.
Back in Iran, Alagha had been trained as a lawyer before he joined
the Iranian secret police, becoming an interrogator – shorthand for
torturer – a top job in that nasty crew. He was a smart one all right
and had managed to get all sorts of innocent folk sent down on his
mere fabrications. So was I in trouble? Was I worried? Was I fuck.

On 21 May 2002, I was in prison. Having been released from
Frankland top-security jail in January that year, a propaganda
campaign by Strathclyde bizzies resulted in my release licence
being revoked and I'd ended back in jail, much to my annoyance.
But the cops' report was based on total fallacies and I was released
pronto by the Home Office six weeks later when they first looked
at the allegations. Point was I was in jail on 21 May 2002. What better alibi did a bloke need?

I wanted to scream out and answer that question. Trouble is
there are no half measures in a no-comment interview. To answer
one question but not the rest is used as casting some doubt on
your integrity. So I had to sit there biting my tongue, frustrated but
happy in the knowledge that Ben Alagha wasn't half as bright or
nearly as thorough as he thought he was.

After the interview, I told my brief about my whereabouts on 21
May 2002.

'You got to be bloody jokin',' he said with a big smile spread
across his face. He knew what I was telling him was a Get Out of
Jail Free Card should it ever be needed. Always useful when a collaborator with the Dark Forces is trying to do you harm.

Home to Glasgow was my next move, happy in the knowledge
that Alagha's plot had come unstuck. But other problems were
waiting for me.

Before the interview with the Met I discovered that the Royal
Bank of Scotland was refusing to have anything to do with my

friends. At the time, I was working as a security consultant and had regular contract with a company called Frontline. The first we realised of this problem was when they were refused an account and had to go elsewhere for the factoring finance arrangements necessary in that business – in spite of the fact that their books were well maintained and totally above board and showed the company to be highly profitable. It was also in spite of one of the bank's top men being happy to accept Frontline's hospitality in attending a fundraising dinner to commemorate the twentieth anniversary of Ken Buchanan winning the World Boxing Lightweight Championship.

Then a pal of mine, with no association at all with Frontline, got the same treatment. Time for me to test it out.

Sure enough, in spite of being well in funds, I got a knock-back. Alagha had set out to get me jailed. He failed in that but he had got to me in different ways. In business, it's not good, not good at all, for such a big prestigious financial institution as the Royal Bank of Scotland to refuse you an account. After all, a student in debt can open an account with them. With my record it was important that showed I all my money up front with nothing to hide. The best way to do that is through a bank account. Now here I was being refused by one of the world's largest banks – in spite of never having banked with them before.

For a while, I thought that Alagha had landed me right in the shit and all by a whispering campaign. Given that I was offence free and very solvent, thank you very much, I can only conjecture that Strathclyde Police had used the bogus allegations from Alagha to have a quiet word in the ear of top folk at the Royal Bank.

A short while later, I solved the problem by going to an independent financial adviser who soon fixed me up with as many bank accounts as I needed – and all legal, of course. Shame I had to put my money through foreign-owned banks, though. His view was that, if the cops had gone whispering to one bank, they'd have been round all the main British banks.

I knew that all the Scottish banks were on the alert since a couple of years earlier the Bank of Scotland had been fined a record sum for not having the proper procedures to monitor money laundering – not good publicity, that.

The irony struck me big time. For the first time in my adult life, I was totally legal with all my money coming from accountable sources yet it was only then that the banks backed off me. Some other former street player trying to go straight, without as many resources, a good means to earn a living and, most important of all, good friends, would have been in the shit. These days, how do you pay a mortgage, council tax, car loans and all the palaver that is part of modern life without a bank account? It might be enough to drive some men back to crime.

Looking back on that episode, it strikes me how, one day, the bold Artorro was honouring me with tales of his past and, the next, the evil Alagha was trying to do me damage. Artorro was a fairly recent friend who I immediately knew could be trusted and it was mutual. Alagha was an old friend who had turned rotten. Probably he was never any kind of friend at all at any time.

People can surprise you good and surprise you bad. Do we ever learn from them? A few years earlier I'd watched another man turn bad. This time with fatal consequences.

19

OVER AND OUT

'Mr G to Mr P,' the radio crackled white noise. 'Mr G to Mr P. Are you reading me?'

I was driving a car through Glasgow's east end. In the back seat was my partner in crime Tam Bagan. We worked as bagmen and equalisers for Arthur Thompson, who some folk saw as The God-father of Glasgow. In the front seat beside me was Thompson's son, named for his father but who everyone knew as Arty Farty, due to a strong and evil flatulence problem, or Fatboy, due to his body shape and disgusting eating habits. We'll call him Fatboy here.

Fatboy was talking into a CB radio in a rigmarole Tam and I had heard a thousand times.

'Mr G to Mr P,' he twittered on again.

'Mr P to Mr G,' the answer came over the wire sounding faint and broken. 'Receiving you loud and clear. Come in.' Mr P stood for Mr Paisley and Mr G stood for Mr Glasgow. When I watched *Reservoir Dogs* years later, I burst out laughing during the early scenes for no other reason than the characters' names – Mr Brown, Mr Blue and so on – reminded me of Fatboy and his pal.

Mr Glasgow was, of course, Fatboy. Mr Paisley was a bloke by the name of Grant McIntosh who, funnily enough, was top dog on the streets of Paisley. For those who don't know, Paisley is a large town so close to Glasgow that outsiders could be forgiven for not noticing where one ended and the other began. It's an old place, some claim older than Glasgow, with a reputation as being tough as fuck. Whatever you want, you can get in Paisley and, if you're not careful, you get a few things you don't want as well.

To be the top man out there, you had to have your wits about you and no mistake. Having heard about Grant McIntosh, I gave him some credit simply for running the show in Paisley. That was credit, not respect. Respect he'd have to earn.

The first time I listened to the Fatboy on that CB doing his Mr G and Mr P act, I listened very carefully. This had to be important for those two players to set up CB radios they always carried with one contact only – each other. So my ears were well pricked up. What a disappointment. It was all about where they were, where they were going, who they might look up – a kind of forewarning of years to come when the guy next to you in the pub uses his mobile phone to tell his missus he's in the pub and ask what's for dinner. Annoying as fuck, in other words, and trivial.

Tam Bagan and I soon reached the view that the Fatboy was a bit of an arsehole wannabe gangster and this CB radio lark was just another one of his games. Grant McIntosh – Mr P – on the other hand, I still gave the benefit of doubt to. It's long been my policy to not judge people till I know them well enough to make up my own mind.

To be fair to Mr G and Mr P, they did have joint enterprises going that were raking in a load of money. One of my regular jobs was to collect large sums of dough from the Paisley mob. McIntosh's linkman was one Ned Kelly – I kid you not – and I became quite fond of wee Ned and his boss. When Ned turned up to make payments, the dosh was always spot on. It would surprise you how the big-name players would keep a tenner back here and there. Not Ned Kelly and, therefore, not Grant McIntosh.

McIntosh was a big guy with bright red hair. He'd been an extremely promising footballer and some said he could have made it professionally. I don't know enough about football or him to comment but I do know that he chose the street. This isn't unusual in the crime career. Joey Pyle, for example, could easily have made it as a boxer but chose the more lucrative game of robbery instead.

Some reckon that Pretty Boy Roy Shaw would have been a contender for the World Heavyweight title if he hadn't taken to robbing security vans single-handed. Among Glasgow street players of my generation, there are plenty of guys who should've been footballers. Mind you, there have been a few footballers who were also street players.

The cops sniffed out that Mr G and Mr P were linking forces and they moved in. This resulted in those two being arrested for what were described as minor charges. The pair of them were held in custody to appear at Paisley Sheriff Court so Tam and I went along. Minor, my arse. It was a full-blown trial and this plain-clothes Drugs Squad cop, called Terence Higgins, no less, was up there giving evidence. At that time, I was still wee and skinny with a head full of hair that seemed too big for my body – young and even younger looking, in other words. This bizzy Higgins looked younger still. No one would have paid him a second glance suspecting he was a cop. No wonder he was able to get close enough to Messers P and G to land them in trouble.

A short while later, both McIntosh and Fatboy got done for much more serious drugs charges and were sent down big time, with Fatboy getting the worst of it. One look at that cop Higgins should have warned them off – told them that the serious mob was on their tail. But greed, ambition and power are terribly corrupting in any walk of life – no less so on the street. Mr G and Mr P probably thought they were untouchable, a state of mind certain to lead you right into the pokey.

Fatboy was dispatched off north to PeterHell – that's Peterhead Prison to you – while McIntosh was left in BarL – Glasgow's Barlinnie Prison. It so happened that I had also been sent down for eighteen months on other unrelated charges and was dumped in BarL in the same hall as McIntosh.

He quickly established himself as the tobacco baron, working the two-for-one system. If someone borrows half an ounce, they repay an ounce – lucrative while you're in jail but pretty worthless when you're free. The guys who usually go for that lark are the small-time hardmen or the top boys who are in for a long spell. McIntosh was neither. Still, it wasn't any of my business why he took to the loan sharking (since that's exactly what being a tobacco baron in jail was all about, except the currency was baccy not pounds). Maybe he just wanted to be in charge.

Yet Mr P had another problem that soon earned him a new nickname – The Ginger Whinger. This one wasn't that hard to work out – Ginger due to his carrot red hair and Whinger because he moaned about absolutely everything. The Mr P tag is long forgotten but The Ginger Whinger, that's alive and kicking years later.

Not long into his sentence, The Ginger Whinger decided to expand his jailhouse empire and extended his role to that of sweetie baron. I'd never come across this before but old Ginger Whinger wasn't so daft, I suppose. This was before the government introduced the mandatory drugs testing that would encourage so many people to avoid their usual dope because it stays in the human system for a long time. Of course, we all now know that so many of those cons have taken to smack with disastrous consequences. But, in the 1980s, there was so much dope floating about the jails that it meant a lot of people were suffering the munchies and were willing to pay top dollar for a sugar hit when they needed it. Add to that the usual lot struggling to cope with the soul-destroying sameness of the stodgy prison diet and he had a nice wee business going. You'd think he'd be happy at that, eh? As if.

The Ginger Whinger was moaning on and on and on. He always talked openly about those he claimed were behind in paying their tobacco debts now he had the sweetie debtors to grumble about too. Debts in jail are even more sensitive than in the outside world. If it got around that some guy couldn't pay back an ounce of snout, others might see it as a sign of weakness and take advantage. If it was that way with tobacco, just think how quickly your reputation could be ruined for owing a KitKat.

The Ginger Whinger was welcome to his cottage enterprises as far as I was concerned. What I didn't like, though, was how he would publicly and loudly slag people off. Not so much the sweetie baron, more the sweetie wife. That's when I decided to take the piss.

One day, when he was out taking exercise, me and a mate raided his cell, going straight to where he kept his sweeties. McIntosh was so sure of his own power that he didn't make much of an effort to hide his goodies. Who would have the nerve to steal from Grant McIntosh? From Mr P himself?

Half an hour later, he came back in and promptly discovered that his sweetie stash was gone.

'YA BASTARDS!' He was standing on the prison landing screaming his head off. 'Ye better return ma gear or you're fucking DEAD MEN.' His 'gear' amounted to a box of assorted Mars Bars, Pan Drops, KitKats, chocolate digestives and Snickers, then called Marathon Bars. His 'gear'? Was this the same man who was going to take over the whole of Scotland in cahoots with Fatboy Thompson?

Jail can do funny things to the most unlikely people. In Mr P's case, all I could say was that it had brought him down to a petty level he'd never stoop to in the real world.

'How the mighty have fallen,' I said to my mate who'd helped me half-inch the chocolate and sweeties.

Outside on the landing there was a roar, 'AH'M FUCKIN' TELLING YE. LAST CHANCE TAE GET MY STASH BACK OR THERE WILL BE BIG TROUBLE.'

From their locked cells other prisoners were shouting back things like, 'Hey, Grant, any Mars Bars left?' and laughing fit to burst. In my cell, I looked across at my partner in crime who smiled as he dunked another one of The Ginger Whinger's liberated chocolate biscuits in his mug of tea. Did we return the goods? Aye, right.

A short while later, The Ginger Whinger was transferred to another jail but he didn't make it to PeterHell where Fatboy had been dumped. PeterHell wasn't the sort of place you'd want to go at that time and it was definitely the hardest jail in Scotland. It was where they put the most dangerous criminals and had housed every hard case for decades.

Fatboy wasn't in PeterHell because he was hard though. OK, he was Arthur 'The Godfather's' son and his old man, helped by his lifelong pal, Paddy Meehan, had helped an associate of his, Teddy Martin, escape from PeterHell in the 1950s. But no one thought that Arthur would break his son out of jail in the 1980s. It was all too obvious. Fatboy wasn't in PeterHell because he was a risk but because he was at risk.

Fatboy had adopted his father's mantle from an early age and went about asking everyone and anyone, 'Do you know who I am?' By doing so, he made sure they knew who he was or, at least, whose son he was. The Fatboy couldn't hold a match to his father but no one had told him that – ever. So he went around threatening people and, in jail, that's lethal. So he was dumped up in PeterHell for his own protection.

It wasn't just the prison system that was trying to protect Fatboy. His old man had taken well care of that. A Glasgow player, Frank 'The Iceman' McPhee, was serving a spell for drug trafficking. Now he was a cold-hearted, dangerous bastard and no one was surprised when they shipped him off to PeterHell. When the Fatboy arrived a short time later, The Iceman was ready. He had a new job as Fatboy's bodyguard.

Grant McIntosh, The Ginger Whinger or Mr P, wasn't to be reunited with his erstwhile partner Mr G in jail, though – lucky break for him. But I would run into him a few years later and see another side to the sweetie baron. And there was to be nothing sweet about it.

20

RED AND GREEN SHOULD NEVER BE SEEN

'Ladies and gentlemen, please raise your glasses.' Grant McIntosh stood in the busy hotel hall holding court. Around him, people took to their feet, the music stilled as a toast was to be given. 'I give you Arthur Thompson.'

'Arthur Thompson,' people echoed back in unison before taking large mouthfuls of booze. It was a champagne do with a free bar, after all, and McIntosh was footing the bill. One question remained unanswered: which Arthur? Father or son? The live one or the dead one?

It was 1991 and McIntosh had been out of jail for a good length of time. He and Fatboy had put their plans to take over Scotland's streets on hold to be acted on as soon as Fatboy was also free. One problem – on the day Fatboy was released in preparation for freedom, he was shot dead in the street outside his father's house.

I was in the secure Wendy House at BarL jail, charged with that killing and a score of other crimes, from attempted murder to kneecapping. McIntosh, most distraught at the Fatboy's death, went to the funeral and afterwards paid a visit to The Godfather's house, The Ponderosa, to pay his respects. That's when old Thompson broke the news. The night before the funeral, someone had killed my best pals, Bobby Glover and Joe Hanlon, and dumped their bodies on the funeral cortege's route.

Old man Thompson was clearly delighted by this move, as was McIntosh. A few days later, The Ginger Whinger set up a celebration party with the drinks on him. So which Arthur was he toasting? His deceased business partner? No chance – it was the old man himself.

All night, as McIntosh got drunker and drunker, he boasted more and more about how he was now in business with Arthur Thompson Senior, giving it Godfather this and Godfather that. Me, I had sussed Thompson out long before and didn't see him so much as The Godfather but more as The Codfather and those who ran with him – or for him – were nothing more than fishwives.

I didn't find out any of that till years later – more's the pity. I knew that McIntosh was doing some work for Thompson, of course. That move might be regrettable in my view but it was no big deal. The party celebrating Bobby and Joe's death, on the other hand, was more serious altogether but I was oblivious to that at the time – otherwise this story might well never have happened. There would've been another tale to tell and there would've been no fairytale ending for McIntosh.

At the time of McIntosh's party, I was well locked up, breaking my heart over my two comrades and working at winning the trial. If I was found guilty, I was looking at spending the rest of my active adulthood behind bars. In other words, I'd a few things on my mind that were more important than The Ginger Whinger.

After the longest criminal trial in Scottish legal history to that date, I was found not guilty on all counts. The media predicted blood on the street on my release as I took over Scotland. The frenzy even reached the southern media with *The Observer* putting me on the cover of their magazine – they had me standing in front of a collage of Glasgow burning. Me? I just fucked off down south.

In truth, I couldn't be bothered with that whole Glasgow scene any more. That, plus I was now free at last to feel for my mates, their wives and their sons. Jail was a hard place to grieve – with the segregated Wendy House the hardest of the lot. If I'd shown any sign of weakness, there would have been screws in BarL who would happily wipe me out, some of them paid by Arthur Thompson. So, free of that shit hole, I was going to allow myself to relax and be human for the first time in many long months.

After seeing to some business in Glasgow, I was spending most of my time in Manchester and London where I'd often hook up with the bold Artorro. One day there in 1995, Artorro took me aside saying he needed my help. No problem but the request was a wee bit different. He wanted me to get back some money that had been stolen – talk about poacher turned gamekeeper . . .

Artorro arranged a meet with the aggrieved guy, Irish Paul, named for obvious reasons, and it all became clear. Irish Paul had been ripped off, having been relieved of a six-figure sum of money in an Edinburgh hotel. Bad as that was, there was worse – he was holding the cash for someone else from across the water. Though he didn't spell it out, it seemed likely we're talking the Republicans here. You didn't lose these guys' money and live. Irish Paul was more than anxious. He was shitting it.

Irish Paul had the name of the rip-off merchant – Brocky, a huge lump of a guy from Paisley who, it so happened, worked for Grant McIntosh. Our paths were going to cross again for the first time since the Great Mars Bar Heist.

After a bit of homework, I set up a meeting in a Paisley pub with Brocky, McIntosh and me. My notion was that The Ginger Whinger should be there because he was Brocky's boss. If the rip-off man wouldn't sort this out himself, then the top man should.

As I headed into the pub on my own, Irish Paul was sitting in a parked car about fifty yards from the front door. The plan was that I'd try and persuade the Paisley guys to come along with me to meet in another place. At that, Irish Paul would clock Brocky and, if he was the robber, he'd give me a thumbs up.

Before I reached the pub door, I noticed someone looking a bit suspicious across the road. To you and yours, he might have just looked like a young guy standing at a bus stop. To me and mine, he looked like a lookout and backup for The Ginger Whinger. Standing in a prime position to see what was going on, he'd be able to get into the pub double-quick or have a pop at me if I got up to badness and made a hasty exit. I might well have been wrong but it would have very reckless of me not to test it out. Reckless? It might have been suicidal.

'Excuse me, mate,' I said, crossing the road from the pub to the bus stop. 'Can you help me?'

'Eh, aye?' he replied, looking straight at me. 'Aye.' No matter how hard you try to avoid it, when you're speaking to someone your eyes automatically search them out. As his did so, it gave me the chance to have a good look at his face. I thought I recognised him but couldn't be sure. What is certain was that he looked startled, baffled, like this wasn't in his script.

'I'm supposed to meet someone in a pub round here,' I went on.

'Aye,' he nodded but was looking away, peering up and down the road as if looking out for a bus.

'Could you tell me where the nearest pub is?' I asked, knowing fine well I'd just walked across from the front door of one and knowing he'd seen me.

'The whit?' His feet were moving, edgy, nervous and he was still intently looking for that public transport.

'The nearest pub, pal – where is it?'

'Look there's one there, mate,' he said, pointing right behind me, 'and there's one just doon the road there.' Pointing in the direction he meant, he turned and lifted his arm, raising his jacket just enough for me to see the bulge under his T-shirt where it overlapped the back of his denims' waistband. He was carrying and I don't mean weights.

Thanking the guy, I left him and started walking back. Much later on, I'd find out that I was right. The bus-stop boy worked for Grant McIntosh and his sidekick David Donnell. They called the guy Babyface because he was so young looking and most of the women fancied him. But looks mean fuck all. Turns out that he was the most mental of all that Paisley mob, which was saying something – a top man, in other words. But that was for later – right then, I was going into the pub on my own.

Some might say that waltzing into that pub in Paisley alone was suicidal. They have a point. But, as well as Irish Paul's motor, there was another car nearby with a couple of my boys in it. I didn't think they'd be needed but insurance is always a good policy.

When I eventually persuaded McIntosh and Brocky to leave the pub, Irish Paul was practically hanging out the car window with both thumbs frantically jabbing the air. As the three of us walked along the pavement, I waved across to bus-stop boy, setting him off looking for the bus again. Then I gave a discreet nod to my guys in their car to get ready. Then I explained the situation to The Ginger Whinger and Brocky, in particular indicating that the money didn't belong to Irish Paul and suggesting who it did belong to. The way I looked on it, I was doing them a favour. No matter how hard you are, who the fuck wants paramilitaries at their door?

There was some squabbling, arguing and a hell of a lot of denial from Brocky and it was getting on my tits. I pulled him round, squared up to him, moved in close so that I had to crane my neck back to look up into his eyes.

'You're well fucked,' I said, nodding over my shoulder to the car where Irish Paul sat for all to see. Brocky was snookered for sure. It was that minute when he could have played along with me or gone for the shooter he'd inevitably be carrying. Instead, McIntosh butted in, saying that he'd sort it. So I gestured towards my car and invited the two of them to come with me and make arrangements.

You'd have thought I'd pulled a Mac-10 on the bastards. Instant paranoia descended and they got as jittery as horses at a slaughterhouse. No way were they going into that motor. No way. They probably thought it was a long goodbye drive, one-way with no return ticket. Brocky looked for all the world like he was ready for the hundred-metre sprint.

'You can run if you like,' I said to him, still keeping close, my neck still craning back so I could look him in the eye. 'But you'll never outrun a bullet.' The man mountain went puce and looked like he was about to puke. I almost stepped back to avoid the multicoloured cascade.

'Paul, I don't want to stick anyone in,' said Brocky, looking down at me and holding my gaze, 'but it's not all down to me.' He then turned and stared right at The Ginger Whinger. It was as good as pointing a finger at his boss. All three of us knew exactly what he was saying.

McIntosh swore that he'd fix the problem and quickly – get the money and make sure it got back to Irish Paul via me. But then he made excuses that he had to go and go right away – probably a very wise man.

'What the fuck did you do that for?' demanded Irish Paul later.

'What?' I asked.

'Let them two fuckers go. That big ginger-haired cunt was there too,' he went on, simply confirming what Brocky had already indicated. 'He was the bastard keepin' fuckin' lookout in the hotel lobby when that bastardin' giant was rippin' me off, so he was.'

Getting Irish Paul to calm down took a while but I eventually managed it, reassuring him that, if Grant McIntosh said he would sort it, he would – he was a man of his word. That's what I believed or I would've sorted it right there and then myself.

Over the next few weeks, I received a number of phone calls from the Paisley mob explaining that the money would be handed over but no one was prepared to turn up with the cash in case they never returned – an understandable fear but I'd no plans for any type of shenanigans.

What I later found out was that McIntosh had had one of his men planted outside that pub too – some guy I had noticed standing at a bus stop, apparently. Maybe it was McIntosh and Brocky who were planning some shooting and assumed, as people do, that I had the same notions.

Eventually, it was agreed that the cash would be paid by banker's draft. Not as good as cash but much safer than a cheque – banker's drafts don't bounce.

One day when I was in London again, I got a call from the offices of one of my companies, DEM Security Services, to say that a banker's draft payable to me for a very large sum of money had just been delivered. Immediately, I instructed a member of staff to jump on the first shuttle to London and bring the draft with them. But, when it arrived, there was another problem – the bloody thing was made out to Paul Ireland/Paul Ferris. What the fuck was that about?

Artorro came to the rescue yet again. He went immediately to a lawyer's office and swore that I often used the name Paul Ireland. The affidavit was then attached to the draft and it was handed over to a third party, a broker to cash. Speed was of the essence and the third party specialised in this type of transaction for a fee of 5 per cent.

Four days later – nothing. I was getting worried and angry – I was suspecting a con. Artorro calmed me down, saying that the third party was well trustworthy and knew the price for any rip-off – and we weren't talking 5 per cent.

On the fifth day, the shit hit the fan. The third party called to say that the draft hadn't so much bounced as bombed. The bloody thing had been stolen from a bank in Paisley. It was worthless. Worse than that, it could've incriminated me in a robbery I had sod all to do with. McIntosh might as well have aimed a loaded pistol at me.

As it happened, I was in the clear because we used a third party. Not that McIntosh would've known that – he'd have expected me to put the draft through my own account. If I had, I would've been in big shit.

Why was he looking to get me in trouble? Did someone grass me up for knocking his KitKats? Worse than that – it was sex.

A while before all this, I had met a woman by the name of Ria. What she told me, only after this grief with McIntosh, was that she used to go out with him. That she had given him the heave and he didn't take too kindly too it. Worse, he'd already been to see Ria's father on several occasions, trying to persuade him that I was no good for Ria.

Sex – isn't it lethal in the wrong hands? Well, it is with big guys who have yet to grow up. Red-haired McIntosh had a serious dose of the green-eyed monster – not a good look.

When I explained the situation to Artorro, I was deeply embarrassed. He had sought my help in an issue that concerned my home territory and had taken my word as far as The Ginger Whinger's trustworthiness was concerned. Not only had I let Artorro down, he had put his finance people in a most embarrassing situation – not good.

Explaining the situation to Irish Paul, I felt like some sort of lying cheat. What was he going to think? At worst, that I had pocketed the money and, at best, that I had been stupid to let Brocky and McIntosh walk away that night outside the pub in Paisley. I have no doubt that, if I had delayed them, Irish Paul and his mates would have inflicted some major violence on them whether or not the money had been paid. I had acted in good faith as a peacekeeper. Now I felt like a right prick.

A few days later, I got a very sad phone call from Irish Paul's wife. It seems he had suffered a severe blow to the skull and was gravely ill in hospital. A couple of days later, she phoned back to say he had died. No one was in any doubt that he had been made to pay a price for the loss of the money. Paid with his life. Died because I had assured him that Grant McIntosh was a man of his word. McIntosh might as well have murdered the guy himself. Why? Because I was going out with his ex-girlfriend.

After the murder of my two mates and my trial for the murder of Fatboy, I had sworn to myself to avoid serious violence at all costs. But this was different – a decent man had died for no bloody good reason. This was payback time.

A short while later, I headed to Glasgow and on to Paisley to see The Ginger Whinger. Glasgow Airport is in fact in Paisley and a short car ride from his haunts. From leaving Heathrow to being in his backyard took me all of an hour and a half. Yet somehow he'd got word of my journey and had conveniently fled the country. I might even have passed the dog as he drove one way and I drove the other.

Brocky had got on his toes as well. But at least he agreed to a telephone chat. It was clear he understood how the situation stood and he promptly left Scotland for England. It was a rule of the street – stay and face out the person you have backstabbed or commit yourself to exile. I'd leave him alone as long as he stayed away.

A few years later, Brocky went down big time for some offence where someone was killed. Eventually, he ended up in the same jail as a good pal of mine, Paul Massey of the Salford Team. Brocky spilled the beans to Paul, telling him that McIntosh had hoped I'd get nabbed trying to pass the stolen banker's draft through my account – exactly as I'd thought.

What of The Ginger Whinger himself? A coward, liar and scumbag for sure, the man was quite happy to see Irish Paul get taken out and to risk his man Brocky getting hurt just to see me go to jail. He's also taken to walking with the devil. A wee while back, he was caught with a load of coke but, amazingly, while it was in the custody of the cops, the coke transformed into speed and it became a much less serious matter entirely. Clever that, eh?

On the street now, he's viewed as a dog. Maybe that's why, when he went very quiet after the Irish Paul incident, he concentrated on another sport that he loves – breeding greyhounds. I suppose it takes a dog to know a bitch.

But sometimes the most unexpected people can surprise you for the better. Sometimes the most unlikely beings can find some common values with you. Like the time I was asked to make some canine connections. Question is would I get bitten?

21

OLD PALS AND DODGY INVITATIONS

Old friends – aren't they great? But, when you haven't spoken to them for a while, they can bring all sorts of changes into your life. This one was about to bring me a challenge in more ways than I could imagine.

It was the summer of 2005 when an old pal, Stephen 'Steph' Menzies, called me up. It was great to hear from him after a good few years. We'd first met in jail, Glenochil, where I spotted him as a young blood constantly giving the screws grief. Don't get me wrong, that's not something I disapproved of back then – quite the reverse. Yet I reckoned Steph was heading for a fall and decided to offer him some advice. Other older cons would just sit back and have a laugh at the stramash – maybe that's how you learn. But that is what had happened to me early doors in jail and I suffered in all sorts of ways just because I didn't know better.

On one occasion, my psoriasis was playing me up and the medic screws up at Longriggend just ignored me – probably as payback for me being an aggressive wee shite. Right, that'll work then, you arse-wipes. Within a week I was the reptile man, my skin splitting every time I moved. I was on fire and it was agony – the only way I got a few seconds' relief was by stripping naked and lying flat out on the stone floor of my cell. Made me feel really at peace with the world – not.

Steph Menzies didn't have psoriasis or any other discernible weakness but they'd get him. As sure as those gates were locked tight they'd get him and good.

In these young rebels I always recognised a wee bit of how I used to be. While I admired their bottle and shared their attitudes, I suppose I came over a bit paternal to them. But, as every parent knows, giving advice to a youngster might be well meant but that's not how it's always received.

As it happened, my approach was well received by young Steph. I tried to show him how a touch of diplomacy can win easier victories than all the aggro in the world. Although that always has its place, especially in jail – it was all about timing.

From that time on, Steph and I were close allies. That kind of bond lasts so, when he phoned me out of the blue, it was as if we'd been chatting just the day before.

As well as looking me up, Steph had a personal security issue he needed some help with. Well, that was my business, then, so anything like that's always welcome. A short time later, he called me from a payphone to put another proposal to me.

'I've got someone who wants to meet you, Paul,' he said, after pointedly telling me that he was in a public phone box. Without spelling it out, he was letting me know that the call couldn't be traced back to him.

'Sure,' I said, thinking it's nice to be nice.

'No,' he interjected, 'this one you'll have to think about.'

'Go on.'

'It's someone who's been in a bit of trouble most of his life,' he explained. 'Someone who wants to walk away from it. Who's looking for a bit of peace.'

'Aye, that'll be a problem,' I offered, knowing I wasn't adding much to the discussion. It was always difficult for a well-known street player to be given the room to retire. And I'm talking about retiring from the media here, not other players – being able to retire from some of them is another story. 'But what does he want from me then, Steph?'

'He's been reading your books, hearing about the film business and all that. And he knew about you before. Wants your advice on how you seem to have managed.'

Is that how my life appeared from the outside? From where I was standing, it was a day-to-day struggle with every day's newspapers bringing with them the prospect of some scandalous claim about me being back at the crime business. It was happening less and less as time passed by, right enough, but not so infrequently that I didn't worry.

'I'm not sure I'm the right guy to advise anyone, Steph,' I eventually said.

'Well, he thinks you are,' replied Steph. 'And he has a great deal of respect for you.'

'Are you no' going to tell me?' I asked.

'What?' he sounded perplexed, thrown. 'Tell you what?'

'No' what, Steph – who.'

'Who?'

'Who is it who wants to meet me?'

'Eh,' I knew Steph's style of talking. He was thinking, still not sure about mentioning the name. 'Eh . . . Johnny Adair.'

At the other end of the line, I held my breath – obviously for too long.

'Paul, did you hear me all right?' asked Steph.

'Oh, I heard you loud and clear.'

Johnny Adair – loyalist paramilitary leader, armed and dangerous – was embroiled in a bloody internal feud and his troops got chased out of Belfast one night in their droves.

Johnny Adair – alleged pal of Thomas 'The Licensee' McGraw – was said to have helped Adair's exiled foot soldiers while their leader was holed up in jail in Ireland. Johnny Adair – fierce anti-Catholic – was wanting to meet with this Catholic, though non-practising Catholic, boy. What do they say? Once a Catholic . . .

Johnny Adair – sworn enemy of all Republicans – was wanting to meet with someone who had spent time with members of the IRA and the Real IRA in jail.

Johnny Adair – so ferocious no one called him by his name any more. They knew him simply as 'Mad Dog'.

This was going to be interesting.

22

MAD DOG DAZE

There had been a few other Mad Dogs before in that northern slice of Ireland still under British rule. It was a top moniker – a hard one to earn and the only way to earn it was through brutality and ruthlessness. Johnny Adair earned it young and had earned it every day since.

For those unfamiliar with the Irish scene, Ireland was split in two – according to the Brits – north and south. Once upon a time, the whole island had been occupied by the British Army. That started to end in 1916 with the Easter Rising when Republican martyrs took over the central post office in Dublin. A few lonesome souls taking on the might of the most powerful army in the world? They knew they were going to perish. It was the principle, right?

Soon afterwards, the island was split with the south being given back to the Irish and the north being kept under British rule. It was the signal for furore between the Republicans who wanted a free united Ireland and the Loyalists who were defending British rule. Republicans and Loyalists. Catholic and Protestants. The north of Ireland and Belfast in particular became a war zone.

Johnny 'Mad Dog' Adair was a Protestant, a Loyalist and a commanding officer of the Ulster Freedom Fighters. The UFF's sole purpose was to do the IRA harm. Mad Dog excelled at that.

At the height of The Troubles, he was attracting the attention of the media. No surprise there – he didn't just act the part, he looked the part too. And there's nothing media luvvies love more than a neat nickname, especially one for street players and men of violence. In one interview, he declared that his sole purpose was to defeat Republicanism and all Republicans and, in that, he included all Catholics. And this is the man who wanted to meet me?

The Republicans had tried to kill Adair several times. The closest they got was in 1993 when a bomb in a chip shop killed nine people – but not Adair.

In 1995 he was jailed for sixteen years for directing terrorism. It was a new law to bag the men who didn't necessarily pull the trigger in all the hits yet he was the only person ever convicted of that offence. It became widely accepted that the law had been created to get him and only him off the street. All he did in court was admit being a commander of the UFF.

But let's not be shy here. You don't get the name Mad Dog by telling other guys to go dish the dirt. Mad Dog Adair had dealt out death, pain and maiming himself. The north of Ireland was a dirty war zone. He played the game to the full.

As much as he was hated on the Republican side of the fight, Mad Dog was loved on the Loyalist side. He was best pals with the Loyalist Volunteer Force founder Billy 'King Rat' Wright, who was gunned down in the Maze Prison right under the noses of armed screws.

As the British government, with Mo Mowlam as the Northern Ireland Secretary, tried to negotiate some peace agreement, they knew that Mad Dog had to be brought on board. Mo Mowlam carried out a most unusual secret visit to Mad Dog in the Maze. In the 1990s, the Loyalists had killed many more people than the IRA who were getting blamed for most of the violence in the British press. The British government liked that but they also knew the truth. They had to get the Loyalists on board and Mad Dog was top of their list.

Whatever was said in that meeting has never been revealed. What is known is that, in 1999, having served less than a third of his sentence, Adair was released early from prison under the so-called Good Friday Peace Agreement. It would never last.

A year later, he was at the centre of a feud between some Loyalist factions. Corpses were left strewn all over the lower Shankill area in west Belfast, Adair's territory, and the new Northern Ireland Secretary, Peter Mandelson, had Adair recalled to prison.

He was released again in 2002 but it took less than a year for yet another Northern Ireland Secretary, Paul Murphy, to sling him back in jail. Whatever your politics, it was plain that the British government, army and security services were terrified of Mad Dog.

While Mad Dog kicked his heels in jail, his wife Gina, aka Mad Bitch, and his supporters and troops were kicked out of Belfast by other Loyalist groups. It was the modern-day equivalent of the retreat to Dunkirk – only, instead of an evacuation over the Channel, it was an evacuation across the Irish Sea to where else but Scotland.

A posse of media and plainclothes cops was waiting for them in the dark that night and trailed them wherever they went. Reports ran in the media the next day about Mad Dog's troops settling in Scotland – no surprise there since many an asylum seeker from Ireland has settled in my homeland. Paramilitaries from both sides of the divide had made new lives for themselves in Scotland and more than a few had taken to the role of street player like a prisoner takes to freedom as they walk through the jail gates in the right direction. No problem.

But there had been rumours that I didn't like. That Thomas 'The Licensee' McGraw had met the party at the ferry and taken them under his wing. That the same Licensee had known the Adair Family for a long time. That Gina 'Mad Bitch' Adair was a close friend of him and his wife Margaret 'The Jeweller' McGraw – had been for years, so they said. Good for them but, to put it mildly, there was bad blood between me and The Licensee.

Rumours are rumours. Printed in the newspapers, they become accepted fact. That is the mindset even guys like me adopt though we try hard not to – even someone who has had many column inches printed about me that I know to be fallacious. Malicious and fallacious sometimes. My mindset wasn't helped by my knowledge that McGraw was a big Loyalist supporter and that his brother-in-law, Snadz Adams, was known to have been an honorary commander of the UDA for many years. Birds of a feather don't just flock together – they also get to know each other, don't they?

Mad Dog's troops and family had hung around Scotland for a while before flitting south to Bolton – not the kind of place you'd expect a bunch of Loyalist paramilitaries to settle but you never really know anywhere from a distance, do you?

A while later, Mad Dog was released from jail yet again and he joined his followers in Bolton. Trouble was he then had a big fall-out with his wife Gina and he left, ending up in Ayrshire. That fact seemed to confirm the reported connection with McGraw. Now he was asking to meet with me.

On the phone Steph explained that all Mad Dog wanted to do was get my advice on how to go about convincing the world he had changed into a peaceful citizen. Some advice was all. Me? I worried that it would be a permanent peace, my last resting place. Besides, did I want to meet with the devil? That's how many of my friends in Ireland saw Mad Dog.

Yet on the phone was Steph, a close and trustworthy friend of mine, reassuring me that he'd be there and absolutely nothing was going down. In the final analysis, I trust my pals. End of story. So the meet was on.

On the appointed day, I arrived at the designated pub in Ayr – early, of course, and with my own security planted all around the place. It wasn't that I didn't trust Steph – I did, absolutely – but there was always the possibility that he was a target in some shenanigans too. The security was insurance. That's all it was – only to be used if necessary.

So I arrived early, deliberately. Standing chatting with Steph, we saw Mad Dog's car pull into the car park and he and two others got out. One I recognised instantly as Mark Morrison, a Scottish guy who bobbed and weaved on the streets and was well known as a friend of Johnny Adair. The other turned out to be a friend of

Mad Dog from Ireland whose name I never got – fearsome-looking bloke, though.

I'd heard enough stories about all the atrocities committed in Ireland by Mad Dog and his like. As I watched the three of them walk slowly and nervously towards me, I felt uneasy – as if I shouldn't be there. But as acid churned in my stomach, I was watching him, looking right into his eyes. He was as wary as Bambi in hunting season.

Terse introductions having been made, we walked together towards the pub. From the side of my vision, I could see Adair's eyes flit from side to side, trying to spot the trap. There was no ambush and he could look as much as he wanted but he wouldn't see my men, my security.

In the pub, the five of us sat at a table. Conversation was sparse and the atmosphere was tense, edgy. I looked across at Adair and wondered about a guy who worries about a possible hit at a meeting he had requested. Then again, I'd been there myself, once upon a darker time.

'I want to say something before we start, Paul,' he broke the dense silence. 'I have fuck all to do with any supergrasses – that cunt McGraw included.' He was off to a good start in my book.

I was laughing, almost chuckling, for a very simple reason – that had been one of the points I'd decided to grill him on before we had any discussion.

But I had another one. 'What about his brother-in-law?' I asked.

He was looking at me blankly, his big shaven forehead wrinkled into a frown.

'Snadz Adams. Isn't he a commander of the UDA? Do you not know him?'

Mad Dog looked across at his mean-looking friend – the man who was never named and who just sat there scanning the room, his right hand hovering over the bulge on the side of his jacket.

'Was he not one of the ones who used to send the movement postal orders?' The big man's voice was friendly enough but his eyes still flickered around the room as he spoke and his hand hovered above his barely concealed shooter. 'Big team of robbers here in Scotland. So big the cuntin' Special Branch were on their tail.'

Adair just looked at him intently, blankly.

'There was one that was called something like Snadz – used to send us a load of money, Johnny. Every week, almost all in postal orders that had been cancelled here but we could cash back home. Then there was that other boy – Jonah. Aye, Jonah, who hadn't been too happy that so much cash was going out. Was grumbling about their team not getting enough.'

'Never heard of them,' said Mad Dog Adair. 'Don't know of any Snadz. And, if he was a so-called commander, it would have been like a toy loyalty badge for points collected. The only real commanders of the Loyalists are in Northern Ireland.' He looked around the room, more relaxed than his mate, buying a wee bit of time rather than looking out for shooters. 'Besides,' he hesitated again and repeated that pretend scanning of the horizon. Then he turned and stared at me straight on. It was the schemie look. The look you'll find in any rundown shit-trodden urban collection of humanity striving to get by. The look that says I might be shite but I'll take you. Any time. The universal look of schemies fighting to get on. Hands up – I warm to that look every time I clock it. Even in Mad Dog Adair. 'Besides, if he has anything to do with that Licensed cunt, then I don't want to know him.'

Ten out of ten for starters. But you have to be fair, I reckon – meet people half way at least. So I put a few of my cards on the table. Like the pals I had made from the Republican movement, my background and upbringing, the fact that I had MI5, MI6 and NCS on my back for a few years. Might still have. They might have been watching us as we spoke. That I knew he was on Republican hit lists – lethal people were actively seeking his whereabouts and not to visit for tea. He just nodded – politely, like – as if he knew all of that, had been well briefed. Or maybe he didn't care. Fair call. No wonder he had been nervous.

Then I asked him a question I was curious about – a question that had occurred to me at the height of my crime career. In spite of being enemies, there are some folk you can't help admire. Did he have anyone like that on the Republican front? Anyone at all?

'Bobby Sands,' he replied instantly.

Now he had my attention. Bobby Sands, for those who don't know, was a Republican who went on hunger strike for the right to be treated as a political prisoner. Nine days into that hunger strike, he was twenty-seven years old. Sixty-six days into that hunger strike, he died a martyr in 1981. I had imagined that he would be one of the most hated Republicans to every Loyalist anywhere.

'And the others who starved themselves to death,' Adair continued. 'How can you not respect someone willing to die – and die slowly – for what they believed in?'

Now I believed that. But this was coming from someone that many people I knew considered to be an uncaring, unprincipled killer. And he was talking about his enemy.

The ice was broken and it was free territory. Adair told me that Gerry Adams, leader of Sinn Fein the political wing of the IRA, had been an active terrorist and top of the Loyalist hit list for decades. Still was. Whatever he had been, Adams was leading the negotiations for peace with the British government. How ironic if the British-supporting Loyalists then assassinated him, ruining the plans of the British government they supported. Politics, it's more vicious than street crime any day.

I also asked him about Michael Stone, a Loyalist fanatic who, in 1988, went berserk at a Republican funeral in Milltown, killing three people. All captured on TV cameras, he was lynched by the Republican crowd before being cut down and rescued by the Brit troops. In custody, Stone admitted to another three killings – all IRA men, he claimed, though the victims' families denied that.

'Stone was never affiliated,' Adair said. 'Bastard was as mad as fuck. Thing is he asked some of our people for weapons for that funeral and some fucker gave them to him.' He looked at the table and shrugged his broad shoulders, more in resignation than anything else – telling the room that it was war and bad things happen in war.

I was beginning to be open to the idea that Mad Dog wanted to walk away from his past. Of course, he never could – no one can entirely – but, if he wanted to try and live a more peaceful life, who was I to stand in his way? Not giving him whatever advice I could would be like keeping him where he was – in big trouble and making big trouble.

To my mind, Adair was in shit, labelled for the rest of his life because he was so committed to Loyalism, Protestantism and that whole sectarian rigmarole that still festers on especially in Ireland and Scotland. Too often, men are still asked what football team they support – meaning Rangers for Protestants and Celtic for Catholics. I openly admitted to being a Celtic supporter and that I was born a Catholic but I wasn't taking any sides in that old war. I actually come from a mixed Protestant and Catholic family and I've been working at my neutrality all my life – though still, occasionally, one or two folk didn't believe me.

'Football?' Mad Dog was looking perplexed after I'd explained the Glasgow football-question phenomenon to him. 'But I don't even know much about the Rangers team. Couldn't even name many of the players.'

Well, that was a start. People would be shocked at that but would they be convinced?

Adair knew how hard it was all going to be and eventually got to the point. 'I need to know that I'll be left here to get on with my life, Paul,' he said. That was the main point of the meeting, I reckoned. If it was, he was going to be disappointed in my opinion. The press and sectarian groups would never leave him alone.

I reminded him that I was apolitical. That there was an unspoken agreement that The Troubles might well be supported by folk in Scotland but, no matter how strongly they felt, The

Troubles weren't to come to Scotland. So any street player I might have met in my criminal career would play no part in harming Adair, even if they hated him. That someone else might pop across on the ferry from Ireland . . . Now that was a different matter altogether.

There was one other point up for discussion. Adair had been approached by Donal McIntyre, the investigative journalist, to participate in a free-access documentary. Free access meant a film crew trailing Adair everywhere night and day for a while. What did I think?

It was a decent question since, the year before, I had done just that. I explained that, before anything else had happened, Reg had met with the film-makers and had a few chats. Only when he was convinced that they were going to make an honest film, that they'd allow him to be involved and that both of us would see the rough cuts and the final film, did we go ahead. Had Mad Dog that type of system going? Of course, he hadn't.

It crossed my mind that Reg and I should make a film of Mad Dog. I'd been setting up film-making facilities anyway and had a few hard-hitting projects in mind. If he really was trying to walk the straight road, it would make for a controversial but fascinating film. In the event, we wouldn't take that film idea any further and Mad Dog did indeed go on to work with Donal. As this book is being written, we're waiting to see the result.

But back then, leaving the Ayr bar, it was a long, slow walk. It had been a tense, terse meeting mostly but the Mad Dog boy had surprised me a few times in his honouring of Bobby Sands, his attitude to football and his conviction that I could simply put the word out and he'd live to collect his retirement pension in Scotland. If only life was that simple.

As we walked to our cars, each giving nods to the men we had planted round the place, there was sense of relief in the air. Mad Dog Adair was relieved he was still alive and, in truth, so was I.

But the nameless man at the table with Mad Dog had set me thinking. At one point, he had revealed he was originally from

Barlanark in the east end of Glasgow. It was a hard area stuffed full of hardmen but, for some reason, that day only one man was in my thoughts.

A certain one-eyed player was on my mind.

The Ross Street San Toi aka the Bowery Boys visit Blackpool to avoid some heat in Glasgow (1946). They are, left to right, John Sawers, Willie Ferris, John Clarke, James Canning and Jimma Hill.

Some weans take time out from playing on the streets of Garngad in 1956. Paul's older brother Billy is on the left at the back. Next to Billy is J. McCrimmon and, in front are J. Toye (left) and P. Kerr.

Mike Yarwood's Rolls in gem raid

BITTER: PC Olds yesterday

Anguish of a hero

CRIPPLED police hero Philip Olds won another bravery award yesterday— and said his life had become "pretty horrible" since he was shot tackling a gunman.

PC Olds, 29, was taken in his wheelchair to London's Bow Street Court to receive a certificate and £560 from the police award fund.

He said: "I do not wish I was dead but I sometimes think it would have been easier if the bullet had gone between my ears."

UPSET: Mike with his dented "pride and joy." Picture: ERIC HARLOW

ARMED raiders stole comedian Mike Yarwood's Rolls-Royce and used it in a gems raid worth £500,000.

By STEVE ATKINSON

The daring theft began at 11 a.m. yesterday when two smartly dressed men stepped from the red Rolls in London's Mayfair.

They marched up to the locked and bolted double-glass doors of exclusive jewellers Kutchinsky's in New Bond Street.

A commissionaire, impressed by the pair's dapper appearance, opened up.

Once inside the two men produced a shotgun and handgun. The commissioner and four salesmen were ordered to lie flat on the floor. Two

more gang members appeared. They smashed an inside display window and grabbed platinum jewellery.

No shots were fired and no one was hurt.

But there was mayhem as the gang sped off in the £42,000 Rolls with a fifth raider at the wheel.

It smashed into several parked cars. Impressionist Mike, who reported the theft from a London hotel car park last Friday, said: "It was my pride and joy."

He added: "Perhaps I should do a take-off of Shaw Taylor's Police Five programme now!"

Scared into bigamy?

SOLDIER John Walker, 41, was so petrified of his girl friend that he committed bigamy rather than tell her he was already married. Divorcee Linda Gander was a powerful and dominant personality who towered above Walker, magistrates at Colchester were told yesterday. His lawyer added: "It wasn't a deliberate act by a shy person but a timid one." Walker, of the Military Corrective Training Centre, Colchester, was fined £500 and £75 costs.

Corgi makes royal slip

THE QUEEN nearly came a cropper yesterday when one of her corgis went out of control.

The royal corgis were a little too impatient to board an Andover for the flight from Aberdeen to London after their Balmoral holiday.

Later at Heathrow, the RAF made sure there was no repeat of the navigational problem.

Officers gripped the dogs—all nine of them—tightly and carried them off the plane one by one.

News EXTRA

Poison alert

EXPERTS were called to a Greek cargo ship anchored off Cowes, Isle of Wight, yesterday after poisonous chemicals leaked from its hold.

Coma girl home

FORMER beauty queen Vanessa Willetts, 23, of Southsea, Hampshire, who was flown from Italy in a coma after a road accident in August, was able to leave hospital for home yesterday.

Training coarse

TRAINEES at a London school for butlers are being taught shooting and kung-fu to prepare them for jobs in America.

Better late . .

LADY BIRLEY, of Seaford, Sussex, who died in June aged 81, leaving £512,864 net wanted her funeral robes as "joyous and as inexpensive as possible."

PET CONTROL: The Queen tries to bring a corgi to heel.

ADVERTISER'S SHOCK ANNOUNCEMENT!

Comedian and impersonator Mike Yarwood isn't joking as he poses with his dented Rolls-Royce which was used in a jewellery heist. ('All That Glitters')

Martin Hamilton, aka The
Lord of the Rings, in one of
his less tortuous moods.
('No School')

Tommy 'TC' Campbell (right) and Joe Steele
(centre) after being freed pending their first
appeal against conviction for the
Ice-Cream Wars murders.
('Bloody Freedom' and 'Child's Eye View')

Grant 'The Ginger Whinger' McIntosh
in his athletic days before he took to
organised crime. ('Over and Out' and
'Red and Green Should Never Be Seen')

Jaimba McLean trying hard not to
look fierce. ('Posted Missing')

Johnny 'Mad Dog' Adair, always keeping an eye open for trouble. ('Old Pals and Dodgy Invitations' and 'Mad Dog Daze')

Gina 'Mad Bitch' Adair poses in her old work clothes. ('Mad Dog Daze')

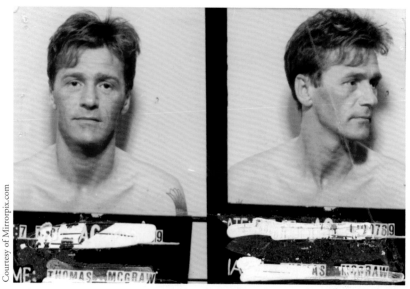

Thomas 'The Licensee' McGraw in a mug shot from a rare arrest. As usual he walked free. ('Mad Dog Daze' and 'Jonah No Pals?')

Blind Jonah McKenzie, with his lawyer, Joe Beltrami (right), is helped away from court. ('Twice Betrayed' and 'Jonah No Pals?')

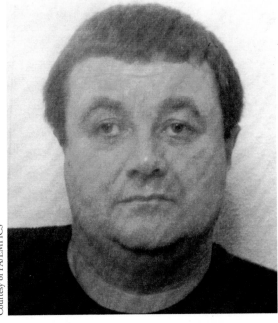

Dennis 'The Menace' Woodman, looking fatter but just as evil, poses for yet another mug shot. His cellmates had better watch out. ('Bad Karma')

Courtesy of Cassidy & Leigh

Courtesy of Photonews Service Ltd

Tommy Adams looking unusually sinister. But why? ('Priceless Love')

One of the notorious Arif brothers ('Wise Is as Wise Does' and 'Jaw, Jaw or . . .')

Courtesy of Mirrorpix.com

Courtesy of Newsquest (Herald & Times) Ltd

Paul 'Krazy Horse' Kerr, brother of Jim Kerr of Simple Minds – would you buy a second-hand car from this man? ('One Simple Mind' and 'The Consigliere and the Conmen')

Tam Bagan, once one of the most feared men in Glasgow, is led away to jail. Now he has found peace. ('Over and Out' and 'Jonah No Pals?')

Ian McAteer – did he really kill Warren Selkirk? Who is so desperate to keep him in jail? ('Spies, Lies and Wee Pies')

Londoner Noel Cunningham, last seen sprinting away from the armoured prison van that was meant to be taking him to jail. ('London Calling', 'Wise Is as Wise Does' and 'Jaw, Jaw or . . .')

Arthur 'The Godfather' Thompson and his wife Rita had a lot to smile about once upon a time – not any more. ('Dan, Dan the Desperate Man' and 'The Clown')

Paul's father, the lion-hearted Willie Ferris, and Paul's older son, Paul Junior. By the time he had become a doting grandfather, Willie had a few tales to tell. ('Old School', 'One Way Ticket' and 'Villains')

Brothers in freedom – a rare occasion, on 21 January 2001, when Paul (front) was able to meet up with his older brother Billy. Paul had just been released from Frankland Prison, Durham, and was vowing to go straight. Billy has since been jailed for murder although he is mounting an appeal.

23

TWICE BETRAYED

'Nice one wi' that blind bastard, Paul,' the young guy said, passing on his way. He was speaking in the same tone that some stranger might use to remark on what a lovely baby you had or how well behaved your dog was or how much he admired your car – except, on this occasion, he was congratulating me on killing someone.

I didn't argue even though I hadn't killed the man. If I'd protested my innocence, I could just imagine him seeing that as a humorous confirmation that I indeed had killed the bloke. It's a Glasgow thing. What was more, I understood why he thought I had killed him. There was a time – several times – when I was tempted.

Looking back now, it's only right to take stock of that man Jonah McKenzie, known as Blind Jonah, for reasons that will become obvious. I believe in listening to people you trust. Too many of those think highly of Jonah. So I'm listening and reappraising. There are a few tales that haven't been told about Jonah, ever – true tales that need to be told. I believe in that.

How does the old saying go? Don't judge a man till you walk a mile in his shoes? Well, let's go for a trek with Blind Jonah McKenzie.

Jonah was a patter merchant as they say in Glasgow – fast with his tongue and always quick with a joke. He was the kind of man who'd prefer to talk and convince rather than wrangle and fight – as long as there was a few quid in it for him, of course.

He was more than just a rip-off merchant though. Many a time, when trouble was about to kick off, the bold Jonah would take to the floor and talk the feuding sides down. But it was always difficult to see that that was what he was about since, most of the time, he'd talk about himself – tales of derring-do, every now and then returning to the dispute and explaining it away.

Loads of people thought of Jonah as a bit of a comedian. In Glasgow, that's not an insult but a compliment. Some of the hardest, smartest guys I've known make people laugh all the time. Let's face it, to take the piss and get off with it on the streets, you either have to be capable or suicidal.

Just because he preferred to talk didn't mean that Jonah couldn't fight. Or that he wasn't brave. He certainly could and he definitely was – but he should've chosen his friends more wisely.

In his young days, he ran with the BarL Team, then just another street mob from Barlanark that included guys like Snadz Adams, Thomas 'The Licensee' McGraw's brother-in-law. One time, they had a battle lined up against a mob called the Shettleston Tigers. Trouble was that the BarL Team were heavily outnumbered. In street terms, that didn't matter a fuck – rather get a doing than lose face. The bold Jonah charged right in. Problem was he was the only one.

As Snadz Adams and the rest slunk away to hide behind their mammies' skirts, Jonah found himself alone and surrounded by the Tigers. They couldn't believe their luck. Jonah McKenzie was a renowned street fighter who had inflicted damage on many of them. Now they had him where he couldn't possibly win.

Jonah stood his ground and fought. Those coming at him from the front paid a price. Even most of those coming at him from the back did too. Then he somehow got wedged against a wall and a few Tigers climbed it, edging along as the others battled Jonah below. When they fell down on Jonah he was poleaxed. They laid him out and laid into him. Finally, as he lay battered, bleeding and unconscious, one leaned over and stuck a knife deep into his eye socket.

Jonah McKenzie died that day – the same day that Blind Jonah McKenzie was born.

You'd have thought he'd have learned his lesson. Being abandoned by your crew to such a fierce mob is surely something most of us couldn't forgive. But Jonah somehow did and he went on to work with Snadz Adams in the BarL Team – armed robbers inc.

We mention the BarL team elsewhere. It was the team of robbers who were so successful that the security services were drafted in to help nab them and failed. Its membership changed from time to time but it featured The Licensee, TC Campbell, Snadz and Jonah. It was the same mob who specialised in post offices and, when the authorities here started cancelling the postal orders they stole, they'd send them to the Loyalist groups in Ireland. There, the postal orders would take longer to be cancelled and they had people on the inside in the Post Office who made sure they were cashed. They'd send them to the likes of Mad Dog Adair's mob – contributing a fortune to that cause. At least Snadz Adams did. TC and Jonah were just interested in what they could use – real money and saleable goods.

Then a special wee job came up. Breaking three men out of Barlinnie. Not easy. But, as ever, Jonah was game.

Archie Stein, Jim Steele and Jonna Boy Steele – the brothers of Joe Steele who, along with TC Campbell, was later to be wrongly convicted of the murder of the Doyle Family – were serving long jail sentences. They were in serious trouble and needed to escape. It was a daring breakout involving armed men in balaclavas breaching the jail's security big time. But it worked and the three men were at liberty.

A short while later, the three met up with Jonah at a pub in Busby, on Glasgow's south-west border, to decide what happened next. It was meant to be a safe pub – it was out of the way and no one was going to grass if they saw a familiar face. People still believed in safe pubs in the early 1980s.

Jonah was chatting away with the men. Some were talking about moving sharpish to Belfast while others just wanted to lie low till the heat died down.

Archie Stein asked the barman for another drink.

'No problem, mate,' replied the pleasant barman pulling another pint, 'but you'd better enjoy it.' He let the final few drips of beer fall from the tap onto the froth. "Cos it's gonnae be your last.'

Every single person in that pub, staff and customers, was a cop. The three men and Jonah were nabbed and huckled right out of the place. Someone had set them up but who? Blind Jonah worked it out – had it well sussed long before most of the rest of us cottoned on.

Only two other people knew about the meet – Snadz Adams and Tam 'The Licensee' McGraw. Snadz might have bottled it from a fight but he was no backstabber. The Licensee, on the other hand – Jonah knew all about him and his cop contacts.

Twice betrayed, Blind Jonah McKenzie finally got the message. That was him finished with the BarL Team. He put it around, as loudly and vocally as he could, that McGraw had set him and the three escapees up that night – that McGraw was a grass who was working hand-in-pocket with bent cops.

'No' just ma opinion,' Blind Jonah would tell anyone who'd listen. 'Ah can prove it. Ah've goat pictures. Pictures don't lie. Well, dae they?'

Jonah insisted he'd been in a flat that was owned by McGraw when he'd photographed two cops, who were well known in the east end, accepting money from The Licensee. Years later, after he'd retired, one of them would do a bit of a homer, fitting a kitchen to McGraw's Mount Vernon home. Later on, he'd turn up running an ice-cream van. Jonah didn't show anyone the pictures as far as I can tell. They might not even have existed. But there is no doubt that those two cops, along with others, had a special relationship with McGraw. Too many other people have since confirmed it.

Right there and then, all Blind Jonah wanted to do was get up McGraw's nose. Upset the man. Get him nervous. Force him into deeper paranoia and make him less likely than ever to sleep at night. And Jonah was using his best weapon ever – his tongue. By all accounts, it worked. Nice one, Blind Jonah McKenzie.

Meantime, the man had to earn a living. We all do. Except, in his case, he was leaving the devil he knew for the devil he didn't know. Blind Jonah thought he was joining The Godfather. Some of us knew better.

Blind Jonah was about to learn the hard way – again.

24

JONAH NO PALS?

Jonah was a junkie, had been for years, but the useful kind of junkie – the type of guy who shot up just to stay straight. And he was disciplined enough to learn about the whole business. A risky way to learn? Sure, but certain folk didn't give a toss about risks other people took as long as they could make a profit out of it – users, in other words, like Fatboy Thompson.

By the mid 1980s, Fatboy was well on his way to achieving one ambition – becoming the biggest smack dealer in Scotland. He'd achieved this by getting rid of his major competitors one by one – usually by setting them up with smack or getting close enough to know when they were doing a run and then phoning the cops. They included guys like Ted Hughes with drugs and John 'The Irishman' Friel with a machine gun and ammo in the boot of his car.

Once they were out of the way, he just took over their customers. It was an old trick, one he'd learned from his father, though, in old Thompson's case, the target wasn't the drug trade but businesses, protection rackets, gun dealing.

Guys like Fatboy didn't get their hands dirty. They expected others to do the work, take all the risks, while they scooped in most of the profits. That's where Blind Jonah came in.

They set up a smack factory in Jonah's flat where he stored, cut and packaged the goods. Fatboy would be in and out of Jonah's flat all the time, making sure the 'staff' were producing the goods and the dosh. What Fatboy didn't know was that he was being watched by the cops.

Fatboy's father, Arthur The Godfather, had sealed a deal with the cops and MI5 years earlier. In return for information on the London teams he worked with and the Loyalists in Ireland he sold guns to, the cops were willing to turn a blind eye to much of Thompson's activities – after all, that was the only way he'd get intelligence on the groups he was informing on. They even said he could deal drugs – within reason. By that, they meant cannabis and a small scale. Fatboy was dealing heroin and large scale. Time to take him out.

The Fatboy had put his own head in the noose when he set me up. I was working for the Thompsons at that time and wanted on thirty attempted murder charges. The Thompsons had arranged for me to hide out in a flat they had down the Clyde at Rothesay on the Isle of Bute. Father and son were the only ones who knew I was there. So it was a bit suspicious when, a few hours after I'd arrived with Anne Marie, my partner at that time, Glasgow cops came bouncing through the door, guns in hand.

Right in front of my eyes, they set me up with a small bank bag full of smack. Although I'd go on to prove my innocence when an independent forensic expert proved that the heroin couldn't have been in the pocket the cops said it was in, they made other gains that night. They found a handwritten note specifying drugs orders, amounts and prices – in Fatboy's writing. Careless? It was enough to make them decide that they were going to take him out only six weeks after that botched raid on me in Rothesay.

The cops claimed they chased Fatboy in his car at speed through Glasgow schemes and he was ditching tenner bags of smack as they drove. Hardly likely. The Fatboy wouldn't take those risks himself. Then they said they found the corner of a porn magazine in the wastepaper bin in his bedroom – the corner from a mag they'd found in Jonah's flat when they'd raided it. Again, as much as I didn't like the Fatboy, that wasn't his style.

While I quickly reached the view that Fatboy Thompson had been set up, he reverted to type – paranoia. He suspected that Jonah or Tam Bagan had set him up – typical of him but no way,

José. I was no great fan of Jonah but he wasn't a grass. Tam Bagan, who had also been arrested, I knew very well and he was more likely to spend time in jail for something he didn't do than point any finger at someone else. Fatboy really was one sad bastard.

At the trial, Jonah made a big deal about being a heroin addict, claiming that the gear found in his flat was for personal use. He even offered to snort the heroin produced as evidence – hardly surprising that the judge declined his offer. But his approach did work.

The fact that Jonah got the expected sentence for heroin dealing, while Fatboy was hit real hard with a twelve-year stretch, added to young Thompson's paranoia. From the outside, it was obviously all to do with who he was. The courts hadn't had the chance to sentence a Thompson for many years.

When Jonah was released from Peterhead Prison, the Fatboy gave him an order to do as much damage to McGraw, The Licensee, as he could. Fatboy had been working in partnership with McGraw, who was meant to pay him wages while he was in jail but, of course, the tight-fisted McGraw hardly passed him a dime. Also McGraw was meant to appear as a witness at Fatboy's trial and, typically, he refused. One way or another, Fatboy reckoned McGraw wanted him out of the way. Maybe he had even helped the cops.

Jonah was pleased enough by the order from Fatboy. He owed McGraw some payback big time and, besides, he didn't like grasses. Jonah set about his task but McGraw had amassed a big team and it was going to take some time. Or was it?

The Caravel pub was McGraw's HQ although it was actually owned by his wife, Margaret 'The Jeweller'. One afternoon, it was packed to the gunnels as usual and no one noticed the Saab rolling up to the door. Out jumped Jonah from the passenger seat and he lobbed in a grenade. Not just any grenade but a NATO-issue one that was capable of severe damage.

As the Saab sped off, some boozer felt a weight bump against his foot and he instinctively kicked it out of the way, deeper into the pub and right into the middle of McGraw, Snadz Adams, Tam

Bagan and Joe Hanlon. If it had exploded, it would have done Fatboy's bidding in one bang. The whole future face of street crime in Glasgow, Scotland and maybe Britain was ticking away at their feet.

Only then did someone notice the grenade, grab it and run out into the street. They lobbed it as far as they could but it landed too close to the pub. Dashing over, the crazy man lifted the grenade again and lobbed it farther and, this time, it landed in the cemetery beside The Caravel.

By the time the cops and the Bomb Squad arrived to defuse the grenade, Jonah's Saab had screeched on to the M8. Pointing it towards Greenock, he opened the throttle and let it ride, fast. He was stopping for no one.

It was a shame for him that he had taken too much of his own medicine that day. The stupid bastard had forgotten to pull the pin out of the grenade before tossing it into The Caravel. Never hire a junkie to do dangerous work – not even a usually capable junkie like Jonah.

A grenade being lobbed into McGraw's pub is not something that would just be forgotten, even if it had failed to explode. McGraw's mob were desperate to get their chibs into the bomber and Jonah was high up on their suspects list.

If the heat was now on Blind Jonah, in Peterhead, Fatboy was furious. Up there, he was in cahoots with a guy called John Gallagher, also known as 'Not a Sausage' or just plain 'Sausage' for short. His strange nickname came from the fact that he had murdered a butcher and a cop in a botched robbery in Bridgetown. It was so botched that he got sod all for the job – apart from a life sentence, that is. Sausage Gallagher and Fatboy had a lot in common – paranoia, cowardice and plain nastiness as long as they ran no risks. It was a pairing made in hell – as Blind Jonah was about to find out.

In PeterHell, Fatboy and Sausage had access to a typewriter and they set about making up false statements. They had a good start in that they were in possession of actual statements to the cops offering information on Ulster Defence Association arms caches, the low-down on some drugs traffickers and so on. The point is that only the names were changed from the actual giver of the statements – Arthur 'Fatboy' Thompson – to the target – Blind Jonah McKenzie. I wish I'd known about this at the time instead of learning about it years later. Thompson Senior would use a similar ploy against me in 1992 when I was on trial for the murder of Fatboy. If I'd anticipated it, I could have blown it out of the water before it happened instead of having to prove the letter was a fake and facing up to a lot of folk who were spreading the poison. That kind of device can be more than a letter or a statement. It can be a death sentence.

The police statements in Blind Jonah's name were circulated on the streets. Some fell for it. Others couldn't believe it. Then someone noticed a quirk in the typing. Certain letters had an extra line at the top. Some folk thought they'd seen that before. They had. In poetry.

Fatboy, believe it or not, had written some poems up in PeterHell. He'd typed them out and, thinking them good enough, he'd circulated them. Now there have been many gifted jailhouse poets, including TC Campbell, but Fatboy wasn't numbered among them. The poems were embarrassing and not just for the childish rhymes and the bad spelling. The typewriter he used put an extra line above certain letters – the same letters as in the alleged police statements in Jonah's name.

The bogus statements did have an effect in that some street players concluded that he couldn't be trusted. That's the start of the end for most players. Blind Jonah himself should have taken it as a warning and got himself new friends. Trouble was he had still to deal with old enemies.

Jonah's partner, Irene, lived too close to McGraw – in fact, she stayed directly opposite the council flat he kept on in Barlarnark in spite of having his fancy, luxury place in Mount Vernon. The Licensee used the place to conduct his business, particularly with the cops, and to keep an eye on what was happening around the streets. It took McGraw a full six years to move into his wonderful house in

Mount Vernon. What the fuck was that about? Did he move some cop allies into the streets nearby first? As a security measure? McGraw is known for being mean except where his own safety is concerned. Want a definition of paranoia? Just watch the man.

Fed up with Jonah publicly fingering him as a grass, McGraw set a trap one night. They caught Jonah at the door of his girlfriend's house and set about him with baseball bats and a Bowie knife. Jonah went down big time with much permanent disfigurement. Worst of all was that one of his hands was crippled. After another attack by the same crew, Jonah more or less lost the sight of his other eye. Almost blind and with one useless hand, things weren't looking good for Jonah McKenzie.

A man has to survive somehow. Following some police raids, Jonah sussed that a major supply of very pure heroin was available from a Maryhill outlet and decided to get his hands on some. After a while, junkies all over Royston and Possil were dying in numbers, killed by overdoses of all to pure heroin. McGraw and his mob put it about that the smack had come from Blind Jonah. Soon he was given a different name – Dr Death. That didn't put some people off. They only wanted to buy from Jonah because his smack was so pure they could cut it heavily and make a big profit. But the truth is that Jonah wasn't selling the death smack. He knew too well how to handle the heroin – unlike McGraw's crew.

A rogue cop had pocketed some of the stash from the Maryhill raid. Approximately ten kilos of very pure smack was then passed on to McGraw's people. These guys thought they knew everything but actually knew fuck all about dealing smack. Pretty soon junkies were dying all over the north and east of the city and the wrong man was getting blamed.

But events took an even worse turn for Blind Jonah. His friends would say that, from the day his second eye was damaged, he lived in constant fear, not a state that he was used to. All he did was take more and more heroin to blot out his terrors and, after a lifetime on the needle, the only way he could do that was to take purer doses.

Jonah wasn't just taking his own gear – he was also hiring him-self out as a human chemical kit to test the heroin for purity. On one of these occasions, he hit the jackpot. It was just too much and he died right there.

'Nice one wi' that blind bastard, Paul,' the young guy said to me, passing on his way a few weeks later. Some people actually believed that I had Jonah fixed up with the killer gear or had him forcibly overdosed. Not true. There was no love lost between us for sure. I started treating Blind Jonah as an enemy when he teamed up with Fatboy Thompson so, when he died, I felt nothing. The only people I feel anything for when they die are loved ones, not hated ones.

Over the years, too many men I respect have told me that they held Blind Jonah in high esteem – a man of good character who fell into bad luck. Bad company more like but then the two so often go together. Then I got thinking of a time when I almost went down for something I didn't do – a time the cops tried to set me up.

I'd been arrested and charged with a car theft I had nothing to do with. At the time, I was doing very well, thank you. What did I need to steal a car for? Not being there shouldn't be too hard to prove, you'd think. Well, not if you're dealing with honest people. I was in big trouble since I'd been ID'd driving the car – a red Astra – stacked full of stolen goodies by none other than the cops.

Any court in land will accept the cops' word against that of a known criminal. Defending yourself against such witnesses is a slippery slope to hell. If your lawyer starts alleging that the cops are lying, the judge is likely to come down on you with more than his gavel. I needed to prove it wasn't me and fast.

To be fair, one of the cops involved refused to ID me and more or less said that he didn't like what was going down – a brave and moral man in my book. Police forces all over could do with more of his type. But others had fingered me even though they only saw the driver from the back while the car was travelling at speed.

As it happened, I was in the city centre buying skiing gear at the time the cops said I'd been spotted in the red Astra. With me was my mate Joe Hanlon, a man whose record was as bad as mine. He made a great amigo but a terrible alibi – especially since he'd somehow managed to shoplift some ski poles and all sorts. This was a man who was loaded but he just couldn't help himself. However, after an approach to the shop, we ascertained that they remembered us because we'd bought so much gear and they could prove when we were in there because of the timing on the receipts and so on. The shop folk stuck to their guns in spite of being constantly hassled by the cops to drop their evidence.

What I didn't find out till later was that someone else had volunteered help. Without being asked to. With no reward. Just because it was the right thing to do.

A bloke called James 'Kinnie' Kinnon had written to my lawyer Peter Forbes from Low Moss Prison to say that it was him who had been in the car, not me. Turns out that not only was this true but the man in question was about a foot taller than me and built like a brick shit house and he had dark hair. How could anyone mistake him for me at five foot eight, average build and fair hair? Because it was no mistake – it was a fit-up.

Kinnie hadn't written to Peter off his own bat. His cousin had persuaded him – his cousin, Blind Jonah McKenzie. Here was a man who considered himself an enemy of mine at that time yet he was doing something that helped me and got one of his relatives into grief. Jonah never told me about this or asked for favour or grace. He did it simply because it was the right thing to do.

Would I kill a man who did that? What do you think?

Drug dealing, violence, robbing – Blind Jonah McKenzie was a villain, that's for sure. But was he bad man? It's not so easy a call, is it? Unless all you consider are the laws of the land. Then what about the cops who claimed to have seen me in that red Astra when I was miles away? What are they – heroes or villains?

For some villains, it's much easier to judge whether they have some good in them or if they are all bad. Let's meet one who is pure evil.

25

BAD KARMA

'The accused has been of great help to the police in solving many major cases,' the plainclothes cop said from the witness stand, looking straight at the judge. 'Each time he has done so at considerable risk to himself and for no reward. I'd ask the court to take this into consideration in considering the disposal in his case.'

Just what every boy needs, eh? A high-ranking police officer speaking on his behalf in court, pleading mitigation. What higher commendation can you ask for? The accused must have been a most upstanding responsible citizen. Well, try this for size . . .

Kidnapper,
Rapist of men,
Sexual sadist,
Robber,
Conman,
Torturer,
Wife beater,
Serial perjurer,
Set-up merchant.

Upstanding responsible citizen? Aye right.

Those who have read our first book, *The Ferris Conspiracy*, will be familiar with the man in question so we apologise to them for relating my first encounter with him. But it needs to be told in brief first, before we bring his story up to date, to support a view I have long held. Once an evil snake, always an evil snake – and that has more to do with the person himself rather than his criminal record.

Dennis Wilkinson, aka Dennis Woodman, aka Dennis the Menace, turned up in my life for the first time in 1992 in the segregation unit of Barlinnie Prison known as the Wendy House. I was facing trial for the murder of Fatboy Thompson, kneecappings, attempted murder and a stack of other crimes. My two best pals, Bobby Glover and Joe Hanlon, had been gunned down and killed while I rotted in jail. It was the most serious situation I'd faced in my life and I was about to be accused of being so sloppy that I'd confessed to murder.

In the Wendy House, only one prisoner is allowed out of their cell at any time and, even then, it's only to go to the toilet, shower room or a for a wee bit of fresh air. And they are always accompanied by a squad of screws.

It was difficult to tell who else was even jailed there. When the screws weren't around, we'd call out to the guys in the next cells to see if we knew them. You could be holed up next door to a life-long pal for weeks and not know it. Some of the men would play chess by shouting through the moves to their opponent and then making the moves for both players on a chessboard in their cell. A bit like postal chess except you're only next door.

I'd played my next-door neighbour a few times and it was eeksy-peeksy between us though I'd claim that I had the upper hand – well, I would. After that, I didn't have the heart or soul to play. I was still grieving big time for my pals and I was facing a trial that could put me away for the rest of my adult life – so there were more pressing things on my mind than knights and rooks.

In the Wendy House, with so little face-to-face contact, you become sensitive to new voices. So I did suss that some guy with what sounded like a Geordie accent had joined us, five or six cells down from me, and he was playing chess with anyone who would take him on. He was crap at the game and the other guys were giving him a body swerve. There's no pleasure in chess if you know you're going to win easily.

Then I got a note from another prisoner called Mark Leech warning me that the new guy was called Dennis Woodman or

Wilkinson and he had been drafted in to get me. Mark had been in loads of prisons and knew all about Woodman's record for suddenly hearing detailed confessions from various guys for the serious offences they were charged with. Meantime, Woodman would get lenient treatment from the courts for his own crimes – and some crimes they were.

Along with a man called Reeves who was on the shoot from Broadmoor, a state hospital that held some of England's most dangerous and unstable killers, Woodman had taken a young man hostage. Holding him captive in his own flat, they'd tortured him till he told them his PINs for his bank and credit cards. Every day, they'd draw the maximum then stay with their captive till the next day when again they'd draw from his accounts. Bored, they decided to torture him some more and then they repeatedly raped him. Bored with that, they shit and pissed on him, forcing him to eat their crap. Eventually, when they had emptied his accounts, they abandoned him. He had 122 weals on his back alone, as well as other major physical damage. But what psychological scarring had they left him with?

Reeves shot across to the Netherlands where he promptly killed a cop and was arrested. When Woodman was arrested for the kidnap and torture of the young guy, a senior cop from Merseyside appeared to plead his case. The man was pure filth yet here was a public servant, paid by the taxpayers, asking a judge to treat him leniently. All the judges he appeared in front of did just that. Do you call that justice?

When a letter arrived for me from Woodman's own brother-in-law warning me about him, I was more convinced than ever. All his family knew about the game he'd been playing – his hearing false confessions for the cops – but his evil didn't stop there. It seems that, before his move to the Wendy House, Woodman had been in Dumfries Prison, awaiting trial for taking a local farmer hostage – old snake, old tricks. But he had stated in his defence that it was all his brother-in-law's fault, when the brother-in-law hadn't been involved at all. Telling the authorities that some innocent guy was guilty of a crime was right up Woodman's street – but his own brother-in-law? How low could he stoop?

The move from Dumfries Prison to Barlinnie in itself was suspicious. My QC, the bold Donald Findlay, didn't let on at the time but he knew then we should be worried, very worried. As he later stated, 'That transfer of Woodman to Barlinnie would need permission from the highest authority.' Bad enough that Strathclyde Police were out to get me – and they were – but what Donald was saying was that the top politicians, the government, were in cahoots with them too. And they didn't even mind working with an evil bastard like Woodman to get me either. That was in 1992. Ever since, I've been confused about who are the bad guys and who are the good guys.

Forewarned was forearmed in this case. My lawyer Peter Forbes got on to Woodman's trail and found out a hell of a lot about him. With Donald Findlay, one of the best QCs of all time, fully briefed, we'd surely deal with Woodman. However, the snake had other ideas.

Woodman claimed that he had been approached by Peter Forbes and offered a huge lump sum and significant annual payments for the rest of his life if he'd drop his evidence against me. Peter, one of the most honest men I've ever met, was shaken to his roots. Not that there was an ounce of truth in Woodman's tales – but even the sniff of a suspicion of such underhanded behaviour hanging over Peter could have ruined his entire career. There was only one way to deal with Woodman and that was to discredit him in court.

When he climbed into the witness box, he looked an insignificant, thin wee bloke. The image wasn't helped by the fact that all his mismatched clothes were several sizes too big for him. I'd later learn that he didn't have many clothes with him in jail and he had been loaned clothes by cops to appear at my trial.

So now the High Court in Glasgow, one of the most eminent courts in Britain, was going to pay attention to a guy who couldn't even organise his life well enough to clothe himself. Usually I'd be sympathetic to a bloke in that situation but forgive me if, this time, I felt nothing but contempt.

If his appearance wasn't a big enough shock, his attitude totally blew me away. The guy actually went head-to-head with Donald Findlay. The lowlife took on one of the sharpest legal brains in the country – a man well known for his court oratory. The cops must have warned Woodman – they wouldn't let him walk into the lion's den without warning him that he might get bitten. As it turned out, Dennis the Menace was now their star witness because they had no other evidence worth a shit.

So there was him swearing on oath that I'd confessed to Fatboy's murder, the kneecapping and all sorts while we were playing chess by shouting the moves to each other several cells away. Like I'd talk about anything with a stranger under those circumstances. If I had played chess with him, half the Wendy House would have heard us exchanging our moves and, if I had confessed to him, they would have heard all that too. And it wouldn't have stopped there – the screws who inevitably would have been hanging about outside the cells would have heard it too.

But a claimed confession is a strong piece of evidence, of course. It would come down to his word against mine and who the jury chose to believe. Woodman just stuck to his story that I'd confessed to him. So Donald Findlay's task was to discredit him in other ways, to make him out to be the liar he was. After two days in the witness box, Woodman had lost the place many times – he began sounding increasingly bizarre but he still hadn't fully cracked. Then he put his foot in the mire – although we didn't know it at the time.

'I swear on the graves of my two dead children,' he squealed, having been asked for the umpteenth time if I had actually confessed to him. This was a blow. He came out with a tragic tale of his two young kids dying in some drowning accident. It was exactly the kind of life story that could swing a jury in his favour. Sympathy is a great weapon in getting people to believe you.

When the trial ended for the day, I headed back to the Wendy House in a really bleak mood. I knew I hadn't spoken to the man before, let alone confessed to him, but I could see the damage his tragic tale might well do. Of course, I should've relied on the ever-thorough Peter Forbes.

Overnight, Peter had managed to contact Woodman's wife. I should say estranged wife because she was chucking him and not just for trying to blame her brother for crimes he had committed himself but because he was a cruel, selfish partner and she'd had enough. Apparently it had been coming for a while and she was very pleased to help Peter in any way possible. Her help was simple but effective. The two kids were alive and well, bless them – they couldn't help who their father was.

Within the first hour of the trial the next day, Dennis Woodman was exposed as a shamefaced liar who had even been willing to lie about his own children's well-being. Donald had proven the man had lied under oath. If he lied about his own children, what else would he lie about? For the first time in what was, at that time, the longest criminal trial in Scotland, I felt confident that justice would be done. It was. I got not-guilty verdicts on all charges on 12 June 1992 at 3.45 p.m. precisely – a date and time I'll never forget since, if it had come out differently, it would have effectively meant the end of my adult life, my free adult life.

Dennis Woodman had lied in court under oath. Was he charged with perjury? Was he stuff! Instead, a top-ranking cop stood on the steps of the High Court after the trial and thanked all the witnesses, 'every one of them' he emphasised and repeated pointedly. That includes Woodman the rapist, perjurer, conman, sexual sadist and torturer. That's British law and order for you.

My 1992 trial was on the front page of every newspaper and lead item of every TV and radio news bulletin for months. And, while he was sitting in the witness box, so was Denis Woodman. Afterwards, a TV documentary called *Dennis the Menace* was made about him. The Scottish tabloids pursued him everywhere, looking for new stories. You'd think the guy would keep his head down and stay out of trouble? No chance.

Woodman did keep well out of Scotland, though. Well, according to the papers I was meant to be the top mobster in Scotland, a killer who escaped justice, brutal, lethal and who didn't like being stabbed in the back. That's who Woodman thought I was and he knew that he had lied about my so-called confession. So, sentenced for the hostage-taking of the Dumfries farmer – with the Merseyside cops again speaking up for him – he was immediately moved to an English jail to serve his time.

From jail, he contacted different tabloids, offering them stories on how I had taken out hit contracts on him in prison. Pure crap because, if I had, he wouldn't have been in any state to phone anybody. I've never seen a phone in a coffin, have you?

The truth was that Woodman had cheated and lied all his life and he was still cheating and lying so he got into big trouble with other cons. It's the same in every prison, anywhere. He got into so much trouble that he was soon shifted to the nonces and ponces unit where he belonged. But he didn't stop hearing 'confessions'. After his efforts at doing me, I'm told he played the same game successfully against at least another seven men. That's at least seven men he put away for crimes they didn't commit. In total, it looks likely that Woodman has done that nineteen times.

When he was released, Woodman started a range of low-level cons, something he'd done most of his life. Divorced from his wife after the shenanigans of my 1992 trial, he also somehow found another woman – a young, attractive woman by all accounts. Christ knows how but then I'll never fully understand women – that's part of their attraction for me.

Woodman was doing all right working some scam to do with photocopiers and contracts. Then he got caught bang to rights. Jailed yet again, he was worried that his new wife might be tempted to see other men so he hired a private detective to check up on her.

The private detective went to see him in jail a few weeks later. Woodman hadn't wasted his money. His young wife was seeing someone else all right – in fact, she had already started seeing him before Woodman was arrested. That couldn't be true, Woodman protested, since he was a very jealous kind of guy and kept her on a close rein. She looked after their house and her child from an earlier relationship. And she spent a lot of time helping out at the church. She was a very Christian young woman.

Very Christian, the private dick told him. In fact, you could say Christianity was in her. Well, a Christian at least – literally and frequently in her. She was having an affair with the local vicar.

Woodman went mental – absolutely crazy. In the visiting room, he flung himself at the private detective, breaking that old adage of not shooting the messenger. Having been marched out by the screws and flung in a cooling cell, as soon as he was able to Woodman got on the phone howling, threatening and berating his young wife then weeping and begging. Next it was the vicar's turn with all sorts of threats being made, from gangsters carrying out a hit job to grassing him to the media. Finally he phoned the private detective and, before sacking him, he screamed, 'LIAR!' – a bit rich coming from Dennis the Menace, eh?

By the time Woodman was released from jail, his young wife was nowhere to be found. She'd given up their house and moved on but not alone. She hadn't taken to the road with the vicar. The private detective had decided, if Woodman wasn't going to pay his fee, he'd profit somehow. So he took Woodman's young wife. Not only that but she was expecting a child – though whether it was the vicar's or the private dick's is another question entirely. What is certain is that it wasn't Woodman's.

Out of jail with no money, no family, no friends, Woodman was desperate. At one point, he was reduced to selling a leather jacket and a gold chain to a journalist just to get by. Maybe he had an alternative wardrobe – the overlarge clothes he'd borrowed from the cops back in 1992.

I was released from the gunrunning conviction in January 2002 only to be recalled again in May because the papers were full of so-called knife fights between me and The Licensee. Fights that never happened – well, not with me. Woodman stuck his ugly head over the parapet again and tried to flog stories about me. To one journalist he actually said, 'I'll get him to confess to the fight with McGraw and the drug dealing and . . .' When the journalist interrupted and politely pointed out that there was the small complication that I was in Durham Prison and The Licensee wasn't, Woodman went on, 'No problem – I can fix that.' I'm sure he could have – well, maybe not him but his cop handlers who keep turning up at all his trials pleading mitigation on his behalf probably could.

Quite recently, Dennis Woodman ended up in the Scottish prison system and wept and wailed so much, apparently in terror of me, that he was transferred south to England. It's as though he thinks that, by crossing the Scotland–England Border, he magically becomes out of the reach of anyone up north. It doesn't work that way and hasn't for a long time. You don't have to be bright to be a serial perjurer though. Lying is easy.

Last heard of, Woodman's voice had changed. No, his testicles haven't finally dropped. As his poor rape victims know only too well, that had happened a long time ago. It was a small matter of him having had his throat cut from ear to ear. Apparently he was a just couple of millimetres from copping his whack.

Not only did he have an extra smile added, he ended up in jail again. Woodman had cheated some guy on some con trick they were working together and the bloke didn't take too kindly to it. There was no need for me ever to go after Dennis Woodman. He's doing a good enough job of ruining his life himself and it looks like he's heading for an early grave. Should that happen, there might well be a lengthy list of his rape victims, people he's robbed and women he's hurt who'll give a little cheer. Me? It'll not bother me one way or another.

Maybe he did come close to having me jailed for the rest of my active adulthood but he didn't succeed. Besides, I believe what goes around comes around and he is one evil man.

Now, there's a firm in London that journalists keep writing about as the face of evil in organised crime yet those same journalists know very little about them – the firm has made sure of that. Let's pay a visit to the Adams Family and you can make up your own mind.

26

LONDON CALLING

The DJ was mixing the music, both hands flurrying here and there, pulling one disc back and setting another one going. Maybe it was because I was pissed but, right there and then, he was the best DJ in the world. Then I spotted trouble about to erupt.

I was in a pub called Gillies somewhere in London. The reason I say 'somewhere' and not the exact area will become plain in a minute.

It was just before Christmas 1993 and good friends in London had invited me down for a special night out. Since the Fatboy trial in 1992, I had been spending more and more time in the capital and I'd made plenty of contacts and close friends. When the invite came in from my friend Peter, I didn't hesitate and set off down with Jaimba McLean.

The event kicked off in some pub and there were plenty of familiar faces like Noel Cunningham, Spaghetti, who worked with the Adams Family, and several members of the Sabini Family, including Terry and Jason. It was a big mob of over twenty men – it was a mixed crowd, though, with street players, a few straight Joes and some car dealers. To give you an idea of the calibre of people we were in company with, there is no better example than Noel Cunningham. Noel and his brother Dessie were well respected all over England as two of the hardest, most trustworthy guys you could ever meet. Later, poor Dessie committed suicide in jail over his girlfriend ending their relationship while Noel was broken out of a prison van by an armed gang. As we write this, he's still free. Keep on bobbing and weaving, Noel.

Then you had Terry and Jason Sabini. Their great-grandfather came to England from Italy back in the 1880s and called himself all sorts of different names at different times but he was best known as 'Darby' Sabini, King of the Racecourses. Before World War Two, the racecourses were a significant source of income in terms of protection money, pickpockets, illegal gambling and a whole heap more. Darby Sabini ruled every course in England bar none.

Epsom and Ascot were known as the Jewels in the Crown of organised crime back then. Darby Sabini had them in his pocket and kept them there in spite of serious mobs from London, Birmingham and Sheffield trying to take them off him using the only tool they had – violence. Darby Sabini always came out on top in spite of guys like Billy Hill and Jack Spot wanting some action. Yet the Sabini crew, who tended to link in with other Italian families, didn't go in for the big show of violence that some of the other firms favoured. Remember, those were the days when a drive-by shooting with machine guns rat-tat-tatting their deadly way past were almost as common in London as they were in Al Capone's Chicago.

The Sabinis favoured two weapons – razors and their brains – and they won out every time. When their former associates, the Cortesi Family, turned against them, they ended up attacking not the Sabinis but their own allies on one occasion and, another time, in a more successful attack, they all went to jail but none of the Sabinis did. The biggest team in Birmingham at that time was led by Billy Kimber and they suffered a similar result when they tackled the Sabinis.

There was one incident, a shooting in The Southampton Arms (later called The Crescent) pub in Camden in 1922, that was carried out by Sabini associates. Called 'The Lewes Racecourse Fracas' by the press, the story was the motivation for Graham Greene's book *Brighton Rock* and the subsequent film starring Richard Attenborough in the lead role as Pinkie Brown. A classic, some would say it was the first British crime noir film.

For years, Darby Sabini had the Racecourse Bookmakers' and Backers' Association in the palm of his hand. For decades, the cops tried to break that hold and thought they had succeeded. Yet, when two of Sabini's men appeared in court, it was that Association's lawyers who represented them.

Though they claim that they won the battle, the powers that be gave up and more or less left Sabini to his own devices. He retired to Brighton in the 1940s and lived a life of peace till he died. Older faces talked of 'doing a Darby', meaning winning all you need then being able to move on and out to die in your bed. Few succeeded where he did.

Just a few brief details of the Sabini Family. Heritage? You couldn't buy heritage like that and Terry and Jason were definitely chips off the old block.

All these guys were obviously close and they were very welcoming to Jaimba and myself. Of the introductions made, one was to this mixed race, heavy-set guy called Ray who stood out because he looked handy and talked a lot. Every party needs someone to chatter and take the initiative. Ray was one of those. Everyone was friendly and they were all gents, which was just as well because, early on, it became obvious we were heading out on one big session.

After the first pub, we moved on to a restaurant owned by one of the company. We were treated like lords and, as well as having an excellent night, the booze just kept on flowing. The talk was of moving on to another pub. Everyone was in enthusiastic agreement except Spaghetti who made his apologies and left. The man might well have had serious business on that night – not that he'd tell us and nor would we have asked.

Four or five pubs later and, not to put too fine a point on it, we were rat-arsed – still all in a great mood and well behaved but pissed nevertheless. That was when Ray suggested we go to one last pub for a nightcap. He knew the very one, he said, and directed the cars that had been laid on to take us to Gillies. Little did we know, the shit was about to hit the fan.

Gillies was fairly crowded but our big crew still made an impact when we all rolled in. I noticed a few of the customers giving us the mean eye but thought it was just that old pub thing of letting strangers know they were entering foreign territory and they should behave themselves. No problem there or so I thought. Then there were a few nods of recognition between the regulars and some of our crew. No problem there or so they thought.

After a drink or two, I noticed that the DJ was set up on a raised plinth at the other end of the bar and was using a mixing deck. So I decided to stroll over and watch the man at work. From there, I could see Ray speaking to one of the guys who had been in the pub when we arrived. Because of the music blasting out, I couldn't hear a word they were saying but I didn't have to. It was about to kick off big time between Ray and the other guy. That was when Ray was smashed on the side of the face with pint tumbler.

The guy who had hit Ray jumped backwards on to the DJ's platform just a few feet away from me. There he was within striking distance, this guy who had just glassed a guy I had met a few hours before, a guy I hardly knew. But I had been in the guy's company all night and he had treated me well. What to do? The guy who had glassed Ray turned and looked at me then edged towards me. Decision made. I cracked Ray's attacker on the top of his skull with my bottle of beer.

All around me in the pub, my mob were steaming into the regulars. Tables and chairs were flying through the air. Guys were having their heads battered against the floor or smashed against the bar. I had no idea what started it but it had turned into a proper free-for-all – what we call a cowboy night out – and it didn't look like it was stopping any time soon.

The guy I had rapped with the beer bottle was sat on his arse with a funny dazed look on his gob but that was the start not the end of my problems. It was obvious that he was a main man for the Gillies crew and had been watched by all his mates and so had I – as I clattered him with the bottle. Now they were coming for me.

Jumping down from the platform, I bent over a table to lift it. It was a big round fucker and I knew it would be heavy but I couldn't even budge the thing. Looking back, it was probably screwed to the floor by order of the management. I had a sense that this wasn't the first all-out brawl Gillies had housed.

As I was still trying to hoist the table, I looked up in time to see a bar stool – one of those with a thick metal base and feet – come looping through the air in my direction. Looked up just in time to see it flying towards my skull. At the last minute, I ducked my head. Big deal – all that meant was that it landed right on top of my napper. Enough to make eyes water, I tell you, but if it had caught me in the face it would have been a broken nose, mashed teeth and God knows what else besides. It had been a good move but it just didn't feel it at the time.

With blood streaming down the left side of my face, I moved to join in the melee. Just then, one of the opposition pulled a CS gas canister and started spraying the place. Coughing and spluttering, my side headed for the door. I was lucky enough to be caught just behind where the gas was sprayed so I wasn't hit by it so hard and I wasn't for budging.

Eyes streaming and gasping for breath, the opposition headed towards the ladies' toilet. Now I hadn't seen a woman in the place all night but at least their facilities were being put to some use. As that mob fought each other to get through the toilet doors, I hopped to the bar where they had been standing and started lobbing their drinks, glasses and all, at them, sending some of them smashing into their bent heads. Then everything went silent.

Suddenly I realised I was all alone in the pub. Looking across the bar, I caught my reflection in a big mirror. Blood now coursed down my face and over my clothes. My first thought? What a good few quid I'd wasted on my new shirt. I was raging.

Reaching down, I recovered two bar stools from where they lay toppled on the floor and, holding one in each hand, I made my way to the gantry. First I smashed one stool into the bottles and mirror, sending booze and razor-sharp shards everywhere. Then the next section got the same treatment. Moving on down, I did the same again and again, loving that sound of broken glass, letting it sooth my temper. Then I spotted something that drew me up sharp.

A bottle of Captain Morgan's rum hung in the last section. That was my dead pal Bobby Glover's favourite drink. It caught me like a punch to my emotional solar plexus. No way was I going to smash Bobby's favourite drink. It was almost like an act of disrespect. No way. The stools slipped from my hands and I turned away.

At that, the ladies' toilet door burst open and this big fat fucker came growling into the room heading my way. 'Fucking bastard,' he growled, picking up a hefty table leg from the floor. He scanned the room.

'Whatya fuckin' done to my fuckin' pub, you fucking cunt?' he spat, moving my way. Then he spotted the shattered gantry. 'FUCKER! You FUCKING FUCKER,' he bawled, head down, the table leg raised above his head.

Just as I was about to meet him head on, somebody came from behind at speed and pushed me aside, heading past and fast. The bold Jaimba McLean might have suffered a face full of CS gas but that wasn't enough to stop him coming back in to rescue a mate. And he did, big style. So much so, that I almost felt sorry for the big fat guy. Almost.

Noel Cunningham and the Sabinis had followed Jaimba into the bar. 'Let's go, Paul,' Noel ordered, 'the Old Bill are heading this way fast.'

Not needing to be told twice, Jaimba and I were heading out of there in a flash.

Out in the street, a silver Merc screamed up at speed and skidded to a halt in front of us. Acting totally on instinct, I sprinted across and booted the driver's door hard several times, putting a big nasty dent in it and making sure he wouldn't be able to get out that way without calling for the AA.

'Fuck's sake, Paul,' Noel shouted, 'that's our motor.' And sure enough it was.

Once in the car, I sat and watched as Jaimba rubbed his knuckles, raw from the doing he'd dished out to the big man who was a bit upset about the state of his pub.

'Funny thing,' I said to no one in particular, 'that fat bastard looked very familiar.'

Next to me, Jaimba turned and shrugged a 'So what?' sort of shrug.

In the front passenger seat Noel turned and said, 'No wonder – he's one of the Arifs.'

The Arifs – just one of the biggest firms in London, they were sworn enemies of the Adams Family. Adams, the same family who most of the guys I'd been out with allied themselves to. The same Adams Family I was friendly with. The crew who had avoided going to war with anyone . . . especially the Arifs. The same Arifs whose pub we'd just obliterated and the same Arifs who the guy Jaimba had just ripped apart was affiliated to.

Drunk and dazed as I was, I sensed trouble was coming.

27

WISE IS AS WISE DOES

'Here, Paul, wear these.' Jason Sabini handed me a bundle of clothes in his flat. We'd just come from the punch-up in the pub and my face and gear were soaked in blood. Mostly my blood from that crack on the skull with the bar stool.

When I told Jason and the others I had to go right back out because I had an important meeting to go to, they just laughed. Frogmarching me into the bathroom and standing me in front of the mirror, they made me see why. I looked more like someone in the queue at some A&E ward in the centre of Glasgow late on a Saturday night.

A quick rinse down with cold water later, I was climbing into Jason's gear. Good clothes, expensive though not entirely my taste and a wee bit tight. That's what I was thinking, nothing more, nothing less. All rigged up, I took another look in the mirror. 'Very smart,' I said out loud, meaning every word.

In spite of the offer of a car and company, I refused and took a cab alone to the meet in a club called Baluga's. Outside the club, having paid the fare at the window of the black hack, I turned to be faced by a gigantic black doorman. If it hadn't been the middle of the night, the fucker would've been shutting out all of the sunlight.

'Sorry, mate, not tonight,' he said putting out one huge mitt, palm to the front. I've got a lot of time for doormen and bouncers, having run these businesses myself. In fact, at the time, I was running one of the biggest security companies in Britain so I knew how difficult their job was and I wasn't about to cause grief. Besides, I would definitely have come off second best against the big guy.

'Look, I know you're just doing your job,' I reasoned with the bloke, 'but I'm here to meet someone and they're going to be well pissed off if I don't get in.' It sounded like a weak line but it was the truth in every sense.

Big or not, the doorman didn't want to upset who I was there to meet. 'So who is it you're supposed to be meeting?' he asked, not unreasonably.

Before I had time to answer, a bloke came running up the stairs from the club's front door. After he whispered into the doorman's ear and nodded at me, suddenly it was OK and I could go in. I can only guess that the messenger who changed the doorman's tune had been watching on CCTV and clocked me.

My girlfriend of the time, Karen Owens, was there to meet me. She eyeballed me as soon as I walked in, probably because I was running late and she'd been anxious. Smiling, I walked towards her but she wasn't smiling back.

'What the fuck are you wearing?' she asked a horrified expression stretching her face. 'Are you OK, Paul?' Now I was well aware that Karen had high standards when it came to fashion and dress. On every day of my long trial in 1992, she had made sure I had a new suit, shirt, tie, socks, underwear and eau de toilette – every bloody day. For me, it was all about psychology. Telling everyone in that court that I wasn't down. I was on top of the world. But Karen, she enjoyed buying the gear for its own sake. She'd criticised a couple of things I'd worn before but now she was bloody horrified. 'Where did you get those clothes, Paul?' she demanded.

'Who the fuck's that? Norman Wisdom?' I heard some bloke roar behind me before he burst out laughing.

All this was very strange and very fucking annoying. So I let Karen lead me to a bathroom and stood in front of a mirror. Sure enough, Norman Wisdom was looking right back.

Young Jason Sabini might have had a heart of gold but he just had the wrong body size. Small as I am for a street player, he is even smaller. The shirt collar was two sizes too wee, the trousers barely reached my ankles and the jacket sleeves were two inches shy of my wrists. I felt like slapping myself in the head and falling straight over on my side. I might even have done that but my head was aching and the crack in my skull was weeping blood again. Not that any of that mattered. I just stood there looking at myself wondering how the fuck I hadn't noticed when I checked myself out before leaving Jason's flat. That night at that time, I just couldn't work it out and wondered if I'd finally done what so many people predicted – cracked up inside my head as well as cracking my skull.

Later, of course, I realised I'd had concussion. A rap on the napper can do funny things to you. Believe me, I know. You just have to hope it isn't permanent. Thank God mine had passed before my meet – well, if the man was willing to meet with a Norman Wisdom impersonator from Glasgow.

As I walked out of the toilet, a familiar face came up close, wrapped his arm around my neck and said, 'Terry's over there, Paul.' He would have seen everything, of course, that is his way, as it would be mine if the territory tables were turned. So Terry Adams had spotted my state and was still wanting to meet. It reflected well on him and confirmed all I'd heard of him and his family.

A point of note at this juncture. The Adams Family are very private. That I'm going to respect, for reasons you'll learn later. What I will do is tell a couple of tales, never before told, that I know they won't mind me passing on. It beats the conjecture-filled headlines the family have been victims of – journalists making it up simply because they know nothing. Is it any wonder they are shy of publicity?

It was the first time I'd met Terry Adams and there I was looking like Norman Wisdom with serious head injuries.

'You lot up there are mad bastards,' said Terry shaking my hand like an old pal, 'but what is done is done, Paul.' He had obviously heard what had happened at the pub, Gillies. 'You want to go to hospital?' The last sentence was said as he squinted down at the top of my bashed head, a slightly disgusted look on his face. I refused, of course, and we had a drink and got on with the business at hand.

As Terry and I quietly spoke about business and had a few drinks, others would come up and stand by our table. They were probably showing some strength to Terry in case anyone was mental enough to fancy a pop at him. But it had the added bonus that we could hear what they were saying in their loud, normal voices. That's when I heard a familiar voice, the same man who had asked, 'Who the fuck's that? Norman Wisdom?'

'That's that Ozzer Arif's pub just been smashed up,' said the familiar voice, this time addressing Terry. Terry just nodded towards me and the guy blushed scarlet and left. No further mentions of Norman Wisdom were made.

I explained to Terry Adams about Ray suggesting we go there and suddenly he went from quiet spoken and businesslike to fury. Shouting a guy over, he said, 'What the fuck is that daft cunt, Ray, doing taking people like Paul and the rest of the lads to that gaff when he knew there would be trouble?'

It transpired that Ray had issues with one of the Arifs' team and I could see exactly what had happened. With a handy crew gathered for the night out, he'd decided to take advantage and use us as backup in the Arifs' own backyard – without asking. Naughty? That was more than naughty – it was a declaration of war. And here was me thinking it was just a good old London pub brawl.

Terry Adams and I conducted the rest of our business as if the events earlier that night had never happened. With conclusions reached and agreements struck, his mind returned to the trouble that had been caused by the fight at the Arifs' Gillies bar. I couldn't fault him. Adams versus Arifs would have been a bloody feud with many deaths – not just of players but, inevitably, of innocent bystanders too – and it wouldn't have been over in a blink but would've rumbled on for years. Bad? It didn't get much worse.

Terry raised his glass to his mouth and, drinking slowly, he looked at me intently, silently. I wondered if it crossed his mind to have me taken out that night. It wouldn't have taken much. A nod to the three men who stood in the background as we chatted would have been all. One nod and the troubles he had with the Arifs would have been all over – at least that's how some street players would have seen it. The Arifs would have been convinced, especially if he had thrown them a few quid to compensate them for the damage to their bar. A few quid wasn't a problem for the Adams. It was just as easy as a nod. So, I sat and drank, watching him eye-to-eye and waited.

'We'll sort this, Paul,' he eventually said after what seemed like an age but was probably only a minute. 'You're down here as a guest and remember one thing,' he breathed deeply and sighed, taking another drink, 'your might is when you are right.'

Never was a truer word spoken and that was good enough for me. The Adams Family had just said that they believed me, that they were willing to run the risks of that and that they would stand up for me because they believed I had done no wrong.

This was not a scene from some Clint Eastwood spaghetti western. This was real life and the man sitting across from me knew that he and his might pay a terrible price. For who? A man he had just met. Who turned up looking like Norman Wisdom on a bad day. A man from Glasgow that might as well be on the other side of the cosmos. A man who he had had no time to get to know, really know. The easiest kind of man to sacrifice – apart from a man he'd never met at all. We'd spent three hours together yet Terry Adams was willing to risk his life and all his family's lives for me. Why? He believed I was telling the truth. He believed I would always tell him the truth. He was right. But what would the Arifs think?

28

JAW, JAW OR . . .

Bright lights were sparkling behind my clenched eyelids and shooting stars zoomed here and there, curving wide, colourful, lazy loops of raw nerve ends. I knew it was going to get worse. Sooner or later, I'd have to open my eyes. So I did and immediately regretted it.

It was the morning after the pub fight and the council with Terry Adams. If this was the Hollywood version, I'd lie in bed, my six pack glistening in the morning sun as it shone through curtain-free windows and I'd smile and reach out for my woman, standing nearby brewing my coffee with nothing between me and her svelte nakedness than an artfully wrapped sheet.

But this wasn't Hollywood – this was reality. My head ached; dried blood stuck my lips together; I'd wrenched muscles in my shoulder probably trying to lift that fucking screwed-down table; Karen snored next to me though, it has to be said, they were wee cat snores; the bit of light filtering the room blinded my eyes; and, worst of all, I remembered every fucking thing.

What is it with these guys who commit some dreadful crime, usually violent crime, and plead that they can't remember anything because they'd drunk/snorted/smoked too much? That's never happened to me in my whole life though, fuck knows, I've tried. Don't get me wrong, I've forgotten loads of things like shopping lists, people's birthdays, where I've parked my car, even court dates, but that's always when I've been sober. Am I different? Or not drinking enough? Or are so many people just lying and the soor-ploom judiciary swallow it whole?

Some days I would drink to forget, no matter how much it took. Or cost. Or whatever jeopardy it placed my life. Just like that morning in our flat in Crouch End. You know how it goes, don't you?

'Aw NOOOOooooo . . .' So that's your eyes open. After that it gets worse. A lot worse before it's going to get better. Not for the first time, I wished to fuck you could buy Irn-Bru down south. I know you can now – and high time – but imagine then having to get through a mega hangover without it and you're a long way from home.

Eventually I sat up and the pillow came with me, sitting neatly at the back of my napper. There was no Superglue Bandit on the rampage – just the dried blood from my skull sticking to the cotton. It wasn't a good look.

A few hours later and I was almost human again. Almost. Showered, shaved and dressed, I was sitting there across from Karen who was looking immaculate as usual. How do good-looking women manage that? I'm drinking pot after pot of weak tea, which I hate, but would you drink London tap water? A man needs to rehydrate so rehydrate I did. What I really needed was a drink. A belter of a bevvy. But you do this guilt thing, don't you? Well, I did. Can't drink till a certain time in the day as if there's a magic rule for that type of shenanigans. So it was any type of fizzy drink I could find and then tea, tea, tea even though one drink would have cured me and fast. Funny fuckers, folk, aren't we?

The only proper cure for a bit of a hangover is the full Scottish fry-up. Well, north of the Border it's called 'Scottish' but see me? I'm not biased and I easily settled for the full English. It did the business just as effectively.

Just as I was feeling human – waterlogged but human – my phone rang. It was an old London pal of mine, Petchy, just phoning for a chat and chat we did till five minutes into the conversation, Petchy asked, 'Paul, you're not down in London by any chance, old son?'

'As a matter of fact I am, Petchy.'

He then went on to mention some areas that, frankly, meant nothing to me and I told him so. I knew London a bit but it would take more than a lifetime of visits to know it as well as the natives.

'You weren't near a bar called Gillies last night were you?' Petchy asked.

'As matter fact I was,' I replied, wondering how the hell he knew that – why he chose one pub in a city that must have many, many thousands of pubs.

'Fuck sake, Paul, I knew it,' he replied, laughing. 'I knew it was you. I just missed the brawl by minutes as that's where some of my mates drink. Small world, eh?'

Small world indeed. If Petchy had been in there that night, I would have been straight by his side as you do with old mates you bump into. If Ray had started the grief, as he did, then no doubt Petchy would have had the low-down on it and the whole fracas might never have happened. Timing. Sometimes it's with you, sometimes it isn't.

I'd no sooner hung up from Petchy when the phone went again. It was Peter, the guy who'd invited me down in the first place, wanting me to go to a meet. No other explanation offered, no other explanation required.

When I got to Peter's place, most of the crowd who had been there the night before were gathered together with one addition – Spaghetti, the one who'd sloped off before the to-do at Gillies. The fact that he hadn't been there didn't stop Spaghetti holding court, telling everyone what should happen and demanding Ray explain why he had taken us there in the first place.

Ray had obviously been to hospital and had a few stitches where it showed but he was hurting more inside than out. 'We otta go and sort those bastards,' he declared to the meeting. 'They took liberties with us last night – pure liberties.' His view was that he hadn't been there to start anything – it was the other guy who'd approached him and glassed him.

'Leave it out, Ray,' one of the men said. 'You knew you had issues with that geezer.'

'Yeah and you knew he'd be in there – he's always fuckin' in there,' said another.

'But we weren't there on business,' insisted Ray. 'We was all suited and booted and well Brahms, yeah. It was obvious . . .'

Noel Cunningham had been listening silently from the edge of the group but now he had had enough, 'Ray, you have no fuckin' idea what you have done, you daft cunt. You have just started a fuckin' war that we can well do without.'

That was that. All the other guys agreed and I could feel the heat on Ray. As a matter of diplomacy, I hadn't said a word during this discussion. This was their territory, their people, so who the hell was I to put in my tuppence worth unasked? Of course, if I had been asked that would've been a different matter. So that was that except it wasn't. There was a small matter of the Arifs' wrecked pub to consider and they weren't going to be pleased.

Behind the scenes, Terry Adams was working hard to cool things down. His family had been there often enough before and too often with that same crew. One of the reasons the Adams were so respected on the street is that they didn't see the point of feuding with other firms. Battling just got in the way of business. What good is there in that?

Don't get me wrong – the Adams were capable, very capable. Put it this way, if there was one crew in Britain I didn't fancy taking on head-to-head, it was the Adams. Not that it ever was necessary or ever will be.

Terry Sabini went and faced up to the Arifs. He told them that what had happened shouldn't have happened. It's the closest you'll get to an apology on those streets. But that wasn't good enough for the Arifs. They wanted the damage paid for with extras – not money but revenge.

'All we want is the Scots mob served up,' said one of the Arifs. It was thinly disguised code for us getting set up to take their wrath. Killed probably. Scots mob? Who did they mean? We didn't go down team-handed – it was just Jaimba and me having a wee night out. Did they think two Scots made a mob? Oh dearie, dearie me.

Later on, Terry Sabini told me what the Arifs had asked for and told me his response. If the Arifs wanted to take out the Scots, they'd have to take on everyone – him included. It was no mean line to draw in the sand and the Arifs knew that. But they were obstinate bastards and I reckoned they wouldn't leave it at that.

A short while later, when I'd gone back to Glasgow, my pal Petchy was on the phone. Naturally we talked about the pub brawl and the fall-out with the Arifs. When war between the Adams and Arifs is in the air, it is the only topic of conversation in London.

Petchy confirmed what I already suspected – Ray was in deep shit for creating the trouble that night. Now he had fallen out with both sides – stupid, stupid man.

Petchy had an in with the Arifs. This is not so surprising since rarely on the street these days do people belong to one team. Petchy didn't belong to anyone. He was very much a freelancer in everything and he was highly respected. In particular, he'd speak to them about wanting 'the Scots mob served up' since he knew exactly what that meant – my head on a platter. Petchy was my pal and he was going to take care of his pal, as you do.

'If you want to pass on a message,' I said to him, deciding it was high time I joined the communication chain, 'tell them I'll pay them a visit.'

I could hear Petchy draw his breath down the other end of the line.

But before he could start advising me that that would me a mite dangerous, I went on, 'But I'll not go till the pub's been refurbished. And it won't be a social call.'

Who did the Arifs think they were, trying to negotiate away my life? Who did they think I was? Did they think Jaimba and I were just two daft Scots? Maybe they're right there, right enough, but they were still asking for trouble.

Petchy tried to calm me and reassure me that it was all down to Ray. That was fair enough but what did the Arifs think? Ray wasn't my problem but the Arifs had decided to make themselves mine. Take that kind of shite on the street and you'll end up looking over your shoulder every two minutes or stretched out on a mortuary slab. I was taking neither option.

'Paul, keep your head down just now,' Petchy said. 'The Old Bill are still all over the place and no doubt waiting for things to blow up. I'll bell you later.'

That's how it was left. My pal looking out for me and me wondering if I'd be making a return visit to London soon. As it happened, I went to London but the visit to the Arifs never proved to be necessary.

Terry Sabini turned up again, giving a message loud and clear. 'It's finished,' he said. 'Ray's the fucking problem here and I told them Arifs to forget about the Scottish firm. They're no mugs and they'd better drop it and fix the fucking pub themselves because the Scottish guys are down here as our guests.' Couldn't be clearer and that's what I call hospitality.

Terry Sabini with the full backing of the Adams had told the Arifs to back off me or else. Told them that, because I was their guest, any trouble I had was their trouble too. It could've resulted in the bloodiest street war London has seen for generations. It would've been costly for both sides. Yet the Adams Family, the Sabinis, Noel Cunningham and others were willing to run that risk. Why? On point of principle. It was the right thing to do. Simple as that.

What had Terry Adams said? 'Your might is when you're right.' Not only true but he lived up to it too. My kind of people.

Years later, in 2004, Terry Sabini contacted me and offered me a table at a charity boxing match he was organising for the following year. Though boxing is not my scene, I was very keen to go not just because the money was going to a good cause but because a wee Scots boxer, Davie Hardie, was making his comeback.

When Davie was just a young man he desperately needed funding. My pal Bobby Glover became his sponsor, though a strange sponsor at that. Usually sponsors insist on putting their company's name on the back of the guy's dressing gown and on his shorts. When a sponsor's boxer appears in a bout, the sponsor gets first access to advertising around the ring. But, when Davie asked Bobby what he wanted put on the back of his dressing gown, Bobby had said, 'Davie Hardie, of course – that's your name, eh?' But Davie persisted and asked what Bobby wanted for his money. My mate just looked at him perplexed like and said, 'Want? Just that you go out and be the best fucking boxer you can be. That'll do me.' That was Bobby Glover for you – top human being.

Davie started off well then fell into bad company, bad ways and worse habits. But, typical of the man, he'd managed to leave all of that behind, got himself fit again and was back in the ring. I would have loved to have been there to shout him on, knowing that Bobby would've done so had he still been alive. But there was a problem.

There are many fine people mad keen on boxing. Many of the top street players in every city in the country will travel anywhere for a good boxing match. But there are also a load of arseholes who only go to be seen and are handy at creating trouble while they're at it.

Mentally, I ran through the list of arseholes who wouldn't want to be in the same hall as me and, believe you me, it was mutual. Before I'd reached the end of the list, I knew I had to let Terry down. 'Sorry, mate, you're going to have to count me out,' I said, 'but I'll give you money for the cause, of course.'

'Payin' dough and gettin' nothin' back?' Terry replied pretending to be all shocked. 'Paul, you're going to give tight-fisted Scots a bad reputation.' We laughed as all the best street players I know do laugh and crack jokes about racial stereotypes, especially when it's their own race.

I explained to him about the other faces who'd be there and the prospect of trouble.

'We'll take care of you, Paul,' he said as I knew he would.

'Thanks, Terry, but on the night I might just be tempted not to want minding.'

'That bad?'

'Aye, some of it is personal. It could go off even if I tried hard to ignore it.'

Terry knew I'd sworn to go straight since coming out of jail in 2002 – that, so far, I had and I wouldn't want to slip back now.

'As bad as the night at the Arifs' pub?' he asked with a laugh.

'Aye and maybe worse,' I laughed back.

'Well, fuck that,' he said. 'You just stay away, Ferris.'

That's how the scene in the Arifs' pub had become known – as some significant event that almost resulted in war. To me it was just a pub fight but obviously, to the local faces, it was a great deal more.

A year after my chat with Terry, the charity boxing night took place. Some newspapers were suddenly filled with reports that I had bought tickets but bottled out because Thomas 'The Licensee' McGraw and his dogs were going to be there. Aye, right. Terry Sabini wasn't selling me a box – he was giving it to me. The money I passed to him was a donation towards the good cause. The Licensee? He'd been losing bodyguards and heavies so fast he was lucky to have someone to go to the boxing with. Tommy No Pals, right enough.

Was he and his crew on my list of arseholes? Absolutely. Was he near the top? Never has been and never will be near the top of anything – unless there's a competition for selling your granny on the cheap. Now that he'd win hands down.

The comparison between McGraw and the men of honour I'd met in London was stark. He'd risk nothing apart from other men's lives whereas they had risked everything – and, as far as some of them were concerned, they'd done so for someone they hardly knew. They will hold my respect forever. Respect – you can't steal it or buy it. Respect needs to be earned – that's why certain arseholes will never have any as long as they live.

The Adams Family are rich in respect for sure and I was about to learn they were rich in other ways too – ways that involved the fairer sex.

29

PRICELESS LOVE

The ground crunched beneath our feet like we were walking on frozen grass. It was just two men going for some fresh air, talking quietly, privately, but, if the press had got hold of it, they'd have given it a Fatboy Hollywood spin – 'Mr Glasgow meets Mr London'.

It was the exercise yard of Full Sutton Prison and I was meeting Tommy Adams for the first time. By rights, we weren't meant to mingle by virtue of him being AA category and me being A. Did that mean the state thought him twice as dangerous as me? I don't think so. I'd had NCS and MI5 on my back. Who did he have? The CI-fucking-A? Punishment for who he is was more like it – that and the fact that they hadn't been able to nab him much before then.

Tommy was in a different wing from me but, curiously, if we timed it right, we could meet up in the exercise yard. So that's what we'd arranged. We had been in Belmarsh at the same time too but there had been no chance to meet up there. It was just two men who considered each other allies, fellow travellers who hadn't had a chance to sit and blether. Now jail time allowed us that. Thank you very much, Home Office.

It was a few years after the incident at the Arifs' pub and I was starting the sentence for gunrunning. Though it was Terry Adams I had met at that time, I knew how the brothers consulted each other on major decisions. Tommy was seen by the outside world as the head of the family but, in truth, he wasn't. All the brothers were their own bosses and they would fall out from time to time as brothers do. But risking a possible war against the Arifs – just after they had dealt with another major crew – would have affected them all. As such, I reckoned that Tommy Adams must have agreed with the stance that his bro Terry took. He had my respect and, at the very least, I wanted to thank him.

Tommy Adams had been travelling in a bugged taxi and his chats about certain crimes went down on tape. That's what they had to do to get him. It was a big success for the cops and they let everyone know it. They'd even released a rare picture of him that made him look like some dense-brained devil. It showed the type of face that would make you shit yourself if you met it on a dark night – a face from your worst nightmares. Thing was I didn't recognise it as being the man I was strolling with.

'Bastards,' he said, without altering his pace. 'It was a mug shot, right, and nobody ever looks good in a mug shot.'

He didn't need to convince me. I'd had some taken that frightened my mother.

'Thing is I sneezed just as the camera clicked. See those half-shut, dead eyes? It's a fucking sneeze.'

As soon as he said it, I saw exactly what he meant. Trouble is they don't put a wee caption at the bottom saying, 'Mr Thomas Adams at the beginning of a sneeze shortly after his arrest.'

'They took hundreds more photographs, of course. The cunts didn't have many photographs of me. They fuckin' well do now.'

Again he was spot on. After my gunrunning arrest the cops even lined up and posed with me. In my court files, I've got more photos of me thanks to the cops than I have at home.

'Most of the others were all right,' Tommy went on, 'but what one did they choose to use? Bastards.'

No street player likes the photos that the cops give to the press but Tommy Adams had more of a point than most. Not only was that pic splattered all over the media during his trial, it was used every time some drunk phoned a tip into a newspaper about the Adams brothers and it had even been used on the front cover of a true-crime book – all without his permission, of course. No one bothers to ask a street player. Why should they? We have no reputation to defend so who cares if they make us look evil or stupid or both? Well, who does care?

At the time, I was in the middle of setting up an appeal against my sentence. The trial judge wanted to whack me away for twenty years till he had to be told in court by his clerk and the silks that ten years was the maximum. He had not been one bit chuffed at that and, of course, gave me the full ten. My lawyer reckoned I could get a reduction. Though I wasn't hopeful, anything would be a bonus and I took some consolation from the fact that other prisoners were in much worse shtook than me – prisoners like Tommy Adams.

As well as being given an eight-year sentence, Tommy had been fined £1,000,000 – kind of puts the old parking tickets into perspective, eh? A court order said that, if he didn't pay the money, he'd be given an additional five years and he'd also have no chance of parole. It meant that, instead of a few years inside, he'd spend a minimum of thirteen years in the pokey and maybe more if he lost the place.

Mind you, I couldn't see Tommy Adams losing the place. He was a kind of gentle giant of the jail. Given his and his family's reputation, as soon as he was brought in through those gates, every arse-licker in the place was at his side. This included a guy called Jason Vella, otherwise known as The Mouth from the South. Those who have read *Vendetta* will realise that he went on to be a right pain for me during my sentence but, back there in Full Sutton, I didn't know that would happen, of course. All I knew is that he claimed to be the original Essex Boy, he had been mentioned in the *Sunday Times* young 'Rich List' one year, he was a drug dealer who had taken to consuming his own product and, oh yes, I recognised an arsehole when I saw one. So did Tommy Adams.

Poor Tommy was surrounded by wankers of every shape and form. He just stayed polite, kept himself to himself and didn't fall for any of their little games that would allow them to say, 'Tommy Adams is a mate of mine.'

Jail is claustrophobic enough as it is. To have a shower like that following you around wherever you went would have driven me mental. So ten out of ten to Tommy Adams for his restraint – I would've melted a few of them within days. Tommy Adams wasn't just the fierce dude the media ranted about – he was bright and disciplined. No wonder the authorities wanted to put him away for as long as possible.

One day, when we met as usual in the exercise yard, I asked him what he was going to do about the £1,000,000 and the threat of thirteen years solid hanging over his head.

'Well, Paul,' he said, without breaking his stride or looking my way, 'I can tell you this. I'll do my time. The fine will definitely be paid and I will be a free man after I get this sentence out of the way.'

Clear and precise, Tommy was old school. If he told me that, then that's exactly what was going to happen. I had no doubt. But, as is the way of prisons everywhere, we both got transferred shortly after this – in my case to Frankland Prison, Durham.

Some time later, up in Frankland, I heard what actually happened. As highly as I thought of the Adams brothers, I didn't reckon that they had close, reliable allies. Very close. Intimate, you might say.

Tommy Adams' wife turned up at the designated government office on the day that the £1,000,000 fine had to be paid. Tommy's release was only weeks away – if his fine was paid. As she was led into a private interview room, she was hefting a couple of heavy-looking, solid Samsonite cases.

'How can we help you Mrs Adams?' the senior civil servant politely asked.

'I've come to pay my husband's fine,' she replied, watching their faces drop.

The authorities didn't want Tommy's fine to be paid. They wanted the alternative – him being locked up for as long as possible.

In fact, they probably thought a cool million was beyond his means. Arse-wipes – they should get out of their offices more often.

'Thing is,' Tommy's wife went on, 'I've only been able to raise half a million.' She touched the bags she had been carrying. 'It's here in cash.'

Let's take a moment to reflect. No matter how successful any street player is, they try to make sure that huge sums of money aren't lying around – I mean, someone might steal it. Then there's the risk of it being found by the cops. What they do is invest the dough into businesses that give them some legitimacy and a profitable turnover. Raising a million quid simply isn't that easy. In fact, it is very fucking difficult but that Tommy's wife had raised £500,000 was, in itself, a massive feat.

'Sorry,' said the suit, 'the court ordered that a million be paid.' He looked down at the two cases. 'This won't secure your husband's freedom. We can't accept it.'

'Yes, you can,' said Tommy's wife calmly. 'Consider it as a down payment – half now, half later.'

'We need the payment in full,' the grey-faced guy in charge said.

'Half now and I'll pay the rest before his release date.'

'No, no, that'll never do,' his grey face had changed to beetroot red. This wasn't something they'd been expecting. 'The fine has to be paid in full by . . .' the civil servant looked at his watch but wasn't allowed to finish his sentence.

'I know,' said Tommy's wife, getting to her feet. 'You keep that,' she said, pointing at the cases, 'and I'll be back with the rest.'

As she strode out of the office, the civil servant sat and stared at the two cases. It was going to be one of those days. It takes a long, boring time to count £500,000, even if it's in large notes. No doubt he got some new member of staff, still soaking wet behind the lugs, to count the dough – no doubt, with at least one if not two witnesses. That kind of money could tempt a saint.

The suit was probably in the canteen dunking his Rich Teas into his mug of char when he was told he was wanted urgently at the front desk. I'll bet he took his time leaving, finishing the story he was telling his workmates, then sucking in his cheeks and straightening his tie saying something trite like, 'No rest for the wicked.' He'd have thought he was joking but there are some who would agree with the wicked bit as far as the criminal justice system is concerned.

All the way down the stairs, he'd have groaned with the pain coming from his piles that had flared up again or from his fallen arches or from the pain in his wrist caused by repetitive strain injury doing the same thing, day in, day out, when serving his time. Office work is not the healthiest pursuit but we insist on putting some powerful people in just that environment. I guess piles is their biggest complaint.

When he saw her face at the other side of the reception desk, he'd have been ready for her. She was going to ask for her money back as sure as he was a member of the Lodge. How could she raise such funds when they'd frozen all their assets? No way could she pay. But he was prepared. He'd tell her that the money was confiscated due to the fact that Thomas Adams owed £1,000,000 in an unpaid fine. It couldn't be returned under any circumstances.

'Mrs Adams,' he gave her one of his special smiles. Well, she was quite a looker and her man was away in prison – away for much longer after today. No harm in chancing his luck.

'Here's your money,' she said, no emotion in her voice or in her expression.

'What?'

'Your money. It's all there,' she nodded at cases, identical to the earlier two.

'Right,' he was looking dazed, as if someone had just punched him on the chin. 'The money,' he looked at his watch and cursed under his breath. 'The money.' He was probably asking himself, after that long paper chase and freezing all Tommy Adams' assets, what they had missed. What indeed?

'I'll need a receipt,' she said, not unreasonably.

'What?'

'A receipt.' She said it calmly, resisting the temptation to let rip and tell him what she thought of him and his like.

'Eh, right – a receipt,' he was thrown, rubbing his brow which was now wet with sweat. 'We'll need to count it first.'

'I'll wait,' and she plonked herself down on a seat, crossed her legs and looked at him, calm written all over her face.

A few weeks later, Tommy Adams was free – time served – fine paid – just as he said he would be.

Up in Frankland Prison, when I heard the tale, I laughed fit to piss myself. I'd loads of reasons for enjoying the story. My friend Tommy Adams was going to be going home earlier than they wanted. He had done what he said would be done with absolute confidence in the exercise yard at Full Sutton. All good but even better was how his wife had conducted herself. No doubt, she was a star.

The media had got it all wrong. It wasn't just the Adams brothers they should have been paying attention to. Tommy's wife had behaved impeccably and with more balls and style than most street players I've known. And I mean the good street players.

It was a good bit of poker offering them half to start with. Who knows they might just well have accepted it and the family would have been half a mil better off. Yet still having the other half stashed nearby, just in case – that was sound tactics.

Drawing in £1,000,000 was another story entirely. How she did that I don't want to know but I was impressed – very impressed. I bet the cops were sickened – very sickened. Well, they will play their games, eh? And the danger of playing games is that they can lose. Best playing it straight, I'd say. But then what would I know about law and order?

In truth, I expected no less from the Adams Family. An honourable crew playing it by some standards, some code, will win every time. Do they teach ethics at cop college? I don't think so, do you?

Let's look at a man who taught himself ethics – the hard way. Harder than you can imagine or wish on an enemy's rabid dog.

Hard at the start because he had parents who died too young. Hard later because he was cast in a dungeon for something he didn't do. He was Scotland's man in an iron mask. There but not there. Till he ripped the mask off and howled at the moon. Eventually, he was heard and set free. Did I say free? He'll never be free till he gets all of his questions answered. Each day, he lives with the knowledge that his questions will never be answered and he'll never be truly free – still in jail, not with gates, locks and bars, but right there in his head.

Here's the tale of TC Campbell after the world declared him innocent and free. A tale of a free man who'll never be free. Shame on us all.

30

BLOODY FREEDOM

'Me? A villain?' said the soft, gentle voice of the man who was once Scotland's most-hated. 'Aye, Ah'm a villain. From when? Oh, fuck me, for ever and ever.'

I was sitting with TC Campbell, as he has come to be known, though his friends just know him as Tommy. Here we'll call him TC so there's no confusion with other Tommies who appear in this book – though, if you ever meet TC, you'll know there's no chance of confusing him with anyone else. The man is an individual, truly unique, who just happened to be wrongly convicted of Scotland's worst murder of the time.

We were sitting together in his Glasgow home and he'd been talking non-stop about the last twenty years of his life. This wasn't just talk for talking's sake though God knows both of us are very capable of that. There was a camera whirring and a mic on the table in front of him. For a change, it wasn't some wandering London crew up to meet the bad boys of Glasgow. I'd formed a production company to make films of street life and I'd thought there would be no better person to start with than TC Campbell – but now I was beginning to wonder.

All I had asked him to do was to tell me – well, tell the camera – what had happened. By the time TC was hardly ten minutes into his spiel, my jaw was hanging loose. I'd thought I knew all about TC's story and I did know more than most of the public. Turns out I didn't know a fraction.

For weeks and months, I lived TC night and day and the

horrors he revealed were wearing me down. How weak is that? I'm getting worn out by hearing from him what he went through. What the hell had it done to him actually living that life?

TC was well known on the streets of Glasgow and, as a teenager, I'd known about him – known about, not known. What I didn't know was that he was friendly with my old man, Willie, from time spent in jail and before. My father ran with a small crew, the Ross Street San Toi aka Bowery Boys, when young. Just five amigos against the world. Later, in the 1960s, the teenage TC had led another small crew, The Gouchos, against teams with hundreds of fully tooled-up members. They had a lot in common, my dad and TC.

When the Doyle household went up in flames in February 1984, wiping out six people, I had other things on my mind like working for Arthur Thompson and being chased for thirty attempted murders. When TC and Joe Steele were convicted of the Doyle murders, I heard the streets grumble that it wasn't them. They were innocent men. The streets knew it first. It would take a long painful time for the radical campaigners to be convinced. Even longer for the media to change their views and twenty-one years for the law of the land to acknowledge what everyone knew – that TC and Joe were innocent.

But back then in the 1980s, it was a very different picture. Then TC and Joe were the most hated men in Scotland. Imagine knowing you were innocent yet having gentle grannies and peace-loving citizens wanting to hurt you, hang you even. Well, what would you feel about men who had wiped almost an entire family including a baby?

I can't pinpoint exactly when I woke up and realised the two men had been jailed large and wrongly for such a heinous crime. It definitely had to do with my experience of being hidden in a flat owned by the Thompsons down on the Isle of Bute yet within hours being raided by the cops. First lesson, Fatboy Thompson, who I worked for, had informed on me.

Back then, I had stood, with my wrists handcuffed together,

watching a cop from the Serious Crime Squad plant heroin on me. Second lesson, a policeman had brought the heroin along specifically for that purpose.

There was also the matter of a bogus gun, an extra shooter that was battered against my nut yet the cops claimed that the cop was never issued with a gun though the others were. Third lesson, the cops will kill you if they can and put your paw prints all over a gun that doesn't exist. Officially.

At the time, they were jailing people for a decade and more for possessing smack. I was young and looking at serious time for something I didn't do. Thank the wee man we called in an independent forensic bod who proved that the heroin couldn't have been in my possession. Proved that the cops had planted the drugs on me. Proved that the bizzies had been busy lying in court.

It opened my eyes to cops as villains – bad villains. If it was true in my case, why couldn't be true in TC and Joe's case? Especially with what the street knew – something you probably know now so I'll be brief.

The night of the fire, Thomas 'The Licensee' McGraw and his pal, George 'Crater Face' McCormack, asked two junkies to torch a door in Bankend Street where the Doyle Family lived. The junkies had agreed to do it but then shot the craw. The Licensee and others had bought a can of petrol at the fuel station nearest to Bankend Street – like you do. There were issues between The Licensed snake and Andrew 'Fatboy' Doyle over the latter's route in his ice-cream van. It was a lucrative round and McGraw wanted it, having tried all sorts of threats and actual violence. Fatboy Doyle refused to budge and fought back. Just the day before, he'd had a run-in with McGraw's brother-in-law, Snadz Adams – and it was literally a run-in as it involved Doyle forcing Snadz's brand-new ice-cream van off the road, causing a lot of damage.

Despite all of this, TC was actually convicted. Though it was accepted by the Crown and the judge that he hadn't been near Bankend Street that night, he was still found guilty of multiple murder. But, back in the 1980s, the streets knew who had been there and knew he had a habit of having folks' doors torched as a threatener.

The media screamed 'ICE-CREAM WAR MURDERS'. The folk who worked the vans scratched their nappers and asked, 'Ice-Cream Wars? What fucking Ice-Cream Wars?' There had been some trouble a few years before but that was small-scale and all over by the deaths of the Doyles. There was no Ice-Cream War in 1984. All you had were some greedy bastards like The Licensee trying to grab every sweet run in Glasgow. That wasn't WAR – that was BULLYING. Now that I can't stand.

Then there was the small matter of the cops lying as they'd have to in order to make sure innocent men were convicted. Well, no need to convince me that some cops some of the time will lie. That wasn't prejudice – that was based on my own experience. Experience that started when I was just a nipper and I watched a cop smash the big glass door of a B&Q store in before rapping me with the same, heavy tool. He'd managed to nab me easily since I had been intent on robbing the place but not that way with all that damage. Why did he do that? Force of habit?

Convinced of TC's innocence but never having met the man, I'd write to him now and then as a mark of support. Often my letters would be dispatched while I was also locked up at Her Majesty's pleasure. Jail letters – that's how we got to know each other.

They were busy jail years for TC. Within a year of being convicted, he and a small group took over Peterhead Prison, a place that was close to TC's heart but in the wrong way. It was TC who invented the name PeterHell.

When the squad took the jail over one night – keys and all – they locked all the guards up in a cell. They had to for the screws' own safety as one of the prisoners was intent on dousing them with petrol and lighting a match. The cons also had the option of jumping on a prison bus and driving like hell out of there. That wasn't in TC's plans either. Why should he run? He was an innocent man. Once the takeover was eventually sussed, what TC wanted was a stand-off between him and the governor. He wanted to make the authorities' lives difficult and awkward and then he would give, in, releasing the captured screws unharmed to prove he was a man of honour. To prove he was an innocent man wrongly jailed.

That night, a large team of screws charged into TC's cell, held him down and beat him to a pulp. They then left him lying on a stretcher in an unmanned room as he called out in agony. Slowly, gradually, the strength leaked from him and he passed out. The face of an angel aroused him – he truly believed that was what she was but it was a female doctor who had eventually been called in by some anxious screw. She might as well have been angel since she saved TC's life.

Having passed out again, he woke to TV heaven. He was in a room full of screens but not one showing a decent programme – TC wondered if he had woken in TV hell. Then he realised he was in a hospital surrounded by worried people in white coats – very worried people. On his wrist, he read on the label 'DEAD ON ARRIVAL'.

Just then he remembered it was his birthday. He would've laughed but for the pain wracking his whole body. They had broken his back and a leg and mashed his jaw and, inside, several essential organs were ruptured and bleeding. His hearing would be buggered forever and migraines would blight his days. It was his birthday all right but it was also more than that. It was the Birth of Freedom. A Bloody Freedom. His fight for freedom. Life was going to get much, much worse for TC Campbell.

Hunger strikes were TC's thing. One lasted over one hundred days and he was moved out of the jail to Law Hospital to die – or, as the official but confidential memo from the government minister said, 'Under no circumstances do we wish to create a martyr.' They were too fucking late. You don't have to die to be a martyr, just caged for life where you might as well be dead.

Lost in delirium, TC was told that a Mafia-style hit contract had been carried out on his friend and campaign manager, John Linton. He roused from his hospital crib and asked for food. He'd eat again. Fight again. As TC said at the time, 'Who wins if I die?

Not me, not Joe, not John Linton, not the Doyle Family, not justice
– especially not justice. The corrupt polis and the killers of the
Doyles will win. Fuck that. Come ahead, you bastards. Any time,
any place.'

Joe Steele did it other ways. He escaped from prisons, enjoyed a
few days of freedom then handed himself in but always after calling the press and creating a blaze of publicity. Just as John Linton
had broken into the House of Commons and left campaign leaflets
in the desk drawers of civil servants and MPs, so wee Joe super-
glued himself to the gates of Buckingham Palace.

'Run, Joey, run,' the prisoners in every jail in Scotland used to
shout with glee when they knew the bold boy was on the hoof
again. Some man.

All through this, TC and I would exchange occasional letters. At
one point, he wrote that it seemed to him that I had been jailed
hundreds of times for different reasons as he sat and rotted in
prison convicted of one crime he didn't do. Hundreds? No – I've
only spent thirteen years in jail. There had been too many – but not
hundreds. Yet it just seemed to TC that, in the outside world,
things were happening – people were moving on sometimes for
better, sometimes for worse but at least they were still moving
while it felt to him that he was stuck, trapped and no matter what
he did, he remained trapped.

Eventually the radicals like Tommy Sheridan MSP and MOJO
(Miscarriages of Justice Organisation) Scotland became convinced
of TC and Joe's innocence. And then the media began to believe it
– ironic really since some might say that, with all the lurid headlines about 'ICE-CREAM WAR MURDERS', TC and Joe were tried
and convicted by media. Now that same media were talking out
on their behalf.

MOJO had a diamond in its ranks – Paddy Joe Hill, one of the
Birmingham Six who'd been wrongly convicted of planting IRA
bombs and who spent decades in jail. As TC is tall and powerful
looking, so Paddy is small and wiry. As TC speaks out softly, gently
and poetically, so Paddy is a motormouth, his Irish brogue going

twenty to the dozen, his rhetoric aiming for the gullet. Yet they had a lot in common – anger and a deep sense of injustice.

I'd heard Paddy go on about how people who have been unjustly dumped in jail never recover – how he'd lost his family, friends, his sense of proportion and all he is left with is his anger. How some mornings he wakens thinking he is still in jail and is throttled by the horror of it all till he realises he's at home in his own bed. All that I'd heard from Paddy and I believed every word.

And, despite this, I somehow thought with TC it would be different. So, when in 2005 the Appeal Courts finally agreed that TC and Joe had been unjustly convicted, it was a time of celebration. But it was also a time of anger too – anger about the forensic linguists who told the court that the cops had lied in a statement they allegedly took from TC, a statement that swung the case. The cops had lied.

One detective, Norrie Walker, who had been in charge of the investigation, had committed suicide shortly after TC and Joe were convicted. Was he the only cop with a conscience? What about his boss, Charlie Craig, a pal of The Godfather and whose name is written over every fit-up in Glasgow for over a decade? He lived easily till he died in bed. What about the cops who lied – thirteen in total according to the linguists? Any troubled souls there? I doubt it, don't you?

TC was a free man and an innocent man in the eyes of the law as well as in the eyes of the people. It was a time for celebration. It was also time to get to know him after those years of writing. I was in for a shock. We were related in more ways than one.

31

CHILD'S-EYE VIEW

'What's that, Tommy?' The young woman pointed under the coffee table in TC's crowded and messy wee flat.

'What?' he asked, a bit thrown since he was about to tell her bad news and he never liked telling people bad news. She was a producer on a TV documentary up in Glasgow and she was meeting TC with a view to him participating in it. They'd met a few times and, as with most folk, she easily relaxed in TC's company early on. That's the way the man is.

'That,' she said, pointing again, 'with the wooden handle?'

'Oh, that,' TC bent over and picked it up. 'That's just a hatchet.' At the time, TC had been released on bail pending his appeal. He'd been out a few months and they weren't quiet months. In his legal position, he had to be careful. Any minor indiscretion and he'd be thrown back into pokey and this would be accompanied by outraged media coverage. No one knew that better than TC. No one hated prison more than TC. But he'd drawn the line on allowing anyone to hurt him or his. 'There's a wee story about that axe,' said TC with a smile. He wasn't wrong.

When TC and Joe were released from prison pending their appeal, it was in a wave of publicity. That's all they got – publicity, a few quid benefits and shown the door. TC went back to a wife and young child who were also on benefits – back home with nothing. They'd locked him up for twenty years, now they accepted that he might well be innocent – that's the only reason people get released pending appeal – and they dumped him, leaving him worse off than when they'd snatched him from the street two decades before.

The media queue for interviews was long and insistent. They particularly wanted to interview TC and he could've started asking for payments. That would've helped. Yet TC would have none of that. It was important that the truth got across. Who better to tell the truth than him?

Just as quickly as it had sprung up, media interest died. They left TC to get on with his life as best he could. That was when his troubles started.

Those troubles meant that he had to move house three times, no longer lived with his wife, had less money than ever and – not to put too fine a point on it – was at risk of murder every minute of every day. The cops knew all about that but would do sod all to help him, of course. Too many of the old brigade would have been quite happy for TC to end up on a mortuary slab. The story he told the young producer about the axe isn't exceptional, not for his life. It was typical and demonstrates how he was forced to live.

One day, he had gone off to some shops when he spotted a group of men behind him. TC might have been in jail for a long time but he'd lost none of his street skills, his canniness. After a couple of tests of delaying and changing route, he noticed the men were still following him. He tried one final test of going into a shop and staying for a long time but, sure enough, as he hit the pavement, the men were still there, waiting for him.

The area TC was in was crowded with people. He quickly reckoned that the men were going to jump him but they wouldn't do it there – too many witnesses. But he wouldn't always have the protection of other people. No matter what direction he travelled home, there would be quiet streets. Besides, he lived in a quiet scheme in a tiny ground-floor flat that had a glass door right into the room that served as both his bedroom and living room. There was something else too.

'Fuck that,' he said to the young female film producer, 'if I didn't get rid of them, I'd be stuck with them forever. I'd done enough time in jail being watched all the time.'

So TC told how he'd wandered slowly up the street, as if aimlessly passing the time, but he knew exactly where he was going. When he reached a shop, he stopped and did some window-shopping before going in.

'Can Ah help ye?' the shopkeeper asked, clocking TC and probably recognising him from the TV.

'Aye, thanks,' TC replied, in his usual friendly way, 'I need an axe.'

'Right – any particular kind?'

'No, no – just give me the biggest one you've got.'

''Fraid this is the best we can do, Mr Campbell,' said the shopkeeper, producing a hefty axe about three-foot long.

'Aye, then, that'll do the business, OK,' said TC. 'How much is it?'

As the shopkeeper wrapped the axe in brown paper, TC counted the money in his pocket. He had barely enough to pay for it and there were still two days to go till his next giro. It would be a hard two days but he'd had harder before.

Leaving the store, TC carried the axe under his coat. If a policeman had seen him with it, he could have been arrested on the spot, regardless of the fact that it was legal and even an underage kid could buy it. In the wrong hands, pieces of domestic equipment are deemed to be weapons. Thing is, on this occasion, the axe was definitely in the right hands.

Sure enough, outside the shop the group of men were there, pretending to talk about the window display of a Pound Shop, like you do – not. TC continued his slow amble then turned down a lane. No point in putting fear into the citizens. Thirty yards down he stopped and slowly turned. There were the men behind him.

'Do you want something from me?' he asked, going face-to-face with his tails. ''Cos I sure as fuck want to give you something.' At that he lifted the parcel out from his coat, ripped the brown paper off in one movement and brandished the axe in the air in front of him. 'Well?'

The men turned and took to their heels – smart thinking. As a young street fighter, TC had few equals.

'And tell the prick that sent you to come see me himself if he wants,' he shouted at the backs of the fleeing men. 'Any fucking time.' TC knew exactly what prick he meant.

Having told the story, TC then went on to tell the producer that he couldn't participate in the documentary. His grown-up children were being hassled, assaulted, terrorised and it got worse every time he appeared on the box or when one of the books he wrote with Reg was published or used in the media. And it got particularly bad when he mentioned that 'prick'. Yet how could he tell his tale without mentioning him?

The producer said that she understood and was very kindly about it all in all. Not like most film people, I assure you, but there were two very good reasons. The producer was a woman called Kirsty Cunningham who is a bit special in the media world in that she believes people come first. In spite of that liberal attitude, she survives in that world full of sharks. She's good, very good, in other words. The other reason was that she was about to tell TC that she couldn't make the documentary about him. They only had an hour, a long time on TV but not nearly long enough to do justice to TC's story. She was absolutely right.

'Hi, Shannon,' I called from TC's front room to his six-year-old daughter out on the veranda. This was some time before TC met with the film producer – a time when he was still living with his wife and his youngest child, Shannon, a great kid, very bright, talkative and relaxed with adults. She reminded me so much of my younger son, Dean, and maybe for good reasons. It wasn't till TC had been released from jail pending his appeal and we had met for the first time that I discovered that he was married to my cousin, Karen Parker.

TC and his first wife, Liz, had been a devoted couple but they were driven to divorce by his imprisonment and the struggle of his appeal. They were still close and TC took a great interest in all of their children but he had married again, a younger woman by the name of Karen. That's all I knew. Sometimes bobbing and weaving and being in and out of jail get in the way of keeping in touch with your extended family. So I suppose that made young Shannon my second cousin or would that be my kids' second cousin? It doesn't matter apart from creating another bond between me and the bold TC.

Shannon was TC and Karen's only child and his youngest and he doted on her. The big man loved all kids. When he was in the Special Unit in BarL – created to house all the hardest prisoners like Jimmy Boyle and TC – he used to play with all the other prisoners' kids, allowing his mates to spend some quality time with their wives. Good of him yet TC also did that simply because he loves kids. There is something distinctly innocent about the man and kids, recognising one of their own, love him to pieces.

Shannon was easy to love too and I always liked a natter with her when I visited. That day, I went out to the small veranda to have a word as usual. I'd ask her about her day and maybe to tease her about something a little – like many bright kids, she loved you to do that so they can tease you right back. It was a first-floor flat and the veranda looked down on to the street, at the side of some houses and farther up to the right, shops and a school – not the most exciting view ever.

'What you looking for, Shannon?' I asked her. A bright child with a rich imagination, I reckoned she'd come up with something funny or, more likely, something I hadn't noticed. She didn't turn her head but kept staring out, gripping on to the veranda rail.

'Bad men,' she said, no emotion in her voice. Now, I knew all about what had been going on but also knew TC and Karen worked hard to protect Shannon.

'What?' I asked, thrown by her answer.

She turned and looked up, her sweet wee face all glum. 'Bad men,' she repeated and turned to stare out again as if stopping looking would mean the bad men would come.

Confession time. I bottled it – retreated right back into the living room where, only yards way, TC sat and watched over his young daughter. I gestured with my head and eyes meaning, 'What was that about?' Quietly, so Shannon couldn't hear, TC explained.

A few months after he'd been released, he had been walking to the local shops to pick up a prescription for Shannon who was ill. As he crossed the shops' car park, a beast called Billy McPhee came at him carrying two blades. He'd jumped out of his boss's jeep. His boss, Thomas 'The Licensee' McGraw, sat and watched. Even with surprise, youth and weapons on his side, McPhee couldn't take TC. Forty-five minutes later, after several assaults and even more new blades, McPhee was tiring and the bold TC was going to have him. Suddenly he got whacked on the back of the skull. McGraw, seeing the state of his heavy, had finally come out of his motor and had smashed TC from behind with a golf club.

This happened in broad daylight, with over forty reliable witnesses, yet no one was charged. Bad enough as that was, it didn't stop there. Wee Shannon had seen the damage done to her father and, in spite of TC and Karen's best efforts, it upset her. Then it got worse.

Billy McPhee, Gordon Ross and a pack of other vultures – all The Licensee's men – started circling. Not TC or even Karen – just Shannon. They'd catch her on her own and tell her they were going to kill her father, showing her knives and saying what part of his body they were going to stick the blade in.

McPhee and company are villains – just as Tommy and I are villains – but do you think for one minute that we think we're the same as them? The same as grown men who would mentally torture and terrorise a young girl? There are villains and villains. I'd rather torch myself than be identified with their ilk.

No matter how much TC and Karen tried to protect their girl, the bastards managed to catch her attention just for a few seconds. It doesn't take long to terrify a child if you really want to. Shannon was having nightmares and she was clingy to her dad, never wanting to leave him even for school. She loved school but just loved her father more.

McPhee and Ross are now dead, cut down by hitmen. For the pain and grief they gave wee Shannon alone, they deserved their fates.

The hurt of their child finally got to TC and Karen. He became morose, thoughtful, quiet. She drank too much at times and got angry – with him, of course. They moved house in an effort to get away from The Licensee's mob. It didn't work. After one huge row one night, TC ended up in jail, charged with wife assault. In truth, Karen had assaulted him but old-school TC wasn't about to say so. That was for her to do. She did, of course, but it was a low point – as if they hadn't been through enough.

They separated. Fell back in. Separated again. Meantime TC's cars were getting smashed up. He was being followed everywhere so he needed a car to be safe – well, safer. One was parked in a small space among all his neighbours' motors yet, in the morning, it was only his car that was wrecked. From the damage it was clear what had happened. A big lorry had somehow got into that parking area and rammed his motor to ruin. Once would have been unlucky, twice suspicious but this was the third time one of his motors had been wrecked in similar circumstances. Somebody wanted TC walking the streets.

There's more, much more but, just as with the documentary maker, there's too much for the space we have here. Maybe there's another book from the bold TC Campbell. It would be a book worth reading, a book worth learning from.

Then, of course, he won his appeal. When asked years before what he'd do when that happened, he said he'd build a house at the top of a hill in the middle of nowhere, get all his children round him and spend the rest of his life just being him, living in peace. Reality was a wee bit different.

Sitting in his front room, with the cameras rolling behind me and TC telling his tale, it was obvious he had no peace. When he and Joe Steele were deemed innocent by the Law Lords in 2005, there was no apology from Strathclyde Police. This was in spite of the fact that no less than thirteen cops were found to have lied at TC and Joe's trial – not one, not two, not even one bent senior officer working the case to suit his clear-up rate. Thirteen cop liars and still the word 'sorry' wasn't uttered.

Nor did the cops announce that the Doyle murder case would be reopened. So six people died and no one is convicted yet Strathclyde bogeymen are quite happy to do nothing. Funny fucking business – I thought the public paid the cops to catch killers, not sit on their arses taking the huff.

TC needs answers now. He doesn't want to go on that chase but he just can't help himself. If the new breed of cops announced they would hunt the real Doyle murderers down, maybe he would have some peace. But, by doing nothing, the cops are really saying it was TC who did it. We had the right man and the stupid judges let him go, they're saying. They know that and so does he.

Who runs the cops? I thought it was the public. Citizens like the remaining members of the Doyle Family. Don't they deserve justice?

In his work with MOJO, TC has picked up a great deal about the effects of unjust imprisonment.

'It's great, man,' he once laughed. 'There's me knowing how I feel but now I've got a name for it. Post-traumatic stress disorder – PTSD for short. Game, eh?'

The shrinks all realise that people wrongly jailed suffer the same symptoms as soldiers who have faced extreme situations. I know what they mean. Listening to TC, I could recognise bits of me. Not from getting jailed for things I did – any decent person can do that – but from being hounded and being set up for things I didn't do. Yet I'm lucky. I stayed a step ahead and now I've got my life back.

And TC? As he is fond of saying, 'The beat goes on.'

As we're writing this, TC Campbell is still waiting for compensation. He lives from hand to mouth, week in week out. Money can't repay him for the loss of twenty-one years of his life but it could help him cope, help him be safe.

Strange, isn't it, that, when they found him guilty, they jailed him right away yet, when they found him truly innocent, they did nothing in a hurry? That'll be Scottish justice for you, then.

There's another phrase of TC's, 'Justice just is.'

In his case, justice is just shite. Shame on all those who made it so.

TC is someone who started bad, made it better, only to be hijacked into decades of being the man in the iron mask. Unfortunate? For certain.

Now let's look at someone who had it on a plate and who shit on it from a height – who's still shitting on it now. Simple minded? You bet.

32

ONE VERY SIMPLE MIND

'The fucking cunts have robbed me!' Flecks of white froth flew from the guy's mouth as he spat his words out in anger. 'Taking fucking advantage, the pricks.' More spittle sprayed the air and I edged my coffee cup along the table, away from the danger zone. 'I mean, who do they fucking think they're messing with?' This was one angry man.

Sitting across from him in a cafe in Glasgow's city centre, I was only half listening. You don't need to try hard to hear that someone is furious, do you? The thought occurred to me that he could use one of those anger-management classes, the kind they push at every prisoner in Britain. When will the authorities learn that not every con has an anger problem? Some of us are quite calm as we do our ill deeds – just as some straight Joes aren't tranquil inside and can lose the place big time. Like this guy – except he wasn't entirely a straight Joe, in more senses than one.

A mutual friend had contacted me, asking if I'd meet up with Paul Kerr who had some business I might be interested in. All I knew about Paul Kerr was that he was the brother of Jim Kerr of Simple Minds. Though I like some of their stuff, as it happens, Simple Minds is not my favourite group but that wasn't the point, not the point at all. As far as I was concerned, they were Glasgow guys who'd made their mark in their industry and made it big time and, as such, deserved respect. I hoped some of that might just have rubbed on Paul Kerr so I agreed to the meet. I thought Kerr might be useful to some of my projects. I'd set up a company called Real Productions with a view to making a documentary film based on *The Ferris Conspiracy* and I also had it in mind to make documentaries about TC Campbell. These were to be edgy documentaries with great music, set in the real world, using the actual folk with dramatised slices featuring people straight off the streets.

Obviously I had the stories, the people involved and the people to act but I was short of the music. By then – this was around November 2004 – I'd learned that it can cost a fortune to get the rights to use just one track once. So I thought that maybe Paul Kerr, with his connections to the music industry, had access to copyright-free material or could put me in touch with groups who would be happy to be involved in the films. So I went to the meet intent on listening to his proposals and hoping he'd listen to my request for help. I was soon to discover that listening wasn't one of Paul Kerr's strengths.

'It's about this new band I've got, Paul,' Kerr started off. 'El Presidente.'

'Good name,' I said thinking that he was the one who'd made the name up, thinking that I was congratulating him. In truth, it was the only positive thing I could say since I'd never heard of them though I suppose most people have by now.

'Thanks,' he said, accepting the compliment. 'They are about to make it big – believe me, very big – but somebody is trying to take them away from me.'

So Kerr was coming to me with a problem, not with a business proposition – or was it both?

'I don't know that much about the music industry,' I explained, truthfully. 'I'm just learning a bit about how it works so you're going to have to explain it to me.'

Over the next hour, he did just that, using frequent references to Simple Minds to stake his claim as having some standing in the music business. He said he had been the road manager for his brother's band, organising big shows in London and on the Continent. A mover and shaker behind the group is how he was describing himself. As he explained his problems about El Presidente, Kerr kept returning again and again to Simple Minds as if he needed to be sure that I was impressed by his credentials.

I'm not that easily impressed and I could see what he was doing. However, I'm well used to some folk, when they meet me, relating to the press headlines about me as some big-time gangster rather than a bloke just trying to make an honest living in a couple of businesses he's having to learn about. So I let Kerr's boasting pass for the minute. Besides, how would I know if he was telling me the truth or not?

From what he was telling me about El Presidente, I understood that there had been a sting that had resulted in a takeover. Now, stings I'm well used to. Kerr said that, a year before, he'd been approached by the two brothers behind the band, Dante and Joolz Gizzi, and they were looking for his help because he was the big shot who'd been the mover behind Simple Minds – or so he kept saying. Also he'd been pals with the Gizzis for a long time and they'd had a problem.

Dante and Joolz were looking for help to get a proper CD made. They reckoned that El Presidente was a bit special but that they couldn't open the right doors in the music world. If they had a CD and Kerr was pushing it, they might all benefit.

I imagined this kind of approach was made all the time in the music business. For a group, no matter how good, to get a recording deal, it must be so bloody frustrating with thousands of them competing at any one time – a bit like how it is for writers to get books published although, thankfully, Reg and I haven't had to struggle too much. There must be loads of great writers and musicians that the public never hear of because they never manage to get a foot in the door – what a bloody waste. Anyway, so far, I was following the Kerr man.

Kerr had listened to the band and reckoned they were good so he paid for them to make a CD. In return, he'd own 37 per cent of El Presidente. God knows how this figure came about and I didn't ask him. Kerr's trouble now was that El Presidente had signed with a management team. They had a record deal and were getting big gigs, supporting Oasis among others. They were loved by the music journalists and they really were about to make it big. And he was getting dumped. It was when he reached this point in his story that Paul Kerr started frothing at the mouth.

Mind, I did notice that he suffered a bit from the head-cold-and-weak-bladder syndrome. Constantly sniffing and rubbing at his nose especially after he'd been to the toilet which he did every ten minutes – a big charlie habit if I wasn't mistaken. I'd seen enough of that to recognise it. Maybe if he'd cut back on the marching powder, he'd be calmer with the challenges that life threw at him. Then again, maybe he was just plain mental.

Kerr was offering me half of his share in El Presidente if I could resolve the dispute between him and the band and their new management. Now, before anyone jumps to conclusions, it was no longer normal for me to be asked to go in heavy-handed. However, Kerr probably didn't know that that was not my style now and, in fact, had never been in such matters.

For years, in the 1990s with Premier Security and the like, I had been asked to carry out such negotiations and did so with some success and always with no party coming to grief. Likewise, after my release from prison in 2002, some blue-chip companies had hired me to mediate on such matters and bad debts. They'd pay 10 per cent, 20 per cent – sometimes more – of any amount due and considered that a cheaper and quicker way than pursuing matters through the courts – a process that can take many years in some cases with high legal costs and no guarantee of success.

So I was well used to that role and we shook hands on the deal. In return, he talked about owning the rights for thousands of CDs and said he'd be pleased to help me with those as backing tracks for the documentaries I planned. So, after a short meeting, it seemed that I owned a fair slice of a top group and had free music for my films – a good meeting. Too good? Out on the street on my own, I was fully intent on checking out Paul Kerr and El

Presidente. Well, old Powder Nose might just well have offered me half of nothing.

After leaving Kerr, I went directly to the Thistle Hotel where I had a meeting with former world boxing champion, Ken Buchanan. A mutual friend of ours, Rory Nicoll, had organised some fundraising events for Ken, including a big gala dinner. I'd heard that Ken was really unhappy, believing that he had been cheated out of funds, and I wanted to resolve any issues.

Some years before, Ken had worked with a couple of guys who had spent a year raising funds for him and that also ended in tears with claims that money had gone missing. Now Rory hadn't cheated Ken out of a bean. I know because I kept a very close watch on what was going on. Some of my friends had come up from London – Joey Pyle, Pretty Boy Roy Shaw and others – and they had spent a fortune that night, as had I. No way was I going to allow us to be associated with any petty scams.

After about thirty to forty minutes with Ken, during which everything was resolved amicably, another pal of mine had phoned and I was chatting about the meeting with Paul Kerr. My pal informed me that the El Presidente boys, Dante and Joolz Gizzi, owned a bistro near to the Thistle Hotel. On the spot, I decided to pop in and introduce myself and hear their side of the story.

'Paul, what are you doing here?' Behind the bistro counter the young bloke's face had gone white, bloodless. I didn't think I was looking that rough that day. It was Dante Gizzi and I started to explain the approach by Paul Kerr, making sure that it was clear I was only there to find out if they thought there was a problem.

'Is it OK if my brother joins us?' he asked and, of course, I agreed – better to have two members of the band and be sure what I'm hearing isn't just one guy's opinion.

We sat at one of the tables in the empty bistro, drinking coffee. It was my third cup of the day and I made a mental note to have no more. If I take a lot of caffeine, it has a strange effect on me, sending electric zigzagging pulses all through my body. Who needs drugs when you've got a big jar of Kenco, eh?

The chat was amicable enough but I could see the two Gizzi boys twitching – they were ashen faced, all nervous. They obviously suspected I was pulling what we call the Cilla Black syndrome as in *Surprise, Surprise*. Nothing could have been further from the truth and I reassured them, as much as I could, that all I wanted was their point of view.

They explained the background to El Presidente and their dealings with Paul Kerr which weren't quite the way he had described them. This time there really was no surprise there. They did concede that they owed Kerr something but not 37 per cent. I couldn't be arsed spending time on percentages, management deals, concessions and the like when that had nothing to with me so I told the brothers I'd phone Kerr and did so at the table. When he answered, I made it clear that he should talk directly to the Gizzis himself and passed the phone to Dante.

There was clearly a heated conversation going on. It was all one-way traffic as Dante was quite calm but, even from a few feet away, I could hear Paul Kerr ranting at the other end of the line – probably foaming into the mouthpiece.

Eventually, a distressed looking Dante switched off the mobile phone and passed it back to me.

'Paul, I can't talk to that man,' he said. 'He's just threatened to cut my fingers off.'

Who the fuck had I got in tow with now?

33

THE CONSIGLIERE AND
THE CONMEN

'We don't need nutcases like him on board.' That was rich coming
from Paul Kerr. The man was foaming at the mouth again and,
now that I was used to it, I had my hand firmly over my drink.
Well, you adapt to people's foibles, don't you?

It had been a few weeks since we'd first met. After I'd had a chat
with the Gizzi brothers, Kerr had phoned me up saying that some
lawyer had phoned him complaining that he'd sent heavies round
to threaten the brothers. God knows who the heavies were meant
to be. Me?

My conclusion from that day was that someone was telling
porkies about El Presidente and, although I had only met all three
guys that same day for the first time, my impression was that the
Gizzis were telling the truth. After their initial reaction, the brothers relaxed and we had an amicable and sensible chat – well, until,
that is, Kerr started threatening to cut off Dante's fingers. My suspicions were that the lawyer had contacted Kerr to warn him
about that but, in his naive efforts to keep me onside, Kerr was
speaking with forked tongue again.

A far as I was concerned, there was no business between me and
El Presidente though I wished them luck in their careers. Just as I
was about to tell Kerr that there was no business between us, he
came up with a fat juicy worm that I couldn't resist. Yet, even as
he spoke, I was hoping that there wasn't a nasty hook hidden
inside the worm.

'Know how you're planning to make documentaries?' he asked.

I just nodded.

'How do you fancy making a full feature-length film?'

Now he had my attention.

Kerr explained that he knew a guy called Craig Blake-Jones who ran a company called Box Office Films and who would be interested. I was intrigued enough to arrange for us to meet up at Reg's house. Reg and I work on such projects in partnership so he needed to be brought into the discussions early doors. It was an interesting meeting but the only person who'd gain was Paul Kerr and all he'd get was a new nickname.

We sat round Reg's front room, which must by now have witnessed more confessions, held more street players, been the setting for more true-crime documentaries and news interviews than any other room in Britain. There was going to be a few crimes committed that day too.

Reg and I did our usual – smoked endless fags while wetting our palates with chilled white wine. Kerr, meantime, was having problems with his bladder and nose yet again. Reg started throwing questions at him like: Who exactly was Box Office? What was their track record? What exactly did Kerr expect to get out of it? Kerr in turn talked longer and louder but we weren't letting him away with that. I sat back and enjoyed the joust while Reg kept at him like an irritated terrier, all the time getting more and more pissed off with the lack of answers.

Eventually Kerr left, driving off in his car, and we sat on chatting and drinking.

'Fucking mental, man,' someone said.

'Aye, crazy!' said another and we laughed.

'A right Krazy Horse,' one of us said but God knows who.

'Krazy Horse, that's the man!'

'Aye, Krazy with a K, of course.'

From then on in, it was always Krazy Horse, never Paul Kerr, not till sitting down to write this.

Yet we had to concede that the film industry was one we knew nothing about and, certainly, Krazy Horse knew some people. A hell of a lot of folk seem to cross over between the music and film industries and, obviously, he was well connected in the former. Next we know, a few months later, early in 2005, *The Sun* ran with a front-page story that Robert Carlyle was set to play me in a film of *The Ferris Conspiracy* – it was perfect casting but we were fucked if we knew anything about it.

Krazy Horse had been at his games. He'd given an interview to the newspaper about a Ferris film and the journalist had naturally pushed him about who'd play the lead. Well, *The Sun* paid him for the story and wanted their money's worth, quite naturally. Because Krazy Horse knew Carlyle's personal assistant and her brother, he just mentioned his name. Next day, the big fuck-off headline appeared.

Be clear about this, Robert Carlyle hadn't even been approached about the film at the time Krazy Horse gave the story to *The Sun*. It was a great tabloid story so who can blame the paper for running with it? Not me. But the Krazy Horse was well out of his depth. For a start, the *Daily Record*, the paper that Reg writes a column for, were on to him in a flash. We're sensible people who don't tell lies and he had to say that he knew fuck all about it. Now Krazy Horse was in severe danger of getting egg all over his face. As an escape plan, he somehow managed to convince Robert Carlyle to come to a lunch meeting with me and Box Office a few days later and, of course, Scotland's media were swarming outside the venue.

The most sensible person at that meeting, aside from myself, was Robert Carlyle. Aye, he wanted to make the film and then he negotiated his fee. If he had been surrounded by straight players that film would now be in circulation but, as I watched Krazy Horse at the meeting going more and more to the toilets till he got to the stage that snot coated in white powder was dribbling from his nose, I somehow doubted it. But I had a wee test in store for the Krazy Horse.

'James McIntyre! We don't need nutcases like him, Paul,' Krazy Horse said when I told him I was arranging a meeting and wanted James there. What Krazy Horse didn't know was that James and I had history and calling him a 'nutcase' was a very bad move on Krazy Horse's part.

James McIntyre was once my lawyer and he'd also been the lawyer of most of the top faces in Glasgow and Edinburgh. Young and bright, James was quickly given the nickname Tom Hagan after the lawyer in the *Godfather* films – the one who had crossed the line and was the trusted consigliere to the Corleone Family and, thus, a top man in Mafia terms. But it was only half a joke because James not only spoke and acted the part – he was the real deal.

Faces from all over Scotland would take care of James if he was ever in trouble. Once, a certain party in Glasgow stabbed him deep in the leg, severing tendons and a major artery and almost killed him. It was something that should not have happened and the chib merchant was told that straight. The wound took a great time to heal and meant James was laid off work. The people who made sure he and his family were OK you'd recognise as career criminals – organised people, gangsters some might say.

One time I took a few days' break down in Ayrshire at the estate owned by Lawrence Marlborough, a big-time money man, builder and backer of Rangers FC. I was there in the massive estate house with Tam Bagan, Bobby Glover and Joe Hanlon and, believe me, the party was in full swing. It was an ancient house that looked more like a castle with suits of armour, mounted heads of deer, walls with huge antlers, a real tiger-skin rug and a massive stone-floored entrance hall. You could just imagine the lord of the manor sweeping in with his gowns flowing behind him.

Well into our cups, we decided to explore and came across this tall, wide, ornate wooden seat that looked like a throne. Carved all around the throne were symbols that we all agreed were Masonic – like we would know. Not. Here and there, we discovered secret drawers and compartments. It was one impressive chair and I had an idea.

We'd invite James McIntyre down and, using the chair, we'd go through a ceremony of initiating him into the family. That's Family – as in Mafia Family. Our group was so tight and loyal that that's exactly what James thought we were. In a sense, he was half right. We did consider ourselves to be a family all right but, as for the Mafia stuff, we don't do that in Glasgow.

As soon as I mentioned the idea, everyone agreed but there was one problem – Joe Hanlon. Joe was the fiercest street fighter of his generation but you wouldn't know it in his company. Among friends, he was a relaxed, fun-seeking guy – he was the youngest of us and he loved a laugh. If Joe started laughing, he wouldn't stop. I just knew he wouldn't be able to help himself as we pretended to go through some sombre ritual with James. Joe also had one of those infectious laughs – the kind that's irresistible and you find it impossible not to join in. Screw it, I phoned James anyway.

As it happened, James tried to change his arrangements so that he could make it but couldn't. I hadn't told him about any ritual, of course – just that, if he joined us at the house, it would be to his lifelong benefit and enhancement. A great honour. Just as well he couldn't come, though – all that way just for Joe's giggling to ruin the whole ploy.

James McIntyre had gone native big time. One time, he arrived in court very late. He'd been up most of the night snorting charlie and had taken a straightener before sweeping into the court. As he was trying to find the right papers in his briefcase, the judge leaned over and, not unreasonably, said, 'Do hurry up, Mr McIntyre.'

Jim looked up, grimaced and replied, 'Who the fuck do you think you're talking to?' This was delivered in a tone that was inviting the wigged one to a square-go. McIntyre was in trouble again and not for the last time.

One night the Edinburgh cops got a call that some lunatic in an ankle-length leather coat was strolling near the Royal Mile blasting off pistols at road signs and the like. When they arrested James at his home in the outskirts of the city, they found cocaine in his possession and a cache of arms that would make Al Capone blush.

The Bar Association that governs lawyers didn't take kindly to that and he was struck off. The courts didn't fancy it much either and he was jailed. He was to spend a very irritating time in the pokey as, for a good while, he shared a cell with one Paul Kerr.

'Oh, fucking SHUT THE FUCK UP!'

It attracted my attention, never mind all the other lunchtime diners in L'Ariosto restaurant. I was sitting in a booth with a pal of mine we call The Man Who Knows and had set it up that James and Krazy Horse had a chat in another booth. I trusted James, trust him still, and just wanted his independent appraisal of what the Krazy Horse was proposing.

James wasn't just there as a bright mind, a qualified though non-practising lawyer and a pal. Since leaving jail, he had reinvented himself very successfully as a scriptwriter contributing to many shows including *EastEnders* and *River City*. From a standing start as a disgraced lawyer and ex-offender, he'd worked himself into a business filled with middle-class luvvies with Oxford and Cambridge educations. It was a measure of the man but, also, I reckoned he knew a damn sight more about the film and production business than I ever would. Plus he knew the Krazy Horse.

Paul Kerr had had a wee dispute with a business partner, John Darroch, a DJ, back in 1998. When Darroch and his family were fast asleep in bed, Kerr torched the place. It was a low-life crime that, but for a bit of good luck, could have turned into a murder case – a case like the Doyle murders.

When Kerr and James ended up in the same cell in Saughton, it had driven James to despair. I don't blame him. Imagine being stuck with a guy who talks about himself non-stop – apart, of course, from frequent references to Simple Minds. With all that history, if James McIntyre had emerged from the meeting with Krazy Horse with an even lukewarm but positive appraisal, that would have been a high recommendation. In short, he was the last person Kerr could kid.

'Who the fuck do you think you're talking to? Oh, fucking SHUT THE FUCK UP!' echoed round L'Ariosto, shattering the peace, ruining the stolen, romantic lunches. Krazy Horse stormed out past our booth, his face blood red, his posture all dog with his tail between his legs.

Joining James McIntyre, the first thing I did was to reprimand him for talking and acting like that at a business meeting.

'I know, Paul, I know. But he's such a lying cunt. He was talking down to me, making all of these claims about contacts. I listened for a while and realised I could wipe Kerr's arse with his contacts. The man's got nothing, Paul. He's just a user.'

James went on to apologise for losing the rag but he explained, although he had no need to, that he had got to know Kerr very well while he was banged up with him in Saughton and he'd played the same game then – all smoke and mirrors.

'He got to me so much, Paul, that I used to lie awake at night and consider strangling him in his sleep. Now I think I should have. Our family must be protected at all costs.'

Reinvented as he was, that's still how James McIntyre felt. That we were all linked. That we were family and people like Krazy Horse had to be guarded against.

Of course James was absolutely right. A short while later, I discovered that, in the film business, a load of companies go to private banks in London that specialise in financing the film industry. If a film company can convince the bank that they have a good project coming up, the bank will advance them seven-figure sums. For a bit of paper and a load of patter? Daylight robbery, eh?

I discovered that someone had done just that on the back of the Ferris film and that Krazy Horse was plaguing Box Office, telling them they owed him MORE money. So he has had money from a film about my life while I haven't seen a brown coin? I'm sure Robert Carlyle has been rewarded as richly as me. Later, I was told by Box Office that they had paid him £10,000. Ten grand? Peanuts. What a waste since Carlyle is still keen to do the movie and what a movie it could be.

James McIntyre has moved on from strength to strength. I'm not surprised. As with Tom Hagan, with James, what you get is what you see. And, no, I didn't get that the wrong way round.

El Presidente – well, by publication time, you'll know more about that band than me as they go from strength to strength and I wish them well. As good as they are, I'm quite pleased that Krazy Horse's offer to get me involved with them was all smoke and mirrors. I'm more interested in bands who play from the street – boys who might well be in trouble if it wasn't for music. Bands that keep it real and also write great songs and deliver them with guts and soul as well as skill. Bands like The Ronelles – bloody fantastic. You could jig all night to some of their songs yet they're based on some of the tales in our books. How they do that I do not know – I'm just delighted they do.

Bands like Urbn Ri – that's Irn-Bru back to front – one of their guys had done jail time and decided it would be the last. But the cops don't get the message and keep on raiding them, only to find boxes of musical gear. One day soon, the same cops will be holding back thousands of their fans outside gigs.

Paul Kerr? Well, what do you know? After I broke from him, I discovered he was close friends with a guy called Cass who has been a close associate of The Licensee's for many years. Is that where the 'heavies' who visited the El Presidente boys came from? Since I listened to them and believed them rather than Kerr, had he gone to his pal to arrange a less scrupulous visit? Birds of a feather, eh?

And I reckon that Kerr's well fucked on his claims of ownership of part of El Presidente.

Has he got a new group? No.

Involved in a big project? No.

Making a lot of money? No.

Answering his phone? No.

Still claiming to be a friend of mine? Yes.

Would I cross the road to piss on him if he was on fire? Yes. Just so I could tell him what a backstabbing rat he is.

Dangerous people come in all sorts of guises. We're about to meet one who introduced himself as a saviour.

34

SPIES, LIES AND WEE PIES

'I'll need to meet with Paul Ferris.'

'Why?'

'He's connected. Knows people. He can help me get people to cooperate.'

'What fucking people?' Reg wasn't happy.

'People who know about Ian. Active people. Ferris will know them. He's still connected, isn't he.' It was a statement not a question.

Reg looked out of the booth they were sitting in at Di Maggio's restaurant in Royal Exchange Square. As usual, the place was packed with happy eaters. Groups of young women were having long lunch breaks from their offices, chattering away twenty to the dozen and sneaking extra glasses of wine. In small family groups, kids were eating real pizzas while the adults were having grown-up food, twirling pasta on forks. Here and there, a couple of faces relaxed in manly company, choosing the place because the grub was good and the high booths allowed private chat and they could see who was coming in the front door at any time. Reg nodded at a waiter and turned back to face his company. A man who talked the game but didn't know those faces just yards from him. A man who Reg had decided he didn't trust.

'Ian, we've had this conversation before,' Reg said, pulling out another fag. It was 2004, before Scotland became a nanny state and banned smoking in public places. You could feel it in your water that they'd start with the smokes but they wouldn't stop there.

'Well, it's important,' said Ian Sharman, edging closer in his seat and leaning over the table.

Reg imagined his feet dangling a foot from the floor. This was a very small man but you didn't notice when he was seated. In spite of having met him several times, Reg was always caught by surprise when the man stood up. The size of the man was almost as astonishing as the number of gold rings he wore – almost one on every finger, some with Masonic symbols. And then there was a thick gold bangle. Loads of bling but did he have any zing?

'But you know my answer,' Reg waited for a response. Repeating himself wasn't a way he liked to spend his life.

'But he'll be useful in opening doors,' Sharman went on. 'He's still connected and . . .'

'Do you ever fucking listen, Ian? Or is it just that you don't listen to my answer to this request of yours?'

The waiter arrived and handed Reg the bill. He had the notes ready and laid them on the tray, immediately shuffling his arse over the padded bench and stepping out of the booth.

'Thanks for paying,' said Ian. 'I'll get it next time.'

'So you will,' replied Reg, lifting his bag and heading for the door, muttering to himself, 'Just like you said last time and the time before that, mean prick.'

It wasn't Ian Sharman's reluctance to dip into his wallet that was the trouble – it was his agenda. Yet he was meant to be helping a friend – a friend who needed help. But is that really what he was about?

Sharman was . . . well, he never actually said what he was. An investigator? A private dick? A paralegal? He worked for a big law firm called Levys in Manchester yet he was never there when Reg called. They knew of him all right but never knew where he was. Worse, he didn't possess a mobile phone. It was 2004, for Christ sake. Who didn't carry a mobile phone? Especially when you're investigating claims of unjust conviction. That's what Ian Sharman claimed when he first contacted Reg, on the phone out of the blue. No problem there but then he said he was helping Ian

McAteer. Still no problem. In fact, good news – too few people were looking at McAteer's case.

We've written about Ian McAteer in an earlier book, *Vendetta* – what we said raised a few eyebrows and rattled some cages and quite right too. This tale isn't about McAteer though but, for those who don't know of him, a short summary will be useful.

Ian McAteer was a well-known Glasgow player. He'd turn his hand to most things but earned a regular living moving classy cars around both legally and illegally. In the late 1990s, he was asked by Thomas 'The Licensee' McGraw to give a safe house to a Liverpool guy called Paul Bennett. He did, of course, without question.

This was the same Paul Bennett who had been convicted of drug trafficking along with his uncle John Haase but a royal pardon had been arranged for them by 'jail works' Home Secretary, Michael Howard. The same Haase and Bennett who sent a delegation to my old pal Rab Carruthers in Manchester to ask about buying £50,000 of illegal weapons to trade with the authorities. The same Paul Bennett who had never been arrested since, in spite of being very active.

Ian McAteer knew all about the royal pardon, of course, as every street player did. But he didn't know about the rest of it or the fact that Bennett had just hot-footed it out of Belfast, having started a war among Loyalist groups over drug trafficking. Bennett didn't need a safe house to hide from the authorities as McAteer assumed. He was hiding from the Irish and other street players he had set up as an agent provocateur.

Although he was oblivious to what Bennett had been up to, McAteer was, nevertheless, becoming suspicious. Always a careful man, he became increasingly concerned by the number of times Bennett suggested jobs. He was doing well as it was. What did he want with jobs from that Scouser street player, Bennett? Beginning to suspect a fit-up, McAteer broke from Bennett who headed off down south to Liverpool.

As it happened, McAteer did a great deal of work between Liverpool, London, Newcastle and Glasgow. Then, one night, one of his associates, Warren Selkirk, was found shot dead and left with a bag of dog shit laid on his corpse – a symbolic gesture of disrespect, so the cops said.

After a trial, during which it was conceded that McAteer had not been at the scene of the crime, he was still found guilty of Selkirk's murder. By virtue of satellite readings from his mobile phone, the prosecution claimed he had phoned someone close to the murder scene at the time of the murder . . . claimed that he had ordered the killing . . . conspired to kill. If that seems a bit thin, I agree. But there was much worse to come.

Another of McAteer's associates, George Bell Smith, had given evidence that McAteer had shown him a gun and was boasting of the killing. So McAteer was jailed for life – simply written off as another bloodthirsty gangster – till we started digging the dirt, that is. We exposed a witness trading evidence for the dropping of underage sex charges, a jealous and violent witness – Paul Bennett's hands were all over the case and more. If you want to know McAteer's whole story you'll have to read *Vendetta* – this isn't his story but the story of Ian Sharman, the man who crept in from the cold.

McAteer was appealing against his conviction but he knew it would be difficult. It always is when the court accepts that you weren't at the murder scene but believes you commissioned the killing. It would take considerable detective work and most lawyers weren't equipped for that. He was unhappy with his first lawyer's performance and changed to the large firm of Levys in Manchester. That's when Ian Sharman popped up.

First thing he wanted was to meet with Reg, who'd been digging into the background of the case and had uncovered many dodgy aspects. So it was a fair call that Sharman should want to see him.

At their first meeting, Reg took him through all the details of McAteer's case but he left feeling a wee bit edgy, a bit concerned. By the close of business, Sharman had started to ask questions that didn't seem to have much relevance.

'What's Paul Ferris up to these days?'

'Tell me about McGraw, The Licensee.'

'Who runs Glasgow now?'

It wouldn't be the last time Sharman asked those questions – especially the 'What's Paul Ferris up to these days?' one. Reg would tell him I was writing books, working on making documentaries, doing consultancy work in the security industry (since I still was then) and spending time with my kids and enjoying it all the way. Sharman wasn't convinced. 'What's Paul Ferris up to these days?' he'd ask again. It was beginning to get on Reg's nipples.

Reg and I discussed Sharman, of course – just as we discussed Ian McAteer. The problem was that Sharman *did* appear to be making headway with McAteer's case. He'd interviewed a girl Bell Smith was accused of having underage sex with – by this time, she was a young adult living and working up north. The underage sex case against Bell Smith had been dropped when he gave evidence against McAteer. Sharman had had a go at the cops in Dunbartonshire who had originally charged the guy with underage sex and they admitted that they weren't chuffed that the charges had been dropped because the decision was taken in Glasgow by the Serious Crime Squad who didn't consult them. Sharman then claimed to have challenged the Procurator Fiscal whose responsibility it would have been to bring or drop charges. He'd even got legal access to the cops' and PF's files. Good going – if it was right.

Our dilemma was this: we wouldn't do anything to hinder Ian McAteer's bid to bring all the truth out, of course, yet we didn't want to work with Sharman since we suspected he was in cahoots with the cops and had a secret, sinister agenda. Were we just being paranoid? There's a real danger of that when you write about crime and corruption as we do – you constantly have to check that you aren't seeing something that isn't there. So far, with Sharman, all we had was a bad feeling and an irritation at some of his questions.

Yet I had been trailed by MI5 and NCS for years and these people don't go away. Reg had been digging into the Liverpool story about Haase and Bennett's royal pardon, which was now a sensitive issue especially as there were rumours of bribes having been given to Michael Howard – and this had become an even more delicate matter since Howard had, by then, become leader of the Tories.

Reg had been approached by a number of national newspapers and top independent investigative journalists offering him money just for his files. He refused, of course, but it was no secret that he had got further into the underbelly of the Haase/Bennett story than anyone else. If the media knew, would the secret service? What do you think?

For a long time, Reg and I had the view that Ian McAteer was jailed deliberately for something he hadn't done. The reason was that he'd got too close to Paul Bennett who, since his royal pardon, had floated around the UK and Europe and was involved in big offences. Yet he was never arrested and never charged, while a load of other people were. Was he working for the secret service?

Ian McAteer had given Bennett a safe house in Glasgow for a while but eventually, and independently from us, he sussed the man out. Telling Bennett as much to his face, McAteer split from him, only to be had up for Selkirk's murder very soon afterwards. Want to shut a man up? Making him worry about having to spend his life in jail should do the trick.

The cops were desperate to get McAteer off the street. They will trade charges with some grass to make up false testimony at the drop of a truncheon but even they are most reluctant to drop underage sex charges. Yet that's exactly what they had traded with George Bell Smith. At the time Reg first met Ian Sharman, he seemed to know all about that – strange business since we were about to reveal the whole story for the first time to the public in *Vendetta*. Then again, maybe Sharman wasn't what he seemed?

'There's been a terrible series of events.' It was Ian Sharman's voice at the other end of the line.

'Go on then,' said Reg, pushing his dinner aside and eyeballing an apology to his wife, Gerry, for yet another dinner about to be ruined.

'The Home Office has decided to transfer Ian McAteer to a Scottish prison,' Sharman said slowly, pausing dramatically – another annoying habit of his. Ian McAteer had been convicted in England and he'd been moved about the toughest English prisons since the day he was arrested.

'Ian hasn't asked to move, has he?' asked Reg, anticipating what was coming.

'No, of course not . . .' another dramatic pause 'but you know why, don't you?'

'Why?' asked Reg, just to see what his line was and making a bet with himself he'd get it right.

'A convicted person can't appeal against a conviction unless they are living in the country where that conviction took place.' Sharman paused again while Reg nodded to himself. He'd won that bet.

'Of course, of course – the bastards,' Reg cursed with venom, all the while wondering why they would bother. There were easier ways to keep Ian McAteer in prison.

'And, of course, you know who has men inside Scottish prisons?' More dramatic silence. 'The Licensee.' The pauses were now extremely annoying. 'And you know who The Licensee is associated with?'

'Paul Bennett,' Reg answered to avoid more melodrama.

Then Sharman got to the point, 'You really must write about this in the newspapers urgently. It's the only way to counter the move.'

'I'll need to talk with Ian McAteer.'

'Why?'

'Or his lawyers.'

'But I work for his lawyers,' protested Sharman.

'But, as you've pointed out, you're not his lawyer,' replied Reg accurately. He in turn had to point out to Sharman that he wasn't an investigator but a writer. Now he was being asked to write but how could he when he would be acting on the word of a man he didn't trust? Early on, Sharman had made it plain that he must never be quoted or identified. In fact, he had also said that Levys should not be named and, in spite of being asked why not, hadn't answered the question.

'What's his lawyer doing about this?' Reg asked. 'He should be able to stop it no bother.'

'He can't do anything,' replied Sharman. 'There's nothing the lawyer can do,' he repeated.

Crap. Now it was call his bluff time.

'OK, I'll try and get something in,' said Reg after Sharman had gone on and on about the same points for half an hour. 'It's too late for tomorrow. Maybe the next day.'

'No later,' ordered Sharman, 'by then, it'll be too late to stop them.'

This was a big, smelly red herring. No way would the Home Office take action to move Ian McAteer against his will and then run all sorts of risks of breaching his human rights. No way would his lawyer be powerless to act. Reg wrote nothing and Ian McAteer wasn't transferred to Scotland. It had never been on the cards – never even mentioned. Sharman was caught out big time trying to con us – trying to ruin Reg's credibility by getting him to give some newspaper an untrue story. The question was why.

We strung Ian Sharman along for a while, at the same time quietly advising Ian McAteer to drop him. All you can do is advise – after all, it wasn't our arses stuck in a jail for over twenty years.

Several more times Sharman phoned Reg, calling on urgent coverage in the media of something that he had just discovered, something the cops had just done or whatever. He always phoned at night at a time when he had been asked repeatedly not to since that was when Reg and Gerry always tried to grab a couple of hours' quality time for being together. Smart thinking for a hardworking couple – except when Sharman was at his games.

We strung Ian Sharman along, now telling him less than ever. The top priority was making sure Ian McAteer got justice – everyone has a right to justice. So we kept our lips zipped. Another priority was writing and publishing *Vendetta* with the section on Michael Howard in full. The public has a right to be told what had gone on and that duty fell to us. We'd long since concluded that Sharman was working for someone else. How else could he take on such a complicated case as Ian McAteer's pro bono, gratis, no fees?

Someone was paying his wages and we reckoned it was to prevent the truth coming out about McAteer's conviction and the role of Paul Bennett, a man who clearly was working for the secret services. Given that we explain and expose it more fully in *Vendetta*, they wouldn't want that hitting the bookshops.

For a while, Ian McAteer stuck with Sharman. He was involved in a fight to clear his name so I couldn't blame him. Sharman was obviously complaining to McAteer that Reg was promising to do things and then not doing them – but it was complaining without explaining. We couldn't fully explain our concerns about Sharman to Ian McAteer since it was certain that his prison phone calls were being taped and his mail was being read by the screws.

During this period, Ian McAteer got a friend of his to ask me to meet with Sharman. Curious, I agreed. But, when we met at his hotel as he requested, I knew he was taking the piss – the hotel was right across from Strathclyde Police HQ in Pitt Street, Glasgow. Was that so he had a short walk to work in the morning?

Given that Sharman had been on and on at Reg to arrange a meeting with me for over almost two years, it was curious that, when we eventually did get together, he never actually asked me to do anything. All he did do was tell me over and over again how good he was and then he'd ask odd questions about this street player and that. I told him nothing. However, the meeting was worthwhile – I was now more certain than ever that Sharman could not be trusted.

Vendetta was published at the end of October 2005. By the first week of November, the Metropolitan Police along with the Home Office had launched an inquiry into the whole affair of the royal pardons, Liverpool and trading in guns. Loads of people have been pulled in by the cops and they've also come for me. I've refused on the basis that I can't reveal my sources. No word, of course, if Michael Howard has been interviewed. What do you think?

Then, in July 2006, an interesting letter was passed to us. It was to Ian McAteer from Levys his lawyers. Seems that they have had ongoing problems with Ian Sharman in that he was rarely available to them, they didn't know what he was doing much of the time, they'd had many complaints about him and it sounded like he'd been lying. Sharman was now 'disassociated' with the firm but there was just one problem – he'd gone off with Ian McAteer's file.

Fighting an appeal against murder is hard enough. Fighting a complex case like Ian McAteer's is almost an impossible task. Fighting it without a file – it's like firing a gun when you have no bullets.

Though he denies murder, in other ways Ian McAteer is a villain in this tale – that's in no doubt. But who is the bad man? What do you think?

Good and bad – it's a difficult call sometimes but other calls should be easier. Like when someone is dead or alive. Yet it's a call some people have got wrong about me so many times. Once again I was about to be declared a dead man walking.

35

CURSED

'It says here you're a dead man, Paul.' My pal was advising me what the tabloid headline said.

'Right you are,' I replied laughing, 'and I just thought I had a bad hangover.' If I'd a tenner for every time I'd been declared dead, I'd be lording it up in some big mansion, being attended by servants. Aye, right. 'Who is the Mr Angry this time?'

'Not Mr Angry – Mrs Angry.'

'What?'

'Rita Thompson.'

Now I really was pissing myself laughing. Rita was the widow of Arthur Thompson, the so-called Godfather, and she'd been threatening to wreak revenge on me for years – ever since her man had died of a heart attack. In fact, Tam Bagan and I used to take bets on who was top of her list. I always reckoned that it would be him since he had been brought up by one of Thompson's relatives then turned against him. But it was just pub talk, idle gossip that, in my view, was never going to happen. If it ever had, it would've been years earlier when she was still grieving for her man and had his millions to do what she wanted.

There was also something else that made it less likely now – Rita was dead. She had died, as it happens, on 6.6.6, of natural causes after a long illness. But now someone was claiming to the press that she had left money for a hit job on me.

I know the journalists have to sell newspapers but this really was a scunner. What self-respecting gunman was going to carry out the job after their client had died? These guys aren't in that business on principle or to exude high professional standards. They're in it for one reason and one reason only – money. If they can earn the dough without taking the risks, all the better.

So I just laughed off these most recent threats and here I am still alive and kicking, writing this book. But it must be said that Rita Thompson did hold grudges against me. She still blamed me for the killing of her son, Fatboy, fifteen years earlier. People like Rita don't hold with the findings of a court – like when they found me not guilty. All the bigger shame, then, that her man broke all the streets laws by cooperating with the cops and actually giving evidence against me.

She had also had a hard life by anyone's standards – even those of the wife of a top gangster. Her mother had been killed in a car bomb. Her daughter died from an overdose of too-pure heroin. Her elder son shot dead. Her younger son, born an idiot, now turned an idiot junkie. When her own man died, his empire was crumbling and his days had been numbered for a while before his death. If the heart attack hadn't got to him first, the grieving relatives of some of his victims were all set to take him out. And Rita herself had crossed the line – in avenging her mother's death, she led an attack on the Welsh crew who she held responsible. I'm sure she was right there. That had got her time in jail. She was lucky – it could have been time in the mortuary.

She might have blamed all her woes on me. I blamed her for nothing – she was a wife, a non-combatant, a citizen. Though there were some folk – the wives of Thompson's victims mainly – who wished she'd roast in hell, I had no feelings towards her one way or another.

The date of her death was significant to some people. For me, the date of her funeral also rang true. It was 12 June 2006 – the fourteenth anniversary of me being found not guilty of Fatboy's murder. My freedom anniversary since, if I'd been found guilty, I'd sure as hell still be rotting in jail. But then it wasn't the first time that dates were significant with the deaths of Thompsons. Arthur

Senior had died on the birthday of one of Bobby and Joe's sons and was buried on the birthday of another – sons who still grieve for their dads in spite of having to grow up without them.

Believe in jinxes? Maybe? Then you might just have the grounds for seeing the Thompson Family as cursed.

A couple of years earlier, I had been warned of other threats of hits on my life. These came from a source that some people also believe is cursed – Thomas 'The Licensee' McGraw.

When I was released from prison in January 2002, the press, the police and the ponces of McGraw's camp set out to make life difficult for me – set out to have me locked up again for years in spite of having done sod all wrong.

Was I tempted to fight in the old way, the street way? Fucking right I was. Did I? No need. McGraw's mob had enough problems of their own from all over.

Within the space of a year, McGraw's three main sidekicks and protection had been killed – two were knifed and the other was mown down by a car while he was running away, terrified someone was about to kill him. If losing one was unfortunate and two was careless, what was losing three? Fucking suicidal – or that's how McGraw saw it.

He couldn't get people to work with him, full stop. Meantime, as is his way, he was getting increasingly paranoid about me. Stupid bastard had nothing to worry about. I wasn't playing that game any more – unless someone hurt me or mine, that is.

Yet McGraw needed his driver, his equaliser and his heavy – probably felt like a wean who's lost his comfort blanket without them. Then Reg got word through his sources that McGraw was recruiting again. The papers were full of reports that he'd hired former terrorists from Eastern Europe. Crap. He had gone much closer to home.

According to Reg's contacts, his first port of call had been Liverpool, always a good recruiting centre for well-equipped street players. Apparently he had almost come to an arrangement with a couple of guys but when he mentioned my name as needing sorting out, deal off.

Next stop was Manchester. Some of the Mancunians are a bit more into acting as freelancing agents than the Scousers. You get the impression they would do anything for a bit of money. That's if you don't know them. Many of them also carry shooters like most folk wear watches – every waking hour. But The Licensee's negotiations ended in an angry exchange when my name came up. He offered more money – that's one thing he has plenty of – and was told that his cash would be deposited in a place the sun don't shine unless he left town promptly.

Last stop was London. Now, if you know where to go, that vast cosmopolitan city is a place you can hire anyone to do anything – except, it seems, to kill me. There, he was told that there *would* be a hit – on him – if he didn't fuck off sharply.

As this was being relayed to me, nothing was surprising me. The stupid bastard had gone to places where I was well known. Places I had spent years in the 1990s working with people, bonding with folk – folk like Paul Massey from Salford, Noel Cunningham in London and, of course, the Adams Family.

I'd gone out in the world and proved myself. The Licensee, on the other hand, had hidden at home, taking care of his own wee patch. The only time he went further afield was to a do a bit of exploitation. They knew me down south. They didn't know him – well at least not in the way he wanted them to.

'Paul, I was just phoning to say well done with the books.' It was the Scouse accent of one of the regular players down in Liverpool. 'Fucking great reads – all the boys think so.'

'Yeah, eh . . . cheers.' I struggle every time anybody pays a compliment about the books. Mind you, I'd hate it if not enough people enjoyed them.

'We was just discussing,' he went on, 'who we'd nominate as Liverpool's Licensee.'

'Ha, there's only one of those, thank fuck,' I laughed.

'No but there's not, though. We have at least three of the bas-
tards trading info to the cops to turn a blind eye on their badness.
Cunts so they are. But which one would we choose to call *The
Licensee*? Fucked if we can choose.'

Seems, these days, every city, large town or big patch has its
own Licensee – Nottingham, Bristol, Newcastle, Manchester,
Essex, Edinburgh – that I know from the local guys. Now they all
get called The Licensee, thanks to Thomas McGraw. That's how
he's known out and about in Britain – as the man who made the
model of trading innocent lives with the cops.

I suppose that's a kind of fame. It could be worse. Just as
Rachman became a byword for slum property, so McGraw
could've become a byword for slum morals. It could be called
doing a McGraw.

Power and money – he has them. But reputation? It's all bad.
Who would want to get rich and pay that price? Not me. How
about you?

Knowing you are a villain is usually straightforward. But knowing whether you're a good person or a bad person is often not so
easy. Here's a man who's confused about just that. A man I know
very well – me.

36

A WAKING NIGHTMARE

Fierce waves crashed and roared in my head. My eyes nipped and salt water coated my lips but I wasn't down by the sea – I was walking the streets of Glasgow's east end in the middle of the night, weeping my eyes out – weeping from regret, self-pity and utter anger. A grown man crying? Think that's weak? Think that's wrong? Just as well we didn't bump into each other that night. Just as well for both our sakes.

Regret because I had just beaten Sandra, my partner. Writing these words even now, a few years later, brings back a great shame burning as fiercely as it did that night. Before I go any further, there's something I need to say – Sandra, I'm sorry. I've said that before, of course – said it time and time again and meant it every time but I can't say it enough – Sandra, I'm sorry.

Self-pity because I had no idea how it happened yet I knew that I had just closed a chapter in my life. My life living with Sandra had come to an end. I had done that – me, just me.

Anger because that was the only way I could move, stay alive. Allowing that fury at the whole stinking, shitty mess that was the world for me that night muted the guilt and shame. When you're really angry, there's only room for anger.

How can a man who despises men who are violent to women beat up someone he loves? I never thought I'd ask that question. I started asking it that night and I'm still asking it now. Yet I still have no answers to 'how' – let alone 'why' – it could have happened. All I know is what I remember of that night.

We'd been out for the night with friends down in Dumfries. I hadn't been out of jail too long and I was still enjoying the freedom of being able to do simple things like that. Believe me, you do. Maybe I was enjoying that freedom more than I could handle it. After a few years away, my tolerance to booze wasn't as strong as it once was. I thought it was – and, after all, there was always the occasional prison hooch – but it wasn't.

On the way back, I was niggling about something and Sandra wasn't happy. Can I remember what it was about? No. Can she? No. Does it matter now? No.

By the time we were dropped off at her house, more words were had. At this stage, it was just that thing that a lot of couples go through – bad mood rising and no one really knows why. I was drunk and tired and wanted to crash out so I headed for the spare room. It was just another low-key row that couples have – the type of thing that gets patched up in the morning because none of it matters by morning.

Suddenly I was awake, right up on my feet with a start and punching, kicking and flailing out as if my life depended on it – as if some team had crept into the room intent on killing me. But the only person in that spare room at the receiving end of my blows was my woman.

Sandra, I'm sorry.

Then silence. Slowly my eyes took in what I had done – a waking nightmare with nothing that I could do to change it. I'd done too much for no reason so I turned and headed for the street.

It was the early hours of the morning and pitch dark. As I strode away, all I could hear was the clip-clop of my shoes on the pavement echoing and bouncing off the walls. A lonely noise at the best of times, that night it was my deserved theme tune. I deserved worse. That night, even I agreed with that.

It never occurred to me that I was putting myself at risk. This was the man who checks the doorway of every pub, watches every car when he drives anywhere, looks for familiar faces in crowds and who never gives anyone a time and place for fear of the risks.

Yet here was that same man walking alone through the east end at night. None of that even occurred to me but, if it had, I would have been glad and I would have hoped that the hit man would come and come fast. Hurt? I deserved worse than hurt.

Sandra, I'm sorry.

The tears came. You may not be surprised to know that I'm not someone who's given to weeping. I didn't like it one bit. It made me feel weak and soiled and I stopped it – the anger stopped it. So then I strode out on those streets with the rage singing in my head, hoping I'd meet somebody, anybody, and I'd hurt them as much as I hurt inside. I'd hurt them physically for no reason other than that I hurt.

What fucking right had I to hurt anyone, especially an innocent passer-by? None. What right had I to that anger against others? None. Where did it come from? I don't know but I don't want it back. Ever.

Walking, walking, walking – I've no idea for how long. Then I discovered that I was near a pal's house. A very close pal, one of the few – perhaps the only one – I could talk to that night. What would he think of me and what I'd done? Whatever I deserved.

It was the middle of the night and his lights were all off but he would waken for me and welcome me in. He's that sort of pal. I sat in his front room and told him all. Told him that I was nothing but a lowlife scumbag after all. That it didn't matter what I was trying to do with my life, I was no better than all the men I hated, despised. How could I think well of myself ever again? How could I look Paul Junior and Dean, my sons, straight in the eye and tell them that, above all, they must respect women? Then the tears came – this time flooding my face and grabbing my chest till I heaved for breath and let out a long howl of bloody pain for all that I'd done.

Sandra, I'm sorry.

Later, after I'd had a catnap and a wash and I'd sobered up, I thought back to what I'd been chatting to my pal about. It was still right – for Sandra and young Dean's sake, I had to leave them.

For weeks, I couldn't go near them but I was writing letters. Apologies? I did it early and kept doing it but I knew that saying sorry didn't take away that night – could never take away that night.

Sandra wrote to me, agreeing that we should separate. We'd had some great times, she said, and some bad – like her being left alone with three-week-old Dean while I was hauled off to jail. She was even willing to take some of the blame for that night and, when I read that, I remembered how strong she could be, how loving. But I won't have it. It was nothing to do with her. My fault. My fault. My fault.

Sandra, I'm sorry.

Now Sandra has a new partner and a new life and I'm glad for her. She deserves all the happiness in the world. We're still close friends. I see Dean all the time and he often comes and stays with me.

Me? I'm still worried about me. Why did that happen? Will it happen again? I've studied the whole scene of domestic violence and am appalled by the damage and death men inflict on the women they are meant to love.

Sandra, I'm sorry.

Answers? I have no answers apart from this: unless we face up to male violence against women, we'll never understand it, never change it. I've put a section on my website – the one that the authorities keep trying to close down. I reckon that, for that section alone, they should be paying me a government grant. Then again, how many men in suits go home at night and slap their wives about?

It's a hidden social evil and more of us need to stand up, like alcoholics do at AA meetings, and declare, 'My name is Paul and I beat up my woman.'

Being a villain doesn't make me a bad man. Beating up my woman does.

Through all of this, I wanted to talk to my father, Willie. Of course, he had died and left me to figure out on my own what advice he'd have given me. Now, there was a man who knew the ways of the world – like when to talk and when not to. As we're about to find out, he knew that sometimes silence is the best policy.

37

ONE-WAY TICKET

The back of the bus, they cannae sing,
Cannae sing, cannae sing.
The back of the bus, they cannae sing,
On a cold and frosty morning.

The young school kids were going off to the swimming baths in the school bus. It was always a special treat and they were in such a good mood they were singing a favourite song all the way:

The back of the bus, they cannae sing,
Cannae sing, cannae sing . . .

The driver didn't mind – he liked it when the kids were happy. But, this time, they weren't wrong. He knew that the folk who were sitting at the back of the bus couldn't sing – but they could rob banks, just as they had done minutes before.

I was about seven or eight years old so it was around 1970–71. My old man, Willie, had his own small bus company, Hogganfield Coaches. Three single-decker buses were all he had but he kept them busy dealing with both Rangers and Celtic football support-ers – not an ounce of prejudice in my old man – social club outings, summer Sunday School picnics, runs down to the coast and the regular earner of the school runs. All my father wanted to do was earn money, legally if possible, but he wasn't beyond taking a risk. In his younger days, with the Ross Street San Toi aka The Bowery Boys, he'd developed a reputation as the best getaway driver in Glasgow – skills he hadn't lost.

He'd had a bit of tax trouble a wee while before that saw him being sent to jail – just a short term in Barlinnie but long enough to hatch a plan. These other two guys got friendly with him and had heard all about his reputation as a driver. They were planning to rob a bank, a stone's throw from where they were sitting. It was in a sheltered location, quiet, and it carried a fortune – especially on the Barlinnie screws' pay day since their wages were paid in there. Would he like to drive the second getaway car? The standard approach in such a robbery is for the robbers to drive away fast from the scene in one car, dump it, change motors where no one can see them and go off unnoticed in that second car while the cops are still hunting the first.

'I'll do you better than that,' said the old man, 'I'll get you a getaway bus.'

At first they took some convincing but, when he explained to them that the cops would never stop, never mind search, a bus full of weans, they thought he was a genius.

Out of jail, the three men followed through on the plan. On the day, it went like clockwork. My old man, with a bunch of kids heading to the baths, stopped dead on time at the designated spot, let the two robbers get on and hid them out of the way up at the back of the bus.

Once the kids were dropped off at the baths in Calton, my father drove the guys on to another location. Later that night, they met up and he was paid his wages – and very handsome they were for half an hour's work.

All three men swore not to spend any of the money for at least six months. They wouldn't go out on expensive meals or buy their wives fancy presents. They'd do absolutely nothing that might make the cops suspicious of their new-found wealth. My father was an old hand and knew the score so, when he came home, he placed the money in a thick brown envelope right at the back of a drawer.

No one in my family, not even my mother, knew a thing about what my father had been up to, of course. As far we knew, he had gone out to work as usual, doing his usual rounds and, of course, that's exactly what he had been doing – except with two extra passengers.

A few days later, two guys with brand-new, expensive suits and smoking cigars caught the flight from Glasgow Airport to Heathrow. Both were accompanied by their wives wearing full make-up, new dresses, expensive jewellery and fur coats – probably with no knickers. They were full of the joys of life and, all the way down there, the men drank large brandies and the women had G&Ts like they were going out fashion. They were going to spend a few days in London, staying at a top hotel. They had tickets for a big show and the women were going to shop till they dropped. Why should they worry?

They should've paid more attention to the news. It was slap bang in the middle of one of the biggest anti-IRA clampdowns in Britain. Heathrow was hoaching with cops who were paying very close attention to incoming flights, especially those from Dublin, Belfast and Glasgow.

'Excuse me, sir, can we have a word, please?' The cop wasn't wearing a uniform and didn't say he was a cop. Unlike most Glasgow polis of that time, he wasn't a knuckle-dragger, whose neck strained crimson at his collar, and the seams of his suit jacket didn't pull and bulge with his sheer girth. He was of average size, neat and tidy, handsome, some women might say, and he was oh-so-fucking polite. Just another official is how he looked. That was the point, of course. Why scare the targets? He was the cop frontman. The bears were caged in the back room where the suits and the fur coats with no knickers were heading and fast.

Two hours is all it took. Think that's a short time? You're thinking a normal life. You're thinking *Coronation Street* or *EastEnders* on a double-bill night. You're thinking some football match in some big, fuck-off cup that's gone into extra time, maybe penalties. Doesn't that go so fast?

We are talking sweat time – when a second feels like a minute, a minute feels like an hour and an hour feels like a lifetime, a miserable, sad, jailed-up lifetime spent with sadistic pricks who want to punish you. Easy? Fuck off. It's like expecting an untrained asthmatic with panic-attack problems to run a marathon live on TV while being followed at close range by a cameraman on the back of a motorcycle.

A laugh? For those so inclined. But for those left at home depending on them? For them it's a nightmare.

'Fancy a game of Monopoly?' I asked one of my sisters.

'Aye. Aye-aye-aye,' she answered and danced around the floor at our house in Hogganfield Street, Blackhill, Glasgow.

'Me too,' I replied. For years, it was the favourite game of my childhood.

'Ah'll set the board up, Paul,' she wittered on, sounding excited, pleased.

'Fab,' I gave her back. Well, I was only seven or eight and all The Beatles were still alive and still performing. Very soon, for a while, I'd be wearing Bay City Rollers gear. Which do you prefer?

'Will I set it up here, Paul?'

Without turning round and knowing she'd have chosen the usual place since we played Monopoly most days, I replied, 'Aye, please, and I'll deal out the money.'

SKERRUNCH. On the page it looks like something from a *Batman* comic yet I've heard it so many times and I can't find a better way to describe the sound of wood shattering. It was our front door coming in, making way for the cops fast behind it.

Down in Heathrow one of the Glasgow women had seen her husband being led away by men in suits.

'Oi, whit the fuck are yese daein' wi ma man, ye cunts?' she'd growled, totally spoiling the effect of all that dough she'd lavished on her fur coat.

The good-looking, mild-faced frontman stepped forward between her and her husband. 'Madam, we are conducting an investigation into travellers with possible IRA links. I'm sure in your husband's case it will just be routine.' Behind him her man overheard and his face turned chalk white and his jaw hung down.

In the police interview rooms, they had the men empty their pockets. Nothing much of interest apart from huge sums of money, all in used Scottish banknotes – so much money the cops weren't about to let the men walk till they got an explanation of where it had all come from.

One of the robbers was a staunch Protestant of the Orange Order brigade. When he heard that he was suspected of being a member of the IRA, he took great offence and personal hurt.

'Ah'm no' any fuckin' papist,' he'd said to the London cops who must have been struggling to understand him. 'See me? Ah'm loyal and true to the Queen. An' Ah'm no a fuckin' terrorist either. Ah'm a fuckin' bank robber, so Ah am.' You can take the man out of Glasgow but some bits of Glasgow are just going stick to his shoe. In the back of that school bus in Glasgow, maybe he couldn't sing but, by Christ, he was singing now.

He then proceeded to sing the whole song about the robbery, including the involvement of the other robber – at that time stuck in an adjacent interview room with other London cops. Yet why he gave them unnecessary details, like my old man's part in the heist, remains a mystery that only the singer can tell.

Now the cops were coming through our front door in Blackhill.

'Enjoying your game, son?' a big uniformed polis asked me. Even then I hated anyone other than my old man calling me 'son'. But it was the polis so what do you say?

'Aye.'

'Could Ah just have a look at that a minute?' The cop was talking about the game and I wasn't too chuffed. I'd just landed on Park Lane, a good earner, and was about to buy it. In fact, I had the notes counted out in my mitts. A big bundle of notes. Real notes. Real money.

That morning, I'd watched my father leave for work. A bit late and rushing, he'd been searching for something in a drawer and he'd left it slightly open. Always a curious kid, I decided to have a wee look at what was in there and found the big brown envelope full of cash. Much better than that stupid Monopoly money, eh?

I was really pissed off because the cops confiscated not just the money but the Monopoly game as well. That game was never returned. Maybe it's up in some polis canteen for their troops to amuse themselves while they should be out patrolling their beats. Then again, maybe they were just being bad bastards to a couple of wee kids.

It turned out that my old man hadn't been so careless as to put all his substantial ill-gotten gains in one place. Tearing our house apart, eventually the CID found a huge sum of money up in our loft. When the case came to court, it transpired that substantially less had been found than my father had stashed. Funny that.

My old man stood there in court blushing with anger, knowing the police had lined their own pockets. Years later, when he was telling me about this, I could feel my own hackles rise with anger.

'Did you not say something? Put the bastards in it?' I asked him.

'Tempting,' he conceded, 'but why would I do that? Less money in my house meant less jail time for me. I got five years as it was. That was long enough away from you weans and your mum.'

Long enough, indeed – too long. Yet I could see that he was right. Anyway, who'd believe him that the cops were thieves? He'd probably have got extra time just for his cheek in making that claim.

So Willie Ferris got back to his family sooner and the police got to line their pockets. Tell me, who do you think were the bad guys there?

38

VILLAINS

'Didn't you suspect there was something wrong with that guy who grassed you up in London?' I'd asked my father one time over a quiet drink in his and my ma's house.

'Aye, truth to tell, I wasn't that sure about him,' he replied putting his beer down. 'Maybe that's one time I should've swung the lead rather than keeping quiet, eh?'

He was referring to the tale of his mate who had been cornered by the mob up that lane and was refusing to say where the Ross Street San Toi aka The Bowery Boys were, despite having had a doing, in spite of the lead being swung closer and closer to his skull. That small group are all dead now. None made it to be Mr Bigs. None became infamous. Yet all died rich in the love of their families, friends and the principles they lived their lives by.

'It was a big robbery,' I went on and it was. It was so big that the bank started getting hit by other players almost on a monthly basis. It became the most robbed bank in the world and made it to the *Guinness Book of Records*. Despite this, my old man was the only getaway driver to leave the scene in a school bus.

'Aye, I know what you're meaning, Paul,' he said. 'You'd drop anyone from the team if you had a slight doubt, eh?'

'Damned right,' I replied, 'and quick.'

'You'd be right, of course, but tell me, son, how do you know that somebody's a grass? Or a man is as tough as he looks?'

'You get an uneasy feeling about the grass. Maybe the hardman too,' I laughed, having got decidedly uneasy in the company of some tough bastards in spite of them being my pals. I knew what they were capable of and it was frightening.

'Intuition, is it? Fair enough but your feelings might be wrong.'

'Yeah, but . . .'

'The only way you can tell if somebody's a grass or somebody's hard is by reputation – their track record. They've got to do the business.'

'Fair enough,' I conceded, 'but, if they don't yet have a reputation as a grass and you only realise what they're like once you've teamed up with them, then it's too late.'

'Precisely,' he smiled, taking a swig of beer, 'that's life sometimes. All I knew about those two was the same as I knew about a couple of bizzies in that team that raided our house, looking for my stash of money.'

'What was that?' I asked and waited as he drank some of his beer.

'That they were fucking thieves.'

'How could you know that about the polis?'

'Same way as the two bank robbers,' he stopped and lifted the bottle of Whyte & Mackay whisky, carefully and expertly pouring himself a double double. 'They'd done it before.' My old man gave a wee chortle and smiled across at me.

He might have been getting on in years. Maybe he needed walking sticks to get around. Yet he was still teaching me good, sound lessons in life. Lessons he'd learned as a kid on the streets and lived his life by. A good life it was too.

'You knew they were corrupt even as they were arresting you?' I asked, remembering how, once upon a time, I thought they were bad guys just for taking my Monopoly game away.

'Aye, those two pricks were villains all right,' he said, raising his whisky in a 'Cheers!' gesture. 'Besides, son,' a twinkle in his eyes and a wink across at me, 'as you well know, it takes one to know one, eh?'

WHERE ARE THEY NOW?

JOHNNY 'MAD DOG' ADAIR – last heard of, he'd taken up with mental Lotto chav, Mickey Carroll.

ADAMS FAMILY – still at the top and as private as ever.

JAMES ADDISON – still free as a bird and last heard of in Rotterdam.

ARIF FAMILY – continue to work the licensed trade in spite of some bad experiences.

ARTORRO – want to hear a story? The man's got a few.

BROCKY – last heard of in jail in England for a job where a man was killed.

TOMMY 'TC' CAMPBELL – after twenty-one years of being deemed a multiple murderer, now deemed innocent. The state are fighting dirty to avoid paying Tommy any compensation. Having convicted him as an Ice-Cream War killer and stolen his adult years, now they deny he was ever involved in the business. Who are the crooks?

RAB CARRUTHERS – rest in peace.

NOEL CUNNINGHAM – slipped out of an armed prison wagon and ran to freedom. Still free today.

EL PRESIDENTE – getting on with the business they are good at – making music – and free from one interfering, powder-snot nose.

FRANK THE YANK – never been heard of since. Let's hope he's not in the bottom of the River Clyde.

MARTIN HAMILTON, 'THE LORD OF THE RINGS' – serving life for torturing a young man and woman. Keeps complaining that people write nasty things about him. Wonder why...

PAUL 'KRAZY HORSE' KERR – accused in the newspapers of ripping off punters for T-in-the-Park tickets – all for the price of a night on the charlie. Last heard of, he'd been charged with threatening behaviour towards the Gizzis and released on bail.

THOMAS 'THE LICENSEE' McGRAW – had a book written about him, *Crimelord*, which he denied cooperating with – that'll be why he was frequently spotted with the author. McGraw died unexpectedly of natural causes in 2007.

GRANT 'GINGER WHINGER' McINTOSH – still keeping company with dogs.

JAMES McINTYRE – scribbling storylines for soaps for a living but none of them are as fantastic as his own life's tale.

DANDY McKAY – long since dead.

JAIMBA McLEAN – retired from the street business but I'd still not mess with him – or get between him and his bingo.

PAUL MASSEY – in a secure prison in England for an offence he never committed. If they can't get him fairly, they'll try any bloody way.

MOBINA – never seen again – probably in some alcoholic daze somewhere.

ONITY – his nose eventually stopped bleeding. He's given up sniffing the ivory dust and hasn't yet found the nerve to try rhino horn.

JOEY PYLE – the man. When we're long gone and forgotten, they'll still remember Joey Pyle.

JASON SABINI – a big thank you for the outfit – I owe you a shirt and a jacket.

TERRY SABINI – a successful boxing promoter and top man. He'd be welcome in Glasgow anytime.

THE SHARK – still got all his teeth and more wits than most of us put together.

IAN SHARMAN – where he goes, no one knows – till it's too late.

ROY 'PRETTY BOY' SHAW – last seen eating crystal brandy glasses.

ARTHUR THOMPSON – dead and buried in an unmarked grave, just yards from his house, The Ponderosa.

RITA THOMPSON – dead and buried beside her man. The Ponderosa is now up for sale.

DENNIS 'THE MENACE' WOODMAN – who cares?

MIKE YARWOOD – had a nervous breakdown when he started to believe he was his voices and he began to lose his lifelong fight against stage fright – a shame and waste of great talent. Let's hope he has learned to keep his cars well locked up.

INDEX